D1438000

The Sharpest Point
animation at the end of cinema

edited by Chris Gehman and Steve Reinke

YYZ Books/Ottawa International Animation Festival/Images Festival

Library and Archives Canada Cataloguing in Publication

The sharpest point: animation at the end of cinema / edited by Chris Gehman and Steve Reinke.

Co-published with the Ottawa International Animation Festival and the Images Festival.

Includes bibliographical references and index.

ISBN 0-920397-32-8

1. Animated films—History and criticism. 2. Animation (Cinematography) 3. Computer animation. 4. Digital video.
I. Gehman, Chris, 1966-   II. Reinke, Steve, 1963-   III. Ottawa International Animation Festival
IV. Images Festival

NC1765.S45 2005   791.43'34   C2005-904179-X

Graphic Design by Franci Duran and Kika Thorne, F. Duran Productions
Printed in Canada by Kromar
Managing Editor: Robert Labossière
Copy Editor: Bridget Indelicato, bridget_indelicato@yahoo.com
Cover image: LeCielEstBleu's *Puppet Tool*; **Page 288:** still from Jim Trainor's *The Moschops*

YYZ Books
We gratefully acknowledge the support of The Canada Council for the Arts and the Government of Canada through the Book Publishing Industry Development Program (BPDIP) for our publishing program.

 401 Richmond Street West, Suite 140, Toronto, ON M5V 3A8, Canada, www.yyzartistsoutlet.org

Ottawa International Animation Festival
Managing Director: Kelly Neall
Artistic Director: Chris Robinson
Founded in 1975 by the Canadian Film Institute, the Ottawa International Animation Festival is the largest festival of its kind in North America and one of the most respected animation festivals in the world. Bringing art and industry together, the now annual festival attracts production executives, artists, students, and animation fans from across Canada and around the world.

 2 Daly Avenue, Suite 120, Ottawa, ON K1N 6E2, Canada, www.awn.com/ottawa/

Images Festival
Executive Director: Scott Berry
Established in 1987, Images is an established and influential integrated media arts festival, dedicated to the moving image in all its forms. We curate programs of film, video, installation, performance, new media and web-based art works that approach their subject in formally, conceptually, and aesthetically unconventional ways.

 401 Richmond Street West, Suite 448, Toronto, ON M5A 3A8, Canada, www.imagesfestival.com

---

The Canada Council   Le Conseil des Arts
for the Arts   du Canada

 Canadian   Patrimoine
Heritage   canadien

Additional Support from:

Sheridan
Sheridan College

Concordia University

Toronto Animated Image Society

Table of Contents

Acknowledgments

This book emerged partly from the recognition that moving image theory and scholarship was only beginning to grapple with animation, and partly from the recognition that there are many artists working with animation today in a variety of contexts whose work has not received the recognition it deserves. The project has been supported in a number of different ways by several organizations and individuals.

First, we must acknowledge the invaluable contribution of Rob Labossière of YYZ Books, whose organization and oversight helped to shepherd a complex and multifaceted project through from early in the editorial stages to completion. Sally McKay and Kerri Embry were our initial liaisons at YYZ, and we thank them for their efforts in getting this book funded and getting the editorial process started. Thanks to copy editor Bridget Indelicato for catching all our mistakes and inconsistencies. And to lightning Barb Webb, without whom we simply would not have been able to index this book.

The generous support of the Canada Council for the Arts, through its Media Arts section, made the publication of this book possible. The additional support of the Ottawa International Animation Festival, and specifically Managing Director Kelly Neall and Artistic Director Chris Robinson, was also absolutely indispensable. The Images Festival in Toronto assisted us in finding the final bits and pieces needed to complete the funding puzzle: Thanks are due to the efforts of Executive Directors Petra Chevrier and Scott Berry, Development Director Shannon Cochrane, Artistic Director Jeremy Rigsby, and Michael Zryd, President of the Images Board of Directors. The School of Animation, Arts and Design at the Sheridan Institute of Technology and Advanced Learning provided vital financial support, for which we thank specifically Dr. Michael Collins. We also acknowledge the generous assistance of the Toronto Animated Image Society (in particular Michèle Stanley), the Mel Hoppenheim School of Cinema at Concordia University (thanks to Richard Kerr), and the Department of Image Arts at Ryerson University (thanks to Don Snyder).

Our thinking about the contemporary position and role of animation has been informed by conversations with a number of colleagues. These include Jonathan Amitay, Roberto Ariganello, Ellen Besen, Marc Glassman, Pierre Hébert, Mike Hoolboom, Patrick Jenkins, Janine Marchessault, Laura Marks, John Marriott, Susan Oxtoby, Richard Reeves, Chris Robinson, Karyn Sandlos, and Bart Testa.

We also owe a debt of thanks to the many artists and artists' representatives who supplied us with information and images that were invaluable in the preparation of the book. In addition to the artists whose work is represented, our thanks go out to Catherine Belloy, archivist at Marian Goodman Gallery; Julie Quon, archivist at Feigen Contemporary; Hashiguchi Kaori at Gallery Koyanagi; Deirdre Logue, Larissa Fan, and Lukas Blakk of the Canadian Filmmakers Distribution Centre; Wanda Vanderstoop of Vtape; Abina Manning of Video Data Bank; Claude Lord of the National Film Board of Canada; and Eve Goldin and Hubert Toh of The Film Reference Library.
— Chris Gehman and Steve Reinke

Introduction

Chris Gehman and Steve Reinke

This book is intended to bring together several disparate strands of thought about animation as an art, a technological practice, and an object of theoretical investigation, in recognition of the fact that it remains almost a *terra incognita* for serious critical and theoretical writing. We have gathered together writings and images from a wide range of disciplines and practices: animators (in the classical sense); artists (who may work within a gallery/museum context); web designers (who may not distinguish between "art" and "design"); experimental film or video makers (who may not have considered themselves to be primarily animators); as well as curators; art historians; new media theoreticians; and cinema studies academics; many of whom find themselves in multiple camps (or may prefer no disciplinary affiliation at all).

Within the general practices of "film culture" (programming, criticism, and cinema studies—both history and theory), animation remains virtually unnoticed. These fields have tended either to ignore the subject altogether or to bracket it as a special case—generally without returning to the special case for further examination. A typical book from the mainstream of film culture—say, David Thomson's *Biographical Dictionary of Film* or David Shipton's *The Story of Cinema*—despite the encyclopedic claims implied by their titles and their authoritative styles, breezily omit animation and animators from their accounts of "cinema" and "film," along with documentary and experimental film. Those interested in digital media, on the other hand, have tended to accord the animated image a more central position, perhaps because animation became part of new media practice very early in its history, whereas indexical digital procedures ("image capture") have taken much longer to develop.

Only with the publication of recent books by theorists such as Paul Wells, Esther Leslie, and Lev Manovich, whose chapter "Compositing" from *The Language of New Media* (2001) we include here, has this situation begun to show signs of changing. Manovich in particular, with his ambitious claim that the traditional categories of cinema have, in the digital age, become no more than "particular cases" of animation, reverses the usual position of animation in theories of the moving image. Animation has become a kind of black hole or singularity through which all of cinematic practice must now pass, emerging forever changed on the other side. Whether or not this formulation survives, it has thrown up a challenge which existing theories of the moving image, traditionally organized around questions related to the characteristics of the photographic image, can scarcely ignore.

But this is not simply an anthology of theoretical and critical writing: rather, recognizing the fact that the very definition of animation has become unstable in the era of digital media, the book uses the idea of animation as a sort of gravitational centre around which a great diversity of material in a broad range of styles revolves. Not all of the articles included here deal directly with the subject of animation in its narrowest technical sense, but all relate to questions about animation's position in contemporary theory, criticism, and industrial and artistic practice. The range of material in *The Sharpest Point* also reflects the fact that in contemporary culture, art practice, technological development, theory, and criticism overlap and interpenetrate one another. It seemed more valuable to us to allow the perspectives of artists, theorists, critics, programmers and others to appear side by side, rather than segregated into taxonomical boxes. (In this respect, we would be remiss if we did not give a nod to the book which stood alone for so long, and has served as a model for our own: the indispensable and still strangely vital *Experimental Animation*, edited by Robert Russett and Cecile Starr. It is our hope that we have made a book worthy to find itself on a bookshelf next to it.)

The paucity of serious attention from critics, scholars, and theorists partly explains the emphasis in this book on visual artists who work with animation: To put it bluntly, those who are recognized as "artists" and who operate within the "art world" can expect their work to be accorded a certain level of critical consideration, while even the most worthy and ambitious of the non-commercial independent animators who appear by the score in books like Giannalberto Bendazzi's encyclopedic *Cartoons: One Hundred Years of Cinema Animation* (1994) have simply never received the same level of critical attention. For example, William Kentridge has been the subject of extensive critical attention (including an essay by Rosalind Krauss, included here), while the many excellent animators whose work is presented on the cinema, television, or computer screen, rather than in the gallery, labour in obscurity. No single work can begin to address this lack. This anthology includes a number of short pieces by and about independent animators, representing different practices and traditions. Although it is in no way a comprehensive selection, it does give some sense of the extraordinary range of practices that fall into the general category of animation: cameraless direct filmmaking; the digital compositing of graphics, live-action footage, and digitally animated images and text; pixillation of human actors; animation of found objects and images; animation as live performance; and the creation of abstract digital animations using compact executable files, to name a few.

We took our title from a comment made in an interview with animator Pierre Hébert: "Animation should be cinema's sharpest point." The "should" is important: This is a pointed critique from an artist who animates using sharp points, aimed simultaneously at the failure of film culture and media theory to account for animation and at the failure of much animation to rise to its potential. This book concentrates on those instances where part of this potential has been fulfilled and on the questions that they raise.

The World is a Cartoon: Stray Notes on Animation

Steve Reinke

I belong to an online group associated with Maureen Furniss's *Animation Journal*. I haven't posted anything (yet), but I get the group's postings several times per week. It isn't usually a site for debating or developing ideas—it seems to function mostly as a clearing house for information, a way to track down people, films, and facts. Recently though, a problem came along that sparked a sustained and thoughtful debate: what is "experimental animation"?

A frequent—and certainly reasonable—assertion in the online debate was that in order to discuss or conceptualize a thing, it had to be defined. After all, what is a concept but its mental image, its definition? The act of setting up disciplinary/genre/definitional/categorical boundaries was seen as a necessary, preparatory task—a clearing of the ground. But I must admit I have no interest in such a thing. Some preparatory tasks are endless, unproductive, futile. Categorical boundaries shift, fold, interpenetrate, making any clearing of the ground a task which might just self-perpetuate, leading nowhere. For instance: "documentary." As a discipline, documentary scholarship seems as if it will be forever mired in "fundamental" questions. (Luckily, perhaps, the stakes seem lower for animation scholarship. There is, at this time, less of a moral imperative to investigate or discuss animation's relationship to the world. This will surely not be the case in the near future.)

I want to explore the nature of animation, the possibilities contained within the animated image; to establish, after André Bazin's seminal essay "The Ontology of the Photographic Image," something like an ontology of the animated image. Yet, I will exert no effort to define "animation" (let alone "experimental animation"). I run the risk that my refusal is perverse rather than productive. Still, I have some good company. For instance, Lev Manovich's highly influential redefinition of animation is entirely circular, as we'll see below. In fact, some of the most interesting writers on animation provide, at best, partial or inconsistent definitions of animation. Instead, they use animation (or the difference between animation and live action), not as a concept in itself but as a genre or set of techniques from which to devel-

stills: Emile Cohl's *Fantasmagorie* (1908)

op particular concepts: Sean Cubitt's vector, Vilém Flusser's imaginal thought, Jean-François Lyotard and D. N. Rodowick's figural. It is through such concepts that it becomes possible to claim that animation is now and will continue in becoming the driving force of new media and the moving image: the sharpest point.

In this essay then, this collection of stray notes, I will pursue my vague and, I think, still mysterious question through the work of various theorists, critics, and artists.

Lev Manovich: Myth of Prodigal Return

The most influential recent work which undertakes to redefine animation in this age of digital technology is Lev Manovich's *The Language of New Media*, particularly "Chapter 6: What is Cinema." It is no accident that his project, which begins by investigating the relations between cinema and new media, resolves itself by making claims about animation. Manovich examines these relations along two trajectories. The first trajectory, which I would characterize as conservative, is historical: Manovich "uses the history and theory of cinema to map out the logic driving the technical and stylistic development of new media."(*LNM*, 287) The second, potentially more radical, trajectory goes in the opposite direction: from computers to cinema. It asks: "How does computerization affect our very concept of moving images? Does it offer new possibilities for film language? Has it led to the development of totally new forms of cinema?" (*LNM*, 287)

Manovich's myth begins with an unassailably reasonable assertion. Cinema has been dominated by the live action film: "unmodified photographic recordings of real events that took place in real, physical space." (*LNM*, 294) That is, lens-based recordings of reality. Manovich is at his best, I think, when he deploys a kind of hyperbole that is, nonetheless, razor sharp. Here, vanquishing the dominator, he reduces all of non-animated cinema to "an attempt to make art out of a footprint."

> Yet behind even the most stylized cinematic images, we can discern the bluntness, sterility, and banality of early nineteenth-century photographs. No matter how complex its stylistic innovations, the cinema has found its base in these deposits of reality, these samples obtained by a methodical and prosaic process. Cinema emerged out of the same impulse that engendered naturalism, court stenography, and wax museums. Cinema is the art of the index; it is an attempt to make art out of a footprint. (*LNM*, 294-5)

According to Manovich, whatever the qualities of the digital image, they are not inherently indexical. When indexicality can no longer be seen as a defining quality of an image, what repercussions are there for the ontology of the image? If we move from a lens- to a computer-based production of images, can there still be representations of the world?

> ...the manual construction of images in digital cinema represents a return to the pro-cinematic practices of the nineteenth century, when images were hand-painted and hand-animated. At the turn of the twentieth century, cinema was to delegate these manual techniques to animation and define itself as a recording medium. As cinema enters the digital age, these techniques are again becoming commonplace in the filmmaking process. Consequently, cinema can no longer be clearly distinguished from animation. It is no longer an indexical media technology but, rather, a subgenre of painting. (*LNM*, 295)

Manovich defines animation through a myth of prodigal return. Pro-cinematic machines (kinetoscope, thaumatrope, etc.) relied on hand-painted or hand-drawn images, loops that were manually animated. The cinema proper combined the automatic generation and projection of images. Once the technology stabilized, cinema cut all references to its origins in artifice. Animation was banished as "cinema's bastard relative, its supplement and shadow." (*LNM*, 298)

With the burgeoning digital technologies of the 1990s, the prodigal returns: Marginalized techniques of animation reclaim their apparent birthright. Manovich offers a definition of digital film that becomes (morphs into) a redefinition of animation:

> digital film = live action material + painting + image processing + compositing + 2-D computer animation + 3-D computer animation (*LNM*, 301)

> Now we can finally answer the question "What is digital cinema?" Digital cinema is a particular case of animation that uses live-action footage as one of its many elements.
> Born from animation, cinema pushed animation to its periphery, only in the end to become one particular case of animation. (*LNM*, 302)

There are two trajectories here: cinema and animation. Each has three stages: early or pro-cinema, which is allied to animation; the cinema, in which cartoons are ignored and denigrated; and the digital cinema, which is, literally, animation, or, strangely, "one particular case of animation." In the end, animation is triumphant, but at the price of an enormous levelling: It becomes everything. It seems to me that both assertions are equally plausible and, perhaps, equally meaningless: *Cinema has become one particular case of animation. Animation has become one particular case of cinema.* The words "one particular case" may simply function as a rhetorical place-holder to keep his definition from becoming ridiculously bald: *Cinema has become animation. Animation has become cinema.*

Deleuze: Animation's Banishment

If you're looking for mention of animated film in the *Cinema* books of Gilles Deleuze, you don't have to look far. The sole mention comes on page five of *Cinema 1: The Movement-Image.* Deleuze begins with theses on movement derived from philosopher Henri Bergson, in particular from two books that straddle the birth of cinema: *Matter and Memory* (1896) and *Creative Evolution* (1907). Deleuze deploys Bergson to (among other things) tackle a problem which has been central to the theorization of cinema since André Bazin's "The Ontology of the Photographic Image": the relationship of cinema to still photography, particularly in terms of movement and time.

Deleuze's version of Bergson's thesis is perhaps best explained in relation to one of Zeno's paradoxes (an arrow will never reach its destination as the space it traverses is infinitely divisible), and stands with phenomenology as an attempt to reconceptualize time as immanently experienced rather than unfolding in the transcendent. The thesis separates movement from the space it covers. The space that movement covers is infinitely divisible, but the movement is irreducible—it cannot be divided without being destroyed (becoming another movement altogether). The space Zeno's arrow traverses may be infinitely divisible, but the arrow's motion is not. Every movement has an intrinsic quality, a particular, concrete duration [*durée*].

Therefore it is false to say that cinema works with two complementary givens: the individual frame or still image and movement that is "impersonal, uniform, abstract, invisible, or imperceptible, which is 'in' the apparatus." (c, 1) Cinema may be constructed from photogrammes (individual frames), but it is incorrect to think of it as being immobile sections to which abstract time is added. Cinema is not photography + time/movement. Movement is immediately given; it is part of the filmic apparatus, and not a supplement or addition. "In short, cinema does not give us an image to which movement is added, it immediately gives us a movement-image." (c, 2)

Deleuze, via Bergson, goes on to distinguish between privileged instants and any-instants-whatever. The idea of privileged instants corresponds to the ancient view of movement. "For antiquity, movement refers to intelligible elements, Forms or Ideas which are themselves eternal and immobile." (c, 4) The any-instant-whatever is a modern concept. "The modern scientific revolution has consisted in relating movement not to privileged instants, but to any-instant-whatever. Although movement was still recomposed, *it was no longer recomposed from formal transcendental elements (poses), but from immanent material elements (sections)."* (C, 4, italics in original)

The animated film poses a problem for Deleuze, so much so that he questions whether it might not "belong fully to the cinema." This is because animation has the potential to be constructed from privileged instants rather than any-instants-whatever.

> When we think about the prehistory of cinema, we always end up confused, because we do not know where its technological lineage begins, or how to define this lineage. We can always refer to shadow puppets, or the very earliest projection systems. But, in fact, the determining conditions of the cinema are the following: not merely the photo, but the snapshot (the long-exposure photo [*photo de pose*] belongs to the other lineage); the equidistance of snapshots; the transfer of this equidistance on to a framework which constitutes the "film" (it was Edison and Dickson who perforated the film in the camera); a mechanism for moving on images (Lumiere's claws). It is in this sense that the cinema is the system which reproduces movement as a function of any-instant-whatever that is, as a function of equidistant instants, selected so as to create an impression of continuity. Any other system which reproduces movement through an order of exposures [poses] projected in such a way that they pass into one another, or are "transformed," is foreign to the cinema. This is clear when one attempts to define the cartoon film; if it belongs fully to the cinema, this is because the drawing no longer constitutes a pose or a completed figure, but the description of a figure which is always in the process of being formed or dissolving through the movement of lines and points taken at any-instant-whatevers of their course. The cartoon is not related to a Euclidean, but to a Cartesian geometry. It does not give us a figure described in a unique moment, but the continuity of the movement which describes the figure. (C, 4-5)

Deleuze's (partial) expulsion of animation from cinema follows from his extremely limited lineage of pro-cinematic technologies. Gone are the magic lanterns and zoetropes in favour of the snapshot. Emile Cohl's *Fantasmagorie* (1908) would be, in the Deleuzian sense, cinematic, while the work of, say, William Kentridge, in which movement is not a continuity of any-instants-whatever but simply bridges the privileged instants of individual drawings, would not be. (It is no coincidence that Rosalind Krauss reads Deleuze's partial banishment of animation as being a generously inclusive gesture in her often brilliant essay on Kentridge below.)

Sean Cubitt: Graphical Film: The Vector
Sean Cubitt seems to have never met an idea he didn't like. It would not be

inappropriate to describe his book *The Cinema Effect* (2004) in terms generally reserved for action movies: It is an exhilarating ride. We'll limit ourselves
to a few of the ideas—the key ones, of course, but also a few others—in the
chapter which deals with animation: "Graphical Film: The Vector." If there is
a proliferation of ideas in this chapter, there is, mercifully, a single object to
which they are applied: Emile Cohl's *Fantasmagorie* (1908).

We find in Cubitt, I think, a synthesis of Deleuze and Manovich; animation
is no longer banished from cinema, for it is cinema. Yet certain types of animation (the vector-based graphical film, in particular) are privileged
cinematically. It is no coincidence, then, that Cubitt's description of the film
concludes with the Deleuzian assertion that it is not related to Euclidean,
but (presumably) Cartesian, geometry:

> *Fantasmagorie* is a brief line animation in which a mysterious puppet, Pierrot
> or *fantoche*, and his environment change seamlessly. Flowers become bot-
> tles become a cannon; an elephant becomes a house; Pierrot becomes a
> bubble, a hat, a valise. The vector of Cohl's line, as it draws and redraws
> itself, disrespects the frame edge and equally ignores the syntax of layering,
> most notably in the small "screen" that appears on at the left of the image as
> the action with the woman in the hat takes place. Not only does this appear
> to reprise the scenes that we have just watched, but it also lies on an axis of
> depth from which the other characters are debarred. For example, when the
> little Pierrot gets bigger, it is not because he is closer to the virtual eye of the
> rostrum camera, but because he has been inflated. Likewise, the sword-
> wielding giant shares the same plane as Pierrot. However, it is not simply
> that the rules of the cut are being broken: Rather, *Fantasmagorie* obeys
> another set of rules in the same way that the real line is bound by laws other
> than those of Euclidean geometry. (*CE*, 75-6)

Cohl sacrifices editing, storytelling, and staging-in-depth in favour of a uniform line which can perform a series of metamorphoses that is potentially
infinite. Cubitt describes this as a grammatical structure that is primarily
paradigmatic, rather than syntagmatic.

> The rules of syntax govern the structure of meaningful sentences. The struc-
> ture of "My life is an open book" is the same as that of "His cat is a wicked
> creature."... What differentiates them is the [paradigmatic] substitution of
> "life" for "cat." Linguists speak of grammar as the syntagmatic axis and
> imagine it as a horizontal line."... The paradigmatic axis is correspondingly
> the vertical axis, like the reels on a slot machine, allowing us to select which
> word to put into the slots created by the syntax. (*CE*, 76)

It is hard to imagine a film that would be completely based in a paradigmatic, rather than syntagmatic, grammar, but it is surely in animation that the possibility is most likely. *Fantasmagorie* is Cubitt's exemplar of the graphic film as "it is a film within a hair's breadth of being governed by the paradigmatic code of the vector alone." [*CE*, 77]

There are no key frames in *Fantasmagorie*. The metamorphoses do not begin in a particular image (privileged instant) and resolve into another particular image. The movement of the line is never complete. Each frame is an any-instant-whatever. Deleuze's distinction between privileged instants and any-instants-whatever provides a background for Cubitt's categories of pixel, cut, and vector. The most direct precursors for Cubitt's categories seem to be Peirce's increasingly influential concepts of Firstness, Secondness, and Thirdness (concepts also deployed by Deleuze in his *Cinema* books). Pixel corresponds to Firstness, or pure sensation, the referent itself, the Lacanian Real, prior to representation or signification. The cut corresponds to Secondness, the representation of the thing itself, the Lacanian Imaginary, the signified. The vector is Thirdness, the production of meaning, the Lacanian Symbolic, the signifier. The vector is not a representation, it "moves from the presentation of objects to the stimulation of concepts. The vector does not tell us what to expect: it requires us to think. In this way the vector brings us into the realm of the intellect and offers us the delight we take in the pursuit of meaning." [*CE*, 85]

Cubitt sees the vector as a way out of the impasse of representation in a time when the world, as the site of representation's possible referents, has already been negated, lost behind (or within) the Baudrillardian hyperreal. If all is simulation, if the world has been transformed into data, there can be no representation.

> The vector's particular future-directed temporality addresses us no longer as termini but as media: as people who make sense, but only as nodes in interweaving trajectories of signification. It is no longer a matter of recognition, of deciphering what is already encoded. Rather it is a matter of reinterpreting, of adding a new spin to a trajectory that has not yet realized itself. The vector is the regime in which the temporality and the labour of making sense is paramount. If in the pixel we are engaged by an undifferentiated union with the visual, and in the cut by the subjection-objection pair, in the vector we confront the double presence of the screen image as at once object and image, such that what we normally expect to be true of the object—for example, that it possesses a single, discrete, and stable identity— is no longer the case. No longer pointing to an entity separate and opposed to us, but offering itself as a medium, the image becomes a cinematic sign. Like every sign, it implies the existence of other signs. To say of one of Cohl's

lines that it "is" a flower, an elephant, or a house is inaccurate. On the one hand, it is only legible as referring to (conventional images of) flowers, elephants, and houses for brief moments in a trajectory that is never stable. On the other, it is always a line, a signifier, which is what gives it its transformative power. (*CE*, 91-2)

That graphical cinema found one of its clearest expressions early in the history of cinema with *Fantasmagorie* is no surprise. Cubitt radicalizes Manovich's myth of prodigal return. In Manovich, animation's triumphant return, which was marked by a return to manual artifice, has already occurred. For Cubitt, animation is yet to return, but its return is imminent and will be marked by an overthrow of the stupid tyranny of representation and narrative. Thus Cubitt's engagement with animation also involves the inevitable return to the pro-cinematic. He extends Manovich's claims:

> At some point in the near future when historians recognize that the photochemical cinema is a brief interlude in the history of the animated image, representation will become, like narrative, a subcode of interpretation rather than an essence of motion pictures. (*CE*, 97)

If we move from a lens- to a computer-based production of images, can there still be representations of the world? No. There will be no representations (and no world). Instead there will be vectors that move through representation in a process of endless becoming to produce concepts.

Cubitt also makes some claims regarding animators and authorship that I find provocative. I include them below as they seem to me profound and nonsensical in equal measure. They also, incidentally, bring to mind—or, rather, they seem to describe with an uncanny accuracy—Chris Landreth's film *Ryan* (2004).

> The secret consciousness of the vector is this human-mechanical hybrid. Hence we can no longer speak of the author as originator of the cartoon: instead we are confronted with the animator, no longer a subject of the social world, but an exile seeking asylum in the machine world from all demands external to the world itself. (*CE*, 83)

A Rabbit, a Goat, a Mosquito

In Jean Renoir's live-action feature film *The Rules of the Game* (1939), there is a scene in which a rabbit dies. Actually, many rabbits and many pheasants die in the film, mostly in the justly famous hunting scene. But there is one particular rabbit whose death is particularly vivid: It leaps into open meadow, is hit by a bullet, falls, twitches, lies still. So it is that single, par-

ticular rabbit—the one whose death is most real—with whom we are concerned. (But perhaps all slaughters are best narrativized as individual deaths.)

The hunting scene in *The Rules of the Game* brings to mind an equally accomplished and intense hunting scene from a roughly contemporaneous film, Walt Disney's *Bambi* (1942). In *Bambi*, humans (and not just hunters, all humans) are evil and remain unseen. We see their encampment and their fire (which spreads apocalyptically to the forest in the film's last act) and we see and hear their bullets tearing up the forest. And we see their representatives, the demonic hunting dogs (the only creatures who do not talk in the film), attacking Bambi and his wife. But we see only one death, and that from a distance. The nervous pheasant, whose panicked flight sets off the slaughter, falls out of the sky. Otherwise, death is not depicted visually, but through the sound of gunshots and the occasional muffled thud. Still, death is heavy in the film, and traumatic. The film is, of course, notorious for the possibly traumatic effect the death of Bambi's mother has on child viewers. In some ways, hunting and animal death in *The Rules of the Game* is inverted in *Bambi*. The off-screen deaths of cartoon characters can pack an incredible wallop as they raise the spectre of symbolic (and actual) maternal death, while the on-screen death of an actual rabbit is likely to cause a

still: Walt Disney's *Bambi* (1942)

much slighter psychic disturbance, even as it directly raises a complex of moral issues.

The hunting scene in *The Rules of the Game* occurs roughly in the middle of the film and is a turning point. Up to that point, the film is largely concerned with character exposition, and afterward it switches into an increasingly narrative mode. It also marks, if not a change in tone, a deepening of affect, an increase of tonal complexity. It foreshadows a scene (the story's climax) in which one of the human characters—the virtuous, innocent one—dies. As Vivian Sobchack points out in her essay "Inscribing Ethical Space: Ten Propositions on Death, Representation, and Documentary" (included in her 2004 book *Carnal Thoughts: Embodiment and Moving Image Culture*), the human dies only in the film, while the rabbit dies in the film and in the world.

> ...the rabbit is not perceived by us solely as a character in the narrative. Rather, it is a real rabbit that we see die in the service of the narrative and for the fiction. The human character who dies, however, does so only in the fiction. Thus, insofar as we are talking about a classic film, even though they eventually survived the actor, both his character and the narrative were immediately survived by him. We cannot, however, say the same of the rabbit. (*CT*, 245)

In this essay, Sobchak is concerned with the ethics of documentary space, using representations of death as a kind of limit case. She establishes two categories: the ethics of making the image and the ethics of looking at the image. Both categories are concerned with the ontological status of the pro-filmic event.

(Ethics is, of course, now that we have dispensed with veracity, the primary concern of discourses of documentary representation. It is, at best, a secondary concern for the live-action feature, where ethics has been limited to the taken-for-granted ground of identity politics. We have yet to develop an ethics of the animated image, apart from issues related to the socialization of children. And an ethics of new media has, so far, been bogged down in a concern all other areas have deemed irrelevant: the veracity of the possibly-no-longer-indexical image.)

Our poor rabbit dies at least two deaths. The first death, and probably the only one to concern the rabbit, is its actual death in the world. We'll call this death pro-filmic. The second death is the one we see depicted on-screen. This death, or this representation, is filmic, or, keeping with Sobchak, cinematic. The man's death is limited to the filmic. It occurs solely in the diegesis of the fictional film. The rabbit's death exceeds the film's diegesis. It occurs within the film's diegesis as a fiction, within the real world as an actual event, within the pro-filmic as documentary and, finally, within the film itself as both fiction and documentary.

> What is important to note here is that the knowledge that informs our distinction between the fate—and fatality—of the rabbit and character is both extracinematic and intertextual. On the one hand, the cinema-specific codes of representation are the same for both the real rabbit and irreal character, and each of their deaths serves a similar and interrelated function in the narrative. Nonetheless, despite these cinema-specific codes (for Renoir, a rigorous realism), a distinction is made between them. Indeed, the textual moment of the rabbit's death gains its particular force from an extracinematic and intertextual cultural knowledge that contextualizes and exceeds the representation's sign-function in the narrative. (CT, 245-6)

If I object to Sobchak's idiosyncratic use of the basic semiotic categories of icon/index/symbol (she seems to reserve "index" for documentary images), I agree with her conclusions.

> The rabbit's death exceeds the narrative codes that communicate it. It ruptures and interrogates the boundaries (and license) of fictional representation and has a "ferocious reality" that the character's death does not. Indeed, it is taken as an indexical sign in an otherwise iconic/symbolic representation. That is, it functions to point beyond its function as a narrative representation to an extratextual and animate referent, executed not only by but for the representation. The rabbit's death violently, abruptly, punctuates the fictional space with documentary space. Nonfictional or documentary space is thus of a different order than fictional space that confines itself to the screen or, at most, extends offscreen into an unseen yet still imagined world. (CT, 247)

The rabbit is martyred to fiction. Its death ruptures the fictional space of the film—its diegesis—and allows the larger world and its concerns to bleed in and contaminate it.

While fiction is ruptured by documentary in *The Rules of the Game*, the opposite happens in Luis Buñuel's *Land without Bread* (1933). It is no coincidence that it also involves the killing of an animal. The film is a human geography documentary of the poverty-stricken inhabitants in a remote area of Spain. It is a parody of voice-of-God expository documentary, and—as parodies should—it follows its models closely. But the voice-over begins to stray from the necessary and expected humanist, objective point of view.

It becomes playful: sadistic and biased. Voice-over is, of course, central to the expository documentary—but in some respects it is also a supplement: It is added in post-production and can be, with some expediency, completely rewritten and re-recorded. It is the images themselves that carry the authority of documentary truth. But the filmmakers of *Land without Bread* find a way to make the images lie, to have fiction intrude into the documentary space.

We see a goat on the edge of a cliff. The voice-over tells us that the land is so treacherous, even sure-footed mountain goats often fall to their deaths. We see a puff of smoke in the bottom right-hand corner of the screen, as if a rifle has been discharged, and we see the goat fall off the mountain. Even if we do not notice the smoke, it is clear that the goat did not slip: It simply topples.

The goat's death is unlikely to make us sad. We are more likely to laugh at the audacity of the filmmakers and the clumsily obvious manner in which they flaunt the basic rules of documentary representation (and morality). (But then Buñuel's celebration of cruelty—it is a distinguishing feature of his work—is, perhaps, always just beyond empathy's reach.)

(As I'm writing this, Lars von Trier's *Manderlay* is premiering at Cannes. The primary controversy concerning the film is that Nicole Kidman almost starred in it, but running a close second is the news that the killing of a goat —an old, sick goat we are assured—has been removed from the film in order that the film does not become about a megalomaniac Danish director who revels in goat-killing.)

Both *The Rules of the Game* and *Land without Bread* are satirical, and both deploy their ruptures to further their satirical ends. When fiction is ruptured by documentary, the fiction may become more concerned with the world: heavier, broader, deeper. When documentary is ruptured by fiction, the documentary is revealed to be the product of a particular subjectivity whose desires determine the shape of the world and the range of representations we might possibly draw from it. As our desires are horrible and petty and base, the result is likely to be comic.

The animated film exceeds both fiction and documentary. These categories no longer mean anything, apart from retaining a link to non-animated films. When we say that Winsor McCay's *The Sinking of the Lusitania* (1918) is an animated documentary, we mean something like: if the same images were live action, we would have a documentary.

The rabbit and the goat become, as they exceed their representational regimes, vectors. The rabbit begins as a fictional rabbit, but ends up really dead and only nominally within the fictional diegesis. The goat begins as a real, documentary goat but gets shot and tumbles into a fictional space of desire.

In Richard Linklater's *Waking Life* (2001), there is (possibly) a mosquito that becomes a vector through its (possible) death. The film was shot and edited on mini-DV as live-action digital video, but was painted over (rotoscoped) to look like, if not become, animation. In a literal way, both digital video and computer-aided animation are exactly the same technology and therefore must share the same representational possibilities: A pixel is a pixel, after all. But as representation is rhetorical as well as technical, it also depends on things such as genre in the determination of representational possibilities. If a digital image of, say, a tree appears to be indexical, there remains the strong possibility that it will be read as being an index and we will have received knowledge of the existence of a particular tree in the world.

The narrative of *Waking Life* is propelled by questions about indeterminate or liminal states. The protagonist initially struggles to find out if he is awake or asleep and dreaming, later if he is asleep or dead. The film also has an indeterminate state as an extra-diegetical thematic concern: whether it— *Waking Life*—is essentially indexical (live action: lens-based) or non-indexical (animation: drawn/painted). One easily discerns the live action "below" the animation. The animation can seem like an embellishment that does not seriously compromise the live action origins of the movie, like adding a filter to video to give it film grain. Sure, some things are added that would not have been on the live-action footage—lightning bolts and flashing lights—but these are obvious supplements: they even seem to float in front of the picture plane (lens-based concept), or to be the uppermost layer (digital painting concept). After all, Julie Delpy is still Julie Delpy and Ethan Hawke is still Ethan Hawke.

In a segment titled "The Holy Moment" (the only segment, if I am not mistaken, to have a title), the protagonist floats into a movie theatre and watches a film of two men talking about, of all things, Bazin and the ontology of the photographic image.

> –Cinema, in its essence—well, it's about the reproduction of reality. Reality is actually reproduced. For him it's not like a storytelling medium. He feels that literature is better for telling a story. Even if you tell a joke, like this guy walks into a bar and he sees a dwarf. That works really well because you're imagining this guy and this dwarf and there's this imaginative aspect to it. But in film you don't have that because you're actually filming a specific guy in a specific bar with a specific dwarf of a specific height who looks a specific way.

So for Bazin, what the ontology of film has to do with—which is also what photography has an ontology of, except that it has this dimension of time to it, which adds this greater realism—and so it's about that guy at that moment in that space. And Bazin is a Christian, so he believes that God—he believes that reality and God are the same, so that what film is actually capturing is God incarnate, creating. At this very moment God is manifesting as this. And what film would capture if it were filming us now is God as this table and God as you and God looking how we look right now and God thinking what we're thinking because we're all God manifest in that sense.
–Mmm. Hmm.
–So film is actually a record of God, or of the face of God, or of the ever-changing face of God. You have a mosquito. Want me to get it for you?
–[Man slaps his own face.] I got it?
–Yeah, you got it.

The character's (flawed) précis of Bazin continues, moving from film as the face of God to a discussion of the holy moment (wherein one looks upon the face of God). The mosquito is an interruption in the discussion that is comical for a number of reasons. First, it simply brings an increasingly lofty, one-sided conversation back down to earth. Reinforcing this fall from the spiritually transcendent to the immanent everyday are the two faces: The face of God becomes the face that gets slapped.

The scene cuts between the protagonist sitting in the movie theatre and the film he is watching, which (until the final moments) is a single medium shot. The camera is hand-held, but relatively static. The mosquito lands on the far side of a head we see only in profile. Barring the insertion of a close-up, we have no way of actually seeing the mosquito. Even within the diegesis of the film-within-the-film, only the Bazin-discoursing character could possibly see the mosquito.

The previous paragraph recounts the scene as if it were part of a live action, lens-based film. If *Waking Life* is essentially live action, with the animation merely a kind of stylistic supplement, a particular question arises: Did an actual mosquito exist in the pro-filmic world? If *Waking Life* is an animated film, the question becomes nonsensical.

The difference in the ontology of the lens-based photographic image of live action and the graphic possibly-digital image of animation lies at the level of the pro-filmic. But, following Bazin, questions concerning the ontology of images are wrapped up in questions of indexicality. In *Waking Life*, the mosquito is a vector, which, by raising questions about the ontological/ indexical status of the film's representations, exceeds the film's diegesis. It seems to me that *Waking Life* inhabits an indeterminate, even liminal, realm in which we cannot say what is animated and what is not.

Of course, it has frequently been stated that this is the usual status of digital images. Generally, though, it seems that this uncertainty is resolved too patly. Both Manovich and Cubitt seem to assert that because digital images are not necessarily indexical, all of (digital) cinema has become animation. As *Waking Life* asserts, perhaps paradoxically through the use of computer animation, lens-based indexical representations have not been so easily eclipsed.

Surface and Line, Line and Letter

Philosopher Vilém Flusser, in a McLuhanesque gambit, divided the world of signs into lines and surfaces, with surfaces becoming ever more predominant over lines. The world of lines, of linear signs, is the world of the alphabet, of language as the printed word. It is a linear world. Each line is a series of points. "[L]ines are discourses of points, and each point is a symbol of something out there in the world (a 'concept'). Therefore, the lines represent the world by projecting it as a series of successions, in the form of a process." (W, 21) Surfaces can, and often do, contain (incorporate) lines, but they do so in a way that makes the line something other than a linear process. TV screens, posters, illustrated magazines, photographs, paintings are all surfaces rather than lines. Both sign systems mean the world, though they, necessarily, mean it in different ways.

> Until very recently, official Western thought has expressed itself much more in written lines than in surfaces. This fact is important. Written lines impose a specific structure on thought, in that they represent the world by means of a point sequence. This implies a "historical" being-in-the-world of those who read and write written lines. But, in addition, surfaces have always existed, and these also have represented the world. They impose a very different structure on thought in that they represent the world by means of static images. This implies an "unhistorical" being-in-the-world of those who make and read these surface images. Very recently, new channels for the articulation of thought have come about (e.g., films and TV), and official Western thought is taking increasing advantage of them. They impose a radically new structure on thought in that they represent the world by means of moving images. This implies a posthistorical being-in-the-world of those who make and read these moving images. In a sense, it may be said that these new channels incorporate the temporality of the written line into the picture, by lifting the historical time of written lines onto the level of the surface. (W, 25-26)

This division of signs into lines and surfaces gives us a powerful way to think about animation and the moving image (and in particular the unfortunate-ly-named category of motion graphics) not bogged down in questions of photographic indexicality. In his writings, which include *Towards a Philosophy of Photography* (1984) and the collection *Writings* (2002), Flusser offers a conception of photography radically different from Bazin's ontology of the photographic image. He claims, for instance, that the apparent index-icality of the photograph is false (or perhaps merely irrelevant), thereby erasing any ontological distinction between lens-based and digital media.

> [P]hotographs are information intentionally produced from a swarm of iso-lated possibilities. Thus, photographs differ in principle from prehistoric images. Prehistoric images are worldviews (copies of the environment). Photographs are computed possibilities (models, projections onto the envi-ronment). This is the reason photographs should be considered posthistorical images. (*W*, 129)

> Photographs are simply the first among the posthistorical images. In the case of photographs, the acquisition of the codes, in which the new con-sciousness articulates itself, is a more difficult task than in the case of more developed images, such as synthetic images. Two aspects of the photograph make it more difficult. First, photos resemble copies more than projections. At first glance, a photo of an airplane does not reveal that, just like a synthet-ic computer image, it signifies a possible airplane rather than a given one. Second, the photograph seems to be made by a photographer operating the apparatus, rather than by a software specialist programming the apparatus. The projecting and computing nature of the photograph is less evident than in synthetic images. Yet this is precisely why learning to photograph in the sense of a posthistorical projection would be extraordinarily emancipatory. (*W*,131)

Let this emancipation be called animation. Or, that which we have been calling animation, without precisely defining it, can perhaps now be charac-terized as the moving image genre best suited to incorporating line into surface. The line-invested surface has the potential to produce imaginal thought, which seems to me roughly equivalent to Cubitt's vector. As Flusser states in his essay "Line and Surface" (1973), "imaginal thought is becoming capable of thinking concepts." (*W*, 30) As lines are incorporated into surfaces, images become discursive.

Two categories developed by Jean-Francois Lyotard in his *Discours, fig-ure* (1971), line and letter, seem to me closely related to Flusser's surface and line, despite the fact they use "line" in roughly opposing ways. Where

Flusser's line corresponds to the linearity of text-based discourse, Lyotard's line is a plastic, graphic line. Rather than opposing language and image, Lyotard sees them as complementary.

> The letter is a closed invariant line; the line is the opening of the letter that is closed, perhaps, elsewhere or on the other side. Open the letter and you have image, scene, magic. Enclose the image and you have emblem, symbol, and letter. (*RF*, 268)

The figural is the force that erodes the difference between line and letter. D. N. Rodowick explains why he finds the "nomadic concept" of the figural central to discussions of digital cinema in his brilliant book *Reading the Figural, or, Philosophy after New Media* (2001).

> Computer-generated and manipulated images are now commonplace, of course. But when these images began appearing in TV ads, music videos, and other venues, it was impossible not to be astonished by how fluidly text was spatialized, thus losing its uniform contours, fixed spacing, and linear sense, and how presumably space was "textualized"; that is, how the Euclidean solidity of the image was fragmented, rendered discontinuous, divisible, and liable to recombination in the most precise ways. Suddenly the image was becoming articulable, indeed discursive, like never before. (*RF*, 3)

So: Cubitt's vector, Flusser's imaginal thought, Lyotard/Rodowick's figural. Through these concepts, animation is now and will continue in becoming the driving force behind discovering the discursive possibilities of new media and the moving image.

Endnotes/Bibliography

C Gilles Deleuze, *Cinema 1: The Movement-Image*, University of Minnesota Press, Minneapolis: 1986.

CE Sean Cubbit, *The Cinema Effect*, MIT Press, Boston: 2004.

CT Vivian Sobchack, *Carnal Thoughts: Embodiment and Moving Image Culture*, University of California Press, Berkeley: 2004.

LNM Lev Manovich, *The Language of New Media*, MIT Press, Boston: 2001.

RF D. N. Rodowick, *Reading the Figural, or, Philosophy after New Media*, Duke University Press, Durham: 2001.

W Vilém Flusser, *Writings,* University of Minnesota Press, Minneapolis: 2004.

Animation as Baroque: Fleischer Morphs Harlem; Tangos to Crocodiles

Norman M. Klein

The Place of Animation in Special Effects

Animation was very much a Baroque form of narrative, highly evolved by the mid-seventeenth century. Steadily, as cinema took charge of visual culture after 1895, it lost its earlier links to theatre and scripted spaces and became associated mostly (and then entirely) with the flat screen. But that was only temporary. After 1955, with Disneyland, animation returned to its roots, as an architectural, sculptural, and graphic narrative.

Today, a much-expanded animation is arguably the primary story grammar for the Electronic Baroque era. Smart bombs are essentially monitored through animation. The desktop on your computer screen is animated. Computer games are animated. The broad principle of user-friendly software is animation—to bring algorithms to life, to anthropomorphize data. We imagine that we have more control because the icons seem to notice us; but with each user-friendly step, we move farther from programming itself.

In much the same way, special-effects cinema is the "uneasy alliance" of animation with industrial melodrama,[1] because animation evolved earlier than 1820, when melodrama essentially was formed. Thus, animation is not a dramatic art, not in our usual sense of the word. It is an "elemental" mode of story, closer to folklore, fairy tales, epic sagas, to its seventeenth-centu-

still: J. Stuart Blackton's *Humorous Phases of Funny Faces* (1906) ry roots (if not older).

Most of all, animation is the story of warring media—where one medium traps another inside it. Puppet shows and *commedia dell'arte* are caught in mid-motion inside a drawing. Sculpture is jump-started to life as theatre. The precise distance from a Bernini sculpture when the flesh turns back to stone is animation. This makes for narrative about uneasy alliances, very much a Baroque sense of story.

As a special effect, animation is a sensory echo—the instant when still images can be sensed. It is momentary, a brilliant pause inside moving pictures. You suddenly notice the strings of the marionette. The drawing climbs briefly out of the movie. Isolated still frames break through the stream inside the projector.

In my book *Seven Minutes*, I review aspects of how animation has expanded since 1928: how it continued to rely on links to music hall and vaudeville, to nineteenth-century illustrated books, to the comics. In other essays, I notice animation expanding into TV viewing, TV commercials, MTV editing back in the eighties. Very early, in Oskar Fischinger's movie commercials (masterpieces from 1929 to the fifties), animation became a primary form of selling a product. It was always interactive marketing, the art of direct address, of making your pitch cleverly. During World War II, SNAFU cartoons and Disney training films showed millions of soldiers how to protect their weapons, avoid malaria and syphilis, watch out for spies. Animation is instructional madness made coherent—controlled anarchy. It maps the unfindable as direct address, very useful for special-effects propaganda, or as spoofs of propaganda; a strangely intimate, non-threatening way to visualize fear (as in animated movies about the risk of crash landing for passengers while they fly on airplanes). It is a carnival about dying, and coming back to life.

Animation never required a fourth wall, not in 1650, and not in 1950. Its proscenium was supposed to look fluid, to allow the viewer into the story; or for characters to escape into the theatre. It was the art of turning Baroque *trompe l'oeil* or anamorphosis into moving images. Animation evolved in an era when the actor often talked back to the viewer. No wonder then that animation was already "virtual" in Ernie Kovacs' TV gags in 1955.

In all its variations, over four centuries (and even further back), one special effect always returned: animation is a string of instants when you sense that this could not be real. It builds stories from moments when both illusion and the "real" are trapped inside the same gesture—or the same gag.

By revealing the illusion in "real" action, animation tells a story about production itself, about the making of; but at the same time, the plot keeps rattling along. As a result, animation often loses character to make a point (an effect). It is consistently less character driven, in order to make the entire screen much more legible: to slip anti-logical fragments in the corners, the background, to reveal the hands of the puppeteer.

These intrusions allow for critiques about the "real." These critiques can be extended to social relationships, to politics, to phenomena. That inspires storytelling where the animated screen is much more exhaustive than in live action, more like multitasking than linear. But it is linear in its way—or multi-linear, many lines competing at once, a flurry of lines.

In the Hollywood film industry, character animation has been shoehorned into movie melodrama all too often. Hollywood animators are trained to think of dramatic character first and foremost, a kind of slapstick melodrama. That is how a feature cartoon must be made, apparently. And I can see the point in one respect: Traces of movie melodrama should be trapped inside the animated dinosaur. But ultimately, the audience comes to see the dinosaur as epic, elemental parody—the battle between industrial myths of free will and epic nonsense. They come to see the uneasy alliance between special effects and drama.

Animation is balletic incoherence suddenly given form and drive, clearly an anamorphic form (from chaos to revelation). The multimedia object flashes to life, very much like *trompe l'oeil*. The tricks with the audience allow for immersive special effects, similar to Baroque sculptural and architectural tricks. It is literally stop-motion, the contradiction between sculpture and "life" brought to a heart-stopping, momentary irony.

Metamorphosis

1900: A chalk line transforms into a man's whiskered face. A hand reaches across the drawing, then erases and redraws the face, aging it, changing its sex, its race. Caricatures of blacks, of Jews, of women's naked thighs appear and dissolve, what was called "lightning hand" at the turn of the twentieth century.[2] In 1907, Stuart Blackton filmed his lightning hand sketches,[3] as did Winsor McCay four years later.[4] The memory of lightning hand reappears in Otto Messmer's *Felix the Cat* cartoons of the twenties. Even as late as the forties, Ward Kimball and other Disney animators performed lightning hand as a racy burlesque for soldiers, where the line drawing turns into a naked woman.[5]

Along with chalk[6]—or ink—any number of substances have been used to indicate the human hand tangibly interfering, leaving textures askew: finger paint on glass; shifting sand; or simply programmers using algorithms to make shapes shimmer without mass. But the effect is essentially the same, in hundreds of animated shorts. The eye senses—almost sees—one substance transmuting into another. It goes from line to protoplasm and back again. And during this transformation, time transforms as well.

While this transforming goes on, another species of special effect makes the look even stranger. Gravity itself seems to disappear. Laws of what goes up cease. An uncanny anti-logic assumes control. Objects lose substance: They become mercurial. Flesh, or metal, flows like water, as in the early "morphing" effect initiated with *Willow*, *The Abyss*,[7] and made standard after *Terminator 2*.

Cartoon metamorphosis may seem to be lost inside an architecture of disunities. However, metamorphosis is far more lyrical than a pyramid of gags. It is the animation walk cycle interrupted, spliced. It is a pause, an Artifice, a mode of *trompe l'oeil* as cinema. In the midst of a walk cycle, a creature changes species. Its body and proportions become exaggerated, with "extremes" on either end. But the frames inside, called "in-betweens," stabilize the action, make the switch more convincing; and also balletic, rhythmic.

Let us say it takes twenty frames to manage this, twenty painted cels. In a midpoint inside this cycle, between the extremes, there is a lapse or hesitation. The picture is suddenly not very readable. For a few frames, the object—the body in this case—does not look like what it was, nor what it will be. This pause is a mode of Artifice, similar to Perspective Awry in the Baroque, a glitch that reveals the apparatus of filmmaking. It is a reveal.

The audience may catch a glimpse of the hand at work—not the hand itself, but the traces it leaves on paper. These traces become an alternative plot point, like noticing the string of a marionette, as part of the story. In Modernist terms, that glimpse is a self-reflexive device. In terms of the Baroque and special effects, it highlights the craft of the animator. Oskar Fischinger's abstract films are essentially reveals as sensory rhythm. But Fischinger's animation, unlike live-action cinema, a stream of reveals—hesitations set to music—can be extended almost indefinitely.

Like anamorphosis or *trompe l'oeil*, they move in a very brief sequence. The reveals move in hyper-extended cycles, literally running into each other. The cycles add up to a narrative of sorts, a visual fable about colliding atmospheres (the god descending to earth; the storm raining indoors). They are condensed magic realism, snippets from Gogol's tales, Kafka's *The Metamorphosis*, or Bruno Schulz's *The Street of Crocodiles*; and of course, the Quays' sumptuous adaptation of Schulz's novel, filled with hesitations as colliding atmosphere. Real meat from the butcher is handled by puppets (an old Švankmajer trick). Screws and dust in the workshop turn in reverse, as if time were going backward. All the automata coexist as a single organism struggling with paramnesia. They perform rituals without purpose, pray at the wailing autopsy wall, pretend to be shop girls, have sexual foreplay with string and grinning manikins and kidneys from the butcher. They play house with an old lightbulb.

In other words, not only does the body morph, but the air itself does as well. It brings us back to the Baroque automaton: A puppet learns to breathe without string, through cams and levers inside its body. Gradually, its gestures evolve, as if lungs were growing. Visually speaking at least, two atmospheres collide; they swarm into each other, like oil through water. The creature seems to breathe our air and another air at the same time.

Composited Space

How does the animator turn this kind of atmospheric palimpsest into story? In simplest terms, the background morphs; it is yet another form of compositing. Imagine Cyrano hopping from the earth's atmosphere to the moon, merely by skipping past a broken yellow line. Depth and mass change hands, as if the background were alive.

How does this tension add up to morphing as story—about the composited space? For clues, we ought to review how animation is drawn. To add life to a drawing, the identity of line should be unstable, to imply movement, breathing. Otherwise, on film, it may coarsen until it becomes bland or unreadable. But it must be firm. Drawing soft outlines around the body may not help, because too often they turn into unlikely shadows on film. Therefore, in life drawing classes, animators are trained to "forget" simple body proportions. Instead, they study "implied mass," lines that show the weight shifting from one leg to another. The model's hip is distorted as he strains to hold pose. That may be distressed even more; the outstretched arm is lengthened. These exaggerated torsos might look very sensual, or merely suggest physical discomfort, the presence of time and gravity. But on film, the results will look fiercely energetic, particularly if clever gaps are slipped into the cycle—as in extremes or hesitations.

Then there is the power of erasure, yet another tool vital to special effects on film, before the drawing is "cleaned up." We look at an animator's sketch pad. To capture implied mass, there is a blizzard of lines. From these, the most "active" (distressed) will be selected. The rest will be erased. The result should leave negative space or mass, which amounts to yet another hesitation, but this version is not chaotic (frozen, entropic, amnesiacal); it suggests controlled stability—no waste. And it implies mystery as well: a phantom presence, as if a hundred pounds were hidden in the dust and scribble.

The drawing becomes allegorical in Walter Benjamin's sense of allegory —a ruin. It is a dialectical emblem, where all that appears natural is simultaneously Artifice. The obvious comparison would be animated bodies that morph, particularly in the X-Men franchise, another Baroque Marvel comic book on film. While the mutants go into morph, their bodies become "events." One persona "shrivels up," but leaves an absence (the person they were). Inside this trace, "craftsmanship" is revealed, "like the masonry in a building whose rendering has broken away."[8]

But animation is shapeshifting not only of the body, but of the space as well; as if body and space were scripted and breathing together. They are a multiple, from colliding atmospheres to dissolving ink-phantom limbs. We imagine the shadow where a picture frame once hung, then sense that the shadow (like *trompe l'oeil*) is actually the leg of a large organism; and suddenly twitches slightly.

All these fragments—bodies, air, background—make a coherent story together, a condensed "epic" about decay or loss; in other words, the loss of control, the loss of the past, the loss of representation. It is a composite in decay, shapeshifting across dimensions, many substances into each other. The morph is solid and absent at the same time. It is like a scar that narrates, a braille of absences. The viewer can practically run a finger across the ridge of a hesitation, very haptic, a touch of all-at-once. The drawings leave an elegant wound as they dissolve to make way for motion.[9]

The morph is also a history of production itself, like many special-effects films: a history of the drawing in decay or erasure; or even of the team who made the effects. In thirties animation, the original drawing was cleaned up, then traced by inkers on to another medium: inked and painted on a cel. In the nineties, it is scanned digitally, then paint-boxed, a morph of production itself, with far fewer strings, often fewer hesitations.

Also, the morph should suggest an uneasy alliance inside the character's body and inside the atmospheres at the same time. Like Dr. Jekyll nervously grabbing his throat, both the space and the body should look as if they might revert back, as if the air is dangerous. The morph is supposed to look unstable, in hesitation, on a journey into antimatter, where many atmospheres meet. *Metamorphosis* then is a story about hesitation and reveals.

We worry when the hidden will surface: the entropy, the molting, melting.

Disney Versus Fleischer On Metamorphosis

This haunted and self-reflexive use of hesitation was not universally admired. Disney, for example, distrusted metamorphosis if it made the animator's drawing too obvious. A revealed scribble weakened the impact of full animation. In the words of Thomas and Johnston, who have become the Boswells of Disney production methods, "When the animator distorts the figure, he must always come back to the original shape."[10] Donald or Goofy can be made to bulge and implode, but never lose their "personality,"[11] never turn into other things in the way Warner's characters did. In thirties and forties cartoons, for example, there are no Disney gags where characters who slam into a wall turn into metal coins, and twirl noisily as they land. That trick, so easily laden with frames that hesitate, was reserved for Tom and Jerry cartoons at MGM.

According to the Disney rule, once a character's body was shown—rubbery, watery, human-like—that substance was irreducible (no hesitation or

still: Walt Disney's *The Band Concert* (1935)

lapse). Walt was convinced that revealing the drawing behind the flesh could wreck the atmospheric effects that he prized so highly. He preferred wind, water, or heat to test the character's endurance. Disney nature made war with the character's body. In *The Band Concert* (1935), Mickey stays intact (no metamorphosis of any kind)—and on the beat—while conducting an orchestra thrown asunder by a tornado. His dogged refusal to morph was the central gag to the cartoon.

Pluto was perhaps the only Disney character allowed to show his scribbles—to have "lapses." For example, in a cycle drawn for the cartoon *Alpine Climbers* (1936),[12] Pluto's body literally takes wing. Lines snarl up until he looks like a bird in a blender, becomes a hesitation. His body appears to dissolve; that is, we see it lost for two drawings out of sixteen. However, in their analysis of this drawn cycle, Thomas and Johnston advise us to turn away from "lapses": "Never lose the personality of the character in either a long shot or a wild action."[13] Other hesitations and lapses were treated in much the same way. At Disney, animators were told to avoid speed lines and rubber-band effects common to thirties cartoons and used frequently by the Fleischers, Tex Avery, Bob Clampett. Disney was emphatic: clean up by shading; keep volumes constant.

Not that Disney hated to see cartoon characters show off their plasticity; quite the contrary. But the stretch and squash that he thought pleased the audience would make "lapses" impossible. For example, characters were supposed to trip broadly, but slowly and gracefully. Goofy in particular often loses his balance so slowly that he seems to be moving in a tai chi exercise. He surfs empty space while he plunges two hundred feet. No matter how awkward the stretch, his body mass remains amazingly constant. His legs knot up like a fishing line, but never lose their mass—never a loose line to remind us of a flat drawing.[14]

For the early sound era, Disney's rival for cartoon special effects was clearly the Fleischer Studios. By contrast, the Fleischer Studios in the early thirties (1931-1933) specialized in metamorphosis, with a simultaneity of effects that is still extraordinary to catalogue; certainly by Disney standards, this seemed to wipe out the coherence of "story." Unlike Disney, the Fleischer animators liked to emphasize "traced memories" when they copied from live movement through rotoscoping (tracing live action into animation frame by frame). They also used allusion in a more self-reflexive way than at Disney—in other words, sight gags about other media than animation; for example, details drawn from vaudeville theatres and Coney Island rides the Fleischers knew. Or even traced memories of New York streets: kosher butchering in a bullfight scene; the Manhattan subway down a rabbit hole.

I suppose much of the difference came out of the Fleischers' love of industrial special effects. The tricks that for Disney revealed "illusion of life" (a caricatural naturalism) for the Fleischers were scientific marvels on display. That meant less commitment to hiding how animation was done.

For example, both studios tried 3-D systems. In the Fleischer version, tabletop models were composited in front of the camera. Miniatures of caves or streets are visually unmistakable; they are much rounder than the cels shot in the foreground. What Fleischer called "3-D" looks much more constructivist than Disney's system a few years later. Disney believed that multiplane should enhance the naturalism of an atmosphere. In Disney's multiplane camera, the cels were placed in slots inches apart, to make them look like atmospheric cutouts in deep focus—smooth from front to back. But in Fleischer (until they tried to copy the Disney look in the late thirties), the solidity of the miniatures is plain to see; it softens the 3-D background severely, leaving the flat drawings—in front of the glass—very crisp and ripe.[15]

Betty Boop Goes To Harlem, By Way of Coney Island

Betty Boop's Snow White [1933] is undoubtedly Fleischer's masterpiece as "lapse," particularly its final sequence in an underworld—both an Orphean journey (i.e., the myth of Orpheus), and an Orphic journey (a silly dance of death set to music). Inside this underworld, "hesitations" govern movement and motivation. For example, the evil queen turns Koko the Clown into a shapeshifting ghost, while her mirror keeps sprouting hands; and a black-face tells her who is fairest of them all. At the same time, Koko as ghost is rotoscoped from a clip of Cab Calloway.

Koko (a leftover from silent animation) was usually the character assigned to such roles. Of all the Fleischer characters, he was rotoscoped the most often. By 1933, that gave him a phantom presence, too often invaded. Graphically, rotoscoping leaves scars—something a bit too human, a bit too lithe, subtle but plain to see. Koko practically inhabited two bodies at once, from a cartoon clown who shuffled (buttery head, sack-like body) to a leaner man who ran gracefully (more angles to his chin; a stiffer spinal column). He was designed to be haunted, wrapped in billowy cloth that was ideal for ghost dancing between bodies, particularly in this, his last extended appearance, his swan song.

Koko sings "St. James Infirmary," while turning into a twenty-dollar gold piece, then into a "shot of that booze."[16] At the same time, to illustrate the line "crap-shootin' pallbearers," the wall behind him is lined with murals of skulls and cows together, gambling. That bears scrutiny, usually requires a few viewings: It is intentionally traced like the wall of a Coney Island Mystery Cave Ride. It is also traced out of a collective imaginary (at least the collective of animators). The skulls of African Americans reenact the greasy underworld of back alley and saloon life in Harlem. But not Harlem as blacks knew it—this is Harlem as the white male Fleischer animators saw it. The skulls resemble the racist extremes in Currier and Ives prints, with Jim Crow white-on-black pickaninny scowls, and the ooga-booga lips common to American cartoons until the late forties.

Trace Memories

The scene is rich enough in allusions to New York—as the animators lived it—to suggest a Trace Memory, like a foldout postcard filled with racy sketches of scenes in the city, a composite of weekend leisure for the boys at the Fleischer Studios. It is their boozy Manhattan caricatured in some detail, as an inside joke. (On Fridays, the animators used to visit hot spots together, particularly Earl Carroll's Vanities, the Ziegfeld Follies, wrestling, and hoochie-koochie dance clubs—and of course the Cotton Club).

Even details on Betty's body were a traced composite—a traced memory of women they saw along the way. Her garter was like those favoured by hoochie-koochie dancers so popular at burlesque and dance parlors.[17] She slouched her back like a flapper at a speakeasy. Her banjo eyes and her bounce were copied from the moves of vaudeville singer Helen Kane. Her head bobbled like a Coney Island Kewpie doll, shaking on a spring.

The "dramatic" plot, such as it is—more a scripted space than a plot—turns a Mystery Cave ride into a blend of Coney Island and Manhattan. It proceeds like a taxi tour, a few drinks at each stop. First, Betty enters during an opening Ziegfeld chorus number, until the queen orders "off with her head" (another hesitation—her thumb and forefinger turn into a guillotine). Then, while tied to a tree, Betty torch sings "Always in the Way," as if she were in a vaudeville "mellerdrammer." But very quickly, she breaks free. Then, while walking downhill, she trips absentmindedly, rolls into a snowball, and slides into an icy lake. While frozen she keeps sliding, passes through the Seven Dwarves' cottage, and into a Coney Island ride. Or should I say an amusement-park underworld/morphworld, even with a potted plant on her coffin, to remind us again of New York apartments, where windowsills were decorated with flower pots.

Meanwhile, the queen is lapsing her way to the cave. She runs the mirror as a hoop over her body, transforms into a hag witch, then forces Koko to shapeshift and freezes Bimbo the Dog. But even this witchcraft fails to kill Betty. In frustration, she turns into a cakewalking, rather cute dragon, with ducks on her head who honk like bird whistles for geese hunting.

The peculiar heat from her morphing into a dragon also melts the underworld, releasing Betty and her friends, as if they were mammoths thawed from the ice. A musical chase ensues, climaxing with hesitations as spectacular as any the studio produced. Bimbo grabs the dragon/witch by the head, and turns her inside out. Her skeleton is visible in black, as if she were wearing tights painted to look like a skeleton for the scary finale onstage. It is easy to run this skeleton gag frame-by-frame on video: her dragon body melts, then seems to run off by itself—lapses bringing hesitation—while the skeleton makes a three-quarter turn. The way she turns resembles gimmicks in theatres—musical finales on a revolving stage.

That finishes off the queen. With a last downbeat, Betty, Koko, and Bimbo flee the cave, and do a May Dance. The lapsed underworld is gone, but the characters show no sign of wear, give no sense that this was any more than a theatrical journey, despite all its allegorical layers—which brings me to broader questions.

The throughline, such as it is, has to be called metamorphic. After all, Betty/Koko's journey is crammed with versions of shapeshifting, body to ghost; frozen death to life, flesh inside out, a world outside caving in. The morph is theatrical; it is Baroque theatrical machines updated, eroded, lingering on the New York vaudeville stage. And it is the moment of wonder surely, as masque. Like many masques circa 1620, that moment fits into a very thin musical sketch, a dance, not much more than a silly allegory; but filled with morbidity and Grand Guignol.

The morph fleshes out the absence of dramatic plot in this cartoon. Instead, the story takes us on a vaudeville tour through the underworld of New York entertainment: cardsharking; running craps on the street; speakeasies in backdoors; boating rides under the sign of death in Coney Island. The "tour" is about uncertainty—modernity and the Depression as the Fleischer team witnessed it. Indeed, from 1931 to 1933, Fleischer cartoons have a peculiar bite to them.

Bimbo's Initiation (1931) is an early example. Bimbo, as if trapped in immigrant panic, is forced to spin into a labyrinth of imprisoning rooms. Some rooms sprout knives that try to stab him; others grow mouths that gulp him; or erase gravity, and force him to crawl across the ceiling. (The comparison with Kafka's Gregor Samsa seems unavoidable, although the Fleischers knew little of European Modernist literature, or Surrealist theatre, film; theirs was a homegrown pathology of urban life.) Bimbo keeps refusing to be a "member" of what seems like a strange Bundist or Masonic order in caricature—hooded men with spent candles on their heads, as if this were the world where dead candles wind up, the coolness after the night-light goes out. (Also, this era witnessed a huge revival of the Ku Klux Klan, even as far north as Maine, particularly from 1922 to 1926, but a symptom of problems in many cities.)[18]

Finally, one of the leaders pulls off his hood, and turns out to be a lady poodle, the sexiest poodle Bimbo had ever seen, "a pip" he calls her. She does a bumptious bump and grind for him. He grins as if he were being tickled from the inside out, lasciviously; his eyes follow her: She is an earlier version of Betty Boop. Then, every one of the hooded KKK Bundists takes off her hood. They're all copies of this voluptuous Betty Boop. Bimbo slaps her ass; she slaps his—a raunchy version of the dance black bottom.[19] Then a gleeful layercake chorus-line finale ends the short in the way most of the Fleischer cartoons of that era ended, like a Victor recording that runs out of threads and simply stops, on a final trumpet or downbeat.

Morbid Parodies of Industrial Special Effects

This is a dark piece of work for kiddies to watch, even for adults. And there were others almost as dark from Fleischer in the twenties, even before the Depression. In two of the most remembered: the world explodes and New York goes cockeyed in *Koko's Earth Control* (1928); and Max gets multiplied industrially and attacks Koko in *Cartoon Factory* (1925). So their apocalyptic cartoons can be periodized, from grim machines to grimmer machines. By the mid-thirties, under the censorship during the Shirley Temple era, their macabre twists continue, but are more about repression, more about guilt than dancing on your grave.

Two cartoons in particular from 1936, *Cobweb Hotel* and *Small Fry*, have since become cult favorites in Weird Cartoon collections. They each are built around nightmare chases like the Boop cartoons—many metamorphic scenes, but here instead of bouncy dance numbers, we see flies tortured, or baby fish forced to swim through inky inversions, as if they were inside a Baroque theatre filled with watery nightmares. While Fleischer employs fewer morphing gags as the thirties goes on, tries to make cartoons that resemble Disney full animation much more, something of the allegory of underworld remains.

I have always assumed that the Fleischers' insistent diablerie came out of the immigrant world they knew from Bedford-Stuyvesant, Brooklyn, as children. They understood the xenophobia of a Jewish neighborhood, living as part of the largest influx of foreign immigrants to hit any American city at that time. In New York, as in Los Angeles today, up to twenty-five percent of the total population were foreign born. This, in itself, is metamorphosis—ethnic cultures caught between, in hesitative shock, in lapse.

This agonizing unease was heightened by economic disasters like the Great Depression; or by class warfare, the strikes, the street fighting. These were localized by the Fleischers, into the look and feel of streets on the way to work, the muddle of urban legends, about gangsters, cops, anti-Semitism, racism, even the rumble of the elevated train; childhood friends caught by the Depression; the taste and service of the food.

Consider how animators draw caricatures of this anxiety. They give a cartoon body more reptilian "attitudes." They exaggerate how heavy (and repressed) or light and sexual cartoon clothing can be. A man or a woman use their arms openly or defensively as they walk through a New York street. The subtleties of an urban case of nerves have their own visual tropes, a rhythm in the shoulders, in the posture, in walk cycles; angling the neck just a fraction to watch out for who may be behind you; staying toward the outside of the sidewalk. It is not really a fear of crime so much as a fear of the mixing of classes and races. It is a comfort zone built out of a mood of uncertainty.

This streetwise anxiety is very evident in the mordant edge of Fleischer cartoons; and it is apparent in a different sense today. I am reminded of the cultural aftershocks in L.A. from 1992 through 1994 (looting, fires, earthquakes, massive recession). And I wonder how Homeland Rule and the War in Iraq, and Bushismo in the cities will show up in the gestures of characters in special effects films to come. In 2003, surveillance is fundamental to the American way of life, and even American entertainment. How indeed today are the shoulders and arms of characters revealing anxieties; how are streets patrolled, how do people shop at night, how does the politics of class and race erase the daily routine? The sheer banality of controlling one's fear is the world drawn by "hesitations."

Imagine how someone tiptoes briskly from their car after parking at night in an empty lot. The walk is usually not an expression of "fear," merely how one moves to establish a comfort zone, when the space feels "lapsed." Then imagine how the movie industry turns these anxious (lapsed) zones into cash, into scripts where computer-graphic monsters, as evil immigrants, destroy middle-class real estate. In the nineties, f/x blockbusters like *Independence Day* were part of a bumper crop of disaster films inspired by the shocks of 1992-1994.[20] Like Fleischer cartoons, they are fables about lapse and hesitation, allegories about powerlessness, about alien presence, about underworlds where the animator builds social imaginaries about collective anxiety

The motivation can be a bit laughable, I admit. Imagine power brokers in the film industry (1993-1994) watching houses burn in Malibu; or their pool spilling over while their best china explodes during the earthquake. Then, after the shaking subsides, or the fires are put out, they head for a local watering hole in West Hollywood perhaps, and decide to greenlight any film that sounds like a special-effects disaster epic. Somehow, lava feels right, anything that shakes like a vengeful mountain god.

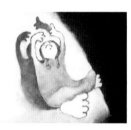

Hesitations: Švankmajer and Leaf

We must do justice to hesitations, as the *trompe l'oeil* of special-effects cinema. For example, Jan Švankmajer's *Dimensions of Dialogue* (1982) is a Baroque (or Surrealist) encyclopedia of hesitations (after seven years of repression in Czechoslovakia, as a dissident). It begins with an Arcimboldo creature (a homunculus made of fruit) eating a hominid made of industrial parts. Through mad pixillation (a technique for speeding up live action), they chop and dice each other ever finer, until they turn into clay sculpture—which segues into the next scene, where clay lovers start off by making love, merging their bodies into hesitations that orgasm.

Then they take a break, reform into bodies, smile. However, one lapse is left behind. A little blob of clay tries to find a home in their bodies, but they kick it away angrily. Finally, the blob becomes the nuisance that sparks a battle to the death between them. The once loving couple literally gouge their clay bodies into a lumpen gravy.

This brown heap acts as a cross dissolve to the third act: Two beefy clay bureaucrats try to communicate diplomatically. Out of their mouths, instead

stills: Caroline Leaf's *The Street* (1976), courtesy of the National Film Board of Canada of words, they present shoes to be tied, bread to be buttered, toothbrushes to be filled, and a pencil sharpener gripped neatly by a highly salivated tongue. However, very soon, they lose track of which object is which. They start buttering the shoes, pencil sharpening everything. At last, hyperventilated, they collapse into doughy lard cakes, like melted bulldogs.

Švankmajer mixes up his "lapses," from clay to everyday objects; that is, by medium, nimbly leaping from food to thimbles to clay to toothpaste tubes. Each substance becomes a robotic piece in a theatre of war—a hesitation to mark the precise instant when social codes dissolve into mindless traces. Then the insanity escalates into oblivion. The key to his condensed fable is the mix of everyday media (clay, meats), the metal junk weirdly stuck inside the organic, with the melee that follows: Arcimboldo vegetables; the chopper/blender effect; clay diplomats with rhino necks and watery green doll's eyes.

Another film rich in hesitation/lapse is Caroline Leaf's *The Street* (1976), done in finger paint on glass, from a story (by Mordecai Richler) set in the Montréal Jewish ghetto during the 1950s. A small boy waits for his grandmother to die so he can get her room, and not have to share with his sister. But his grandmother stubbornly hangs on for months. Meanwhile, neighbours and relatives make sympathy calls, carrying with them a montage of textures: the dense outlines of buildings; the layers of flesh and clothing in a crowded apartment.

Leaf often uses the hesitation as cross dissolve, from neighbours' bodies to buildings; or as fly-throughs before the age of computer, dissolving paint in the path of children running down the street. The neighborhood is soaked in earthy browns and jaundiced yellows, both nostalgic and suffocating. The boy is trapped inside his vigil, then frightened when his grandmother finally dies. To remind him of his greed, the walls of her room are still textured by her presence. The space is infected by memory, as part of a lingering flashback. Finally, the bodies of mourners swarm into the house on the day of his grandmother's funeral. Their noise transfers for the boy into vaguely competing textures, fingerprints of memory crossing each other, against the sheer angles of the house.

Here too the lapses and hesitations—the tension between the organic and the industrial object—make for a bizarre statement, like the Brundlefly in Cronenberg's remake of *The Fly* (1986). Finally, poor Seth Brundle becomes a brooding mutation of metal and rust, with barely a trace of the human left, or even of the fly. He has been mutated into a hybrid that defies both the industrial and the organic, yet is frighteningly compelling, because we sense all those phantom human and fly limbs: the traces of genetic activity; bits of conscious will diffused into uselessness, limping, groaning, and collapsing of its own weight.

Lapses to hesitation become an allegory about the organic disappearing into the industrial, as in the Quays' masterpiece, *The Street of Crocodiles* (1986). The Quays very consciously employ hesitation. In 1995, they said: "What's good about film is that while you're moving through space, it opens up these little parentheses and the imagination drifts off and is flooded by these contaminations ... we love that vague wandering off."[21]

Similarly, the crawl at the end of the film is a clue. It is excerpted from the novel by Bruno Schulz, *The Street of Crocodiles* (1932)—a source as rich in "hesitations" as the film itself (which is mostly a nocturne based on the book). Schulz sets his narrative, a string of evocative short stories, really, in the province of Galicia, in Poland. It is very much a haunted town, haunted first by the decline of a gold rush years before; and second, for the reader today, by its world later wiped out by Nazis. Anyway, the paragraph that the Quays use appears in the chapter entitled, predictably enough, "The Street of Crocodiles." That then is the allegorical setting for the film: a rotting district so embarrassing to the other townsfolk that its precise location is omitted from the map of the city—only a white blank where it should appear.

According to the novel, even the mapmaker had been afraid to visit the Street of Crocodiles. It bears the scars and magical lapses of neglect: cheap jerry-built houses everywhere, suitable now only for the scum of the city. Even the streetcars are made only of *papier mâché*. But like a magic-realist illusion, the coaches run blindly without drivers. As the final quote in the film explains, their only "concession to modernity" are montages cut from yellowing old newspapers.[22]

Not that the city at large is that much better; it feels rather gray and dreary. And thus begin the special effects in the story, about vegetation and the inorganic in revolt: To resist urban sadness, the narrator's quirky father tries to flirt with young women who work at the tailor shop. He then declares himself their "heresiarch," lectures passionately on the biological oddities of the city, particularly the supernatural plant life. One alien species grows in thick colloids that can be preserved with kitchen salt. But that does not preserve their cell structure. So instead, the slime imitates the nuclei of whatever lies nearby.

The streets become infected, a perfect host for a very exuberant mildew that can turn a room into hothouse. In some rooms, an even stranger mulch attacks furniture, until table legs start to grow like trees. The branches climb the walls, and strain against the limbs of the house. The groans of lumber suggest a building about to have a heart attack. Therefore, the furniture itself is victimized by modernity. The joists are crippled like beggars' children.

Brute matter comes to life, and starts to morph into pieces of flesh. But rather than an allegory about animism, it is more about morphing atmospheres and hesitation. All living things languish somewhere between discovery and annihilation, fail to connect.

Schulz's technique is similar to Vertov's theory of intervals. More to the point, it resembles Deleuze's description of René Clair's use of Vertov, for the film *Crazy Ray*:

> The desert town, the town absent from itself, will always haunt the cinema, as though possessing a secret. The secret is yet another meaning of the notion of interval: it now designates the point at which movement stops and, in stopping, gains the power to go into reverse, accelerate, slow down.[23]

For the Quays, these intervals are enacted, rather than acted, by dolls and a puppet. Each acts almost blindly, as if suffering from faded memory. The dolls' heads sew blindly. The puppet[24] shares in their ceremonies. But they all act as if awaiting orders that never arrive. They pause for cues, tilt their heads, then burst into action anyway. Perhaps they are in the shadow of someone else's story, long gone? Their world is out of scale; they are miniaturized inside an unknown maker's creation. The sewing factory has rusted. No humans seem to work there anymore. The cordage machines spin like ancient film projectors. Occasionally, die-hard spectators show up on the corners of the screen (as in all Quay films). But the voyeur seems no more certain of the direction than the others; he too is a puppet—a very important distinction for stop-motion animation. Puppets are another species of "character" than dolls. The puppet's face is weathered, historicized: thoughtful, greedy, scheming. The doll, on the other hand, is merely a remnant of a childhood desire; it is a carrier, much blanker in expression, and clumsier in its expressive movement.

Animated Puppets

The puppet and the doll are very much survivals from Baroque animation. Švankmajer is the son of a puppeteer in Prague. Quite possibly, the Quays knew poet Rilke's essay on dolls. Rilke remembers the scrawny, expressionist wax dolls, made by Lotte Pritzel, from a show in 1913. "The doll was so utterly devoid of imagination that what we imagined for it was inex-

haustible.... The doll was the first to make us aware of that silence larger than life which later breathed on us again and again out of space whenever we came at any point to the border of our existence."[25]

As computer-generated imagery has increased, the fascination for stop-motion puppetry has grown. The poses, the blind movement of stop-motion animation puppets serve as psychological "lapse." In their housing, they are neither present nor absent—as in Starevich's films (1912), which essentially begins the trajectory that lead to the Quays' work. There, each body that is animated leads you closer or farther from memory—from insects to onion skins to Pulcinella dolls. We observe their source, and watch them blindly follow. They occupy two places at once: the production (the hand of the maker) and the space on film, but in Quay, the space seems to refuse to tell the tale. They are stop-motion "parentheses." They are "contaminated" by a lost narrative. Movement proceeds very slowly and precipitately, the way water leaves a leaky jug—but always with hesitation, gravity in pause. As in Švankmajer, the anatomical scenes use cut organs from the butcher, and scenes where heads are transferred from one body to another.

Interiors and Miniature

Most of all, *Street of Crocodiles* is an extraordinarily rich interior allegory.

still: The Brothers Quay's *Street of Crocodiles* (1986), courtesy of Atelier Koninck/Zeitgeist Films

The "lapses" jump from phantom memory to phantom film production, a journey through an underworld inspired by Schulz's Kafkaesque magic realism, by Švankmajer's Surrealist hesitations, by the rusting of industrial sites (from Pennsylvania where the Quays grew up, to London where they work). Finally, the uneasy memory of the lost Jews of Poland seems represented here as well, a diorama "contaminated" by the Holocaust.

And yet the structure of the scenes is astonishingly coherent, always about inversion, entropy, losing memory: the neglected industrial warehouse; the cordage and blinking windows as the movie projecting without memory; the puppet without strings unable to remember; the amnesiacal dolls pretending to act sensually; the autopsy as prayer; sexual foreplay with plaster manikins; screws unscrewing; ice melting; automatons blindly gesturing. From practically every angle—place, character, and plot coexist as lapsed hesitation.

Most surprisingly, this interiorized film (and the Quays' work generally) was embraced in the nineties by the MTV generation. The Quays produced a number of commercials,[26] even some for MTV.[27] A video for the band Tool clearly plagiarized the Quay technique, as homage; the same for a video from Nine Inch Nails. As many student computer animators have told me, they want their digital films to be haunted also.

They want the algorithm to also function as expressionist lapse, as interior journey about being caught between. Thus, stop-motion puppets serve a warning about the disembodied sensibility that the computer represents, and the poetics of loss that it should reveal, but rarely does as yet. We can find a prophetic allegory in hesitations—morphs about bad faith, corporate politics.[28] Dozens of morphing programs are for sale, from about nine hundred dollars to as low as twenty dollars, most of them extensions of "feature based image metamorphosis" software developed in the early nineties.[29] The technique has escaped from its animation ghetto, and now is vital—not only for mainstream narrative cinema but also for banking, architectural planning, engineering, advertising, fax machines, interface design. The name Morph (originally a character on BBC in 1981-1983) has taken on a pioneering meaning, as in *Morph's Outpost on the Digital Frontier* (since 1993), for "business, education and entertainment."[30]

The technology quickly outraced the vocabulary. Nineties morphing already resembled (and operated as) an allegory about accommodation, an attempt to turn our 2-D sense of decay into 3-D global fantasies. Perhaps this was a "natural" evolution: one could argue that computer-graphic morphing was always an epic form of evasion. It was an empty display of worlds in collision, of new species of identity that are perhaps no newer than the assembly line, a few frills added to the workplace. But most of all, morphing suggests that we can author our own modernity, not only survive the shocks easily, but run ahead of them—ultimately a very conservative message.

Like special-effects compositing in other forms, Fleischer's style of morph shows us the city imploding. The pauses mid-morph are cracks in the street, *détournements*,[31] the point where myths of outracing modernity fall apart, and we see the crisis of identity (at work, at home) more clearly. The morph has been something of an antidote. It is a collage where time and space meet entirely. It may be to our computer culture what the dissolve was to film culture—simultaneously a transition and an erasure.

Endnotes

1. See: Robert Lang, *American Film Melodrama: Griffith, Vidor, Minnelli* (Princeton: Princeton University Press, 1989). This is a widely travelled subject, in feminist theory as well. For my summary, see sections on melodrama in *Seven Minutes* (1993).

2. Also called "quick sketches." Film historian Donald Crafton initiated much of the academic study of lightning hand. He expanded his articles on the subject in *Before Mickey: The Animated Film 1898-1928* (Cambridge, Mass.: MIT Press, 1982). The term "lightning drawing" has become fairly standard in critiques of student work at various film schools (at USC and Cal-Arts certainly). In other words, the problems suggested by linear metamorphosis remain fundamental to the field, even today, with the daunting presence of the computer.

3. *Humorous Phases of Funny Faces*, 1906 (Blackton).

4. *Little Nemo*, 1911 (McCay). See: John Canemaker, *Winsor McCay, His Life and Art* (New York: Abbeville Press, 1987), 132. *Little Nemo* was produced by Vitascope, Blackton's company.

5. Interview with Ward Kimball, July 1987.

6. Chalk remains a useful metaphor here, at least as an excuse to play with the poetics of jargon: Chalk can be erased, broken into dust, shaded by hand. It has texture, facture, sound, what can be called "the haptic" (tactile, synaesthetic). The haptic is essential for the animated line, for all special effects, in one of two categories: either it looks anabolic (turning food into tissue) or metasomatic (rocks changing substance). The hesitation/lapse should emphasize one of those two as well, to reveal the mode of production (the animator at work), more than the story. For example, chalk is metasomatic, but primordial ooze is anabolic (micro-organisms in mud). The metallic liquid man in *Terminator 2* remains fiercely metasomatic. The Brundlefly in *The Fly* is hopelessly divided, both anabolic and metasomatic.

7. Apparently Lucas's *Willow* may have been the first Hollywood big-budget feature to employ computerized morphing.

8. Walter Benjamin, *The Origins of German Tragic Drama*, tr. J. Osborne (London: New Left Books, 1977; orig., 1963), 178-179. These are the classic pages, so often cited, discussed in detail by Susan Buck-Morss, by art critics Benjamin Buchloh and Craig Owens.

9. This is similar to what I call "distraction" in *The History of Forgetting* (London: Verso, 1997).

10. Frank Thomas and Ollie Johnson, *Disney Animation: The Illusion of Life* (New York: Abbeville Press), 138.

11. Personality was a very specific term for Walt Disney, as discussed in Thomas and Johnson's *Disney Animation: The Illusion of Life*, and in numerous documents from the thirties. Personality was the point where a character went through a cartoon conflict, reflected in the graphic design, rhythm, colours; also personality was laid out by the story department: certain constants on how this personality responded to being stuck to flypaper, for example (dumb, self-willed, quick to anger, slow to anger, cheerful, paranoid).

But personality also had a second meaning during the thirties (and since, on TV for example, often called a "personality" medium). This was less discussed at Disney, it was simply understood that Mickey or Donald were as familiar as star personalities of the studio era (Gable, Garbo, Laurel and Hardy). A personality always lived outside the narrative diachrony, even while the movie continued. He or she was a living myth, and the details of the myth were written into the story. Thus, star vehicles, in many ways, were a variation of film drama, with distancing devices based on glamour. Disney understood that problem as perfectly as any mogul of his day or our day. He knew that this was his ticket to independence, by licensing his personalities, and keeping them cute enough.

12. Ibid., 148-149.

13. Frank Thomas and Ollie Johnson, *Disney Animation: The Illusion of Life*, 149.

14. See *Moving Day* (1936), *Clock Cleaners* (1937), among the best of Art Babbitt's renditions of Goofy. And then the *Sport Goofy* series directed by Jack Hanna in the forties and fifties.

15. The most widely noticed examples are in *Popeye the Sailor Meets Sinbad the Sailor* (1936), or *Sinbad the Sailor* (1939), because they are in the public domain, and in many video stores, and in colour, which enhances the irony. Many other shorts by Fleischer in the thirties used tabletop miniatures ("3-D Process"), including a Boop in colour, and the two features (*Gulliver's Travels* and *Mr. Bug Goes to Town*). In all of these, the 3-D is only in a few scenes. Generally, fans remember the 3-D Popeyes most of all.

16. Anti-morphs from this sequence were isolated in *Seven Minutes* (London: Verso, 1993), for example, 79, 93.

17. Hoochie-koochie: a pseudo-Egyptian belly dance that was popular at burlesques and "hoochie-koochie" parlors.

18. See Kenneth T Jackson, *The Ku Klux Klan in the City, 1915-1930* (New York: Oxford University Press, 1967).

19. The dog and mouse characters of that era, including Freleng's *Bosko* for Warner's, the early Mickey Mouse of course, as well as Fleischer's *Bimbo*, often show traits that suggest black men. These mannerisms are mixed, of course, with those of white males (the voice, the plots). It is another peculiar coding of black to white, here as a trope where domestic animals mutate almost into humans, but never entirely. It also identifies the deep presence of black dance, music, and theatre in the sources for these cartoons.

20. See Norman Klein, *The History of Forgetting* (chapters on film locations, on the shock waves after 1992, on cinematic responses in police films, on special-effects disaster films, on films reenacting the Rodney King beating).

21. Carolyn Steel, "Space that Breathes," *Blueprint*, Oct. 1995, 42.

22. Bruno Schulz, *The Street of Crocodiles*, tr. C. Wieniewska (New York: Viking Penguin, 1977; orig. 1934). The Quays used a different translation, clearly, since the quote at the end of the film does not match the same passage here, on 110.

23. Gilles Deleuze, *Cinema 1: The Movement-Image*, tr. H. Tomlinson and B. Habberjam (Minneapolis: University of Minnesota Press, 1986; orig. 1983), 83.

24. The puppet's head in *Street of Crocodiles* is often compared to the face of the great installation artist Joseph Cornell, clearly a resemblance.

25. Rainer Maria Rilke, "Dolls: On the Wax Dolls of Lotte Pritzel," in *Essays on Dolls* (London: Penguin Books, 1994), 32-33.

26. Among the Quays' commercials: Honeywell Computers, Skip's Crisps, ICI Woodcare, BBC2, Coca-Cola, Slurpee, Partnership for a Drug Free America, MTV, Nikon.

27. Among music videos by the Quays: His Name Is Alive, Michael Penn, Peter Gabriel (contributed to "Sledgehammer").

28. I decided not to summarize what this warning is, clearly about identity dissolving, the usual debates about public and private space (architectural theory), about the posthuman body (e.g., the writing of Kathryn Hayles, Susan Straight, Donna Haraway).

29. The key essay appears to be: Thaddeus Beier and Shawn Neely, "Feature-Based Image Metamorphosis," *Computer Graphics*, vol. 26, no. 2 (July, 1992), 35-42. In 1992 Siggraph helped to popularize morphing, as it did in 1995.

30. *Morph's Outpost on the Digital Frontier* was a monthly magazine in the nineties. (*Daily Spectrum*, Sept. 11, 1995); (*Wired*, Sept. / Oct., 1993), with contributors from *Multimedia and Videodisk Monitor*; *Envisioneering; Macromedia User Journal*; the firm Gistics. Its founders Craig LaGrow and Doug Millison sponsored a cartoon character named Morph, "the silicon surfing Sherpa," with a touch of nineties graffiti art.

31. *Détournement*: the fissure or suture, the hidden layer behind the surface—a term developed by Situationists in the fifties, to advise walkers through the city how to use their vision more surgically, more radically. [Here, Klein may actually be referring to the concept of the *dérive*. Eds.]

Compositing: From Image Streams to Modular Media

Lev Manovich

The movie *Wag the Dog* (Barry Levinson, 1997) contains a scene in which a Washington spin doctor and a Hollywood producer are editing fake news footage designed to win public support for a nonexistent war. The footage shows a girl, a cat in her arms, running through a destroyed village. If a few decades earlier creating such a shot would have required staging and then filming the whole thing on location, computer tools make it possible today to create it in real time. Now the only live element is the girl, played by a professional actress. The actress is videotaped against a blue screen. The other two elements in the shot, the destroyed village and the cat, come from a database of stock footage. Scanning through the database, the producers try different versions of these elements; a computer updates the composite scene in real time.

The logic of this shot is typical of the new media production process, regardless of whether the object under construction is a video or film shot, as in *Wag the Dog*; a 2-D still image; a sound track; a 3-D virtual environment; a computer game scene; or a soundtrack. In the course of production, some elements are created specifically for the project; others are selected from databases of stock material. Once all the elements are ready, they are composited together into a single object; that is, they are fitted together and adjusted in such a way that their separate identities become invisible. The fact that they come from diverse sources and were created by different people at different times is hidden. The result is a single seamless image, sound, space, or scene.

As used in the field of new media, the term "digital compositing" has a particular and well-defined meaning. It refers to the process of combining a number of moving image sequences, and possibly stills, into a single sequence with the help of special compositing software such as After Effects (Adobe), Compositor (Alias|Wavefront), or Cineon (Kodak). Compositing was formally defined in a paper published in 1984 by two scientists working for Lucasfilm, who make a significant analogy between compositing and computer programming:

> Experience has taught us to break down large bodies of source code into separate modules in order to save compilation time. An error in one routine forces only the recompilation of its module and the relatively quick reloading of the entire program. Similarly, small errors in colouration or design in one object should not force "recompilation" of the entire image.
>
> Separating the image into elements that can be independently rendered saves enormous time. Each element has an associated matte, coverage information that designates the shape of the element. The compositing of those elements makes use of the mattes to accumulate the final image.[1]

Most often, the composited sequence simulates a traditional film shot; that is, it looks like something that took place in real physical space and was filmed by a real film camera. To achieve this effect, all elements comprising the finished composite—for example, footage shot on location, referred to in the industry as a "live plate"; footage of actors shot in front of a blue screen; and 3-D computer-generated elements—are aligned in perspective, and modified so that they have the same contrast and colour saturation. To simulate depth of field, some elements are blurred while others are sharpened. Once all elements are assembled, a virtual-camera move through the simulated space may be added to increase its "reality effect." Finally, artifacts such as film grain or video noise can be added. In summary, digital compositing can be broken down into three conceptual steps:

1. Construction of a seamless 3-D virtual space from different elements.
2. Simulation of a camera move through this space (optional).
3. Simulation of the artifacts of a particular medium (optional).

If 3-D computer animation is used to create a virtual space from scratch, compositing typically relies on existing film or video footage. Therefore I need to explain why I claim the result of a composite is a virtual space. Let us consider two different examples of compositing. A compositor may use a number of moving and still images to create a totally new 3-D space and then generate a camera move through it. For example, in *Cliffhanger* (Renny Harlin, 1993), a shot of the main hero, played by Sylvester Stallone, which was filmed in the studio against a blue screen, was composited with the shot of a mountain landscape. The resulting shot shows Stallone high in the mountains hanging over an abyss. In other cases, new elements will be added (or removed from) a live action sequence without changing either its perspective or the camera move. For example, a 3-D computer-generated creature can be added to a live action shot of an outdoor location, as in the many dinosaur shots in *Jurassic Park* (Steven Spielberg, special effects by Industrial Light and Magic, 1993). In the first example, it is immediately clear that the composited shot represents something that never took place in reality. In other words, the result of the composite is a virtual space. In the second example, it may appear at first that the existing physical space is preserved.

However, here as well, the final result is a virtual world that does not really exist. Put differently, what exists is simply a field of grass, without dinosaurs. Digital compositing is routinely used to put together TV commercials and music videos, computer game scenes, shots in feature films, and most other moving images in computer culture. Throughout the 1990s, Hollywood directors increasingly came to rely on compositing to assemble larger and larger parts of a film. In 1999, George Lucas released *Star Wars: Episode 1*; according to Lucas, ninety-five percent of the film was assembled on a computer. As I will discuss below, digital compositing as a technique to create moving images goes back to video keying and optical printing in cinema; but what before was a rather special operation now becomes the norm for creating moving imagery. Digital compositing also greatly expanded the range of this technique, allowing control of the transparency of individual layers and the combination of a potentially unlimited number of layers. For instance, a typical special effects shot from a Hollywood film may consist of a few hundred, or even thousands, of layers. Although in some situations, a few layers can be combined in real time automatically (virtual sets technology), compositing, in general, is a time-consuming and difficult operation. This is one aspect of the before-mentioned scene from *Wag the Dog* that is misrepresented; to create the composite shown in this scene would require many hours.

Digital compositing exemplifies a more general operation of computer culture—assembling together a number of elements to create a single seamless object. Thus we can distinguish between compositing in the wider sense (the general operation) and compositing in a narrow sense (assembling movie image elements to create a photorealistic shot). The latter meaning corresponds to the accepted usage of the term "compositing." For me, compositing in a narrow sense is a particular case of a more general operation—a typical operation in assembling any new media object.

As a general operation, compositing is a counterpart of selection. Since a typical new media object is put together from elements that come from different sources, these elements need to be coordinated and adjusted to fit together. Although the logic of these two operations—selection and compositing—may suggest that they always follow one another (first selection, then compositing), in practice their relationship is more interactive. Once an object is partially assembled, new elements may need to be added; existing elements may need to be reworked. This interactivity is made possible by the modular organization of a new media object on different scales. Throughout the production process, elements retain their separate identities and, therefore, can be easily modified, substituted, or deleted. When the object is complete, it can be "output" as a single "stream" in which separate elements are no longer accessible. An example of an operation which "collapses" elements into a single stream is the "flatten image" command in Adobe Photoshop 5.0. Another example is recording a digitally composited moving image sequence on film, which was a typical procedure in Hollywood film production in the 1980s and 1990s.

Alternatively, the completed object may retain the modular structure when it is distributed. For instance, in many computer games the player can interactively control characters, moving them in space. In some games, the user moves 2-D images of characters, called "sprites," over the background image; in others, everything is represented as a 3-D object, including characters. In either case, the elements are adjusted during production to form a single whole, stylistically, spatially, and semantically; while playing the game the user can move the elements within the programmed limits.

In general, *a 3-D computer graphics representation is more "progressive" than a 2-D image because it allows true independence of elements; as such, it may gradually replace image streams such as photographs, 2-D drawings, films, video.* In other words, a 3-D computer graphics representation is more modular than a 2-D still image or a 2-D moving image stream. This modularity makes it easier for a designer to modify the scene at any time. It also gives the scene additional functionality. For instance, the user may "control" the character, moving him or her around the 3-D space. Scene elements can be also reused in later productions. Finally, modularity also allows for the more efficient storage and transmission of a media object. To transmit a video clip over a network, for example, all pixels that make up this clip have to be sent over, whereas to transmit a 3-D scene requires only sending the coordinates of the objects in it. This is how on-line virtual worlds, on-line computer games, and networked military simulators work: First, copies of all objects making up a world are downloaded to a user's computer; after this, the server has only to keep sending their new 3-D coordinates.

If the general trajectory of computer culture is from 2-D images towards 3-D computer graphics representations, digital compositing represents an intermediary historical step between the two. A composited space consisting of a number of moving-image layers is more modular than a single shot of a physical space. The layers can be repositioned against each other and adjusted separately. Such a representation, however, is not as modular as a true 3-D virtual space because each of the layers retains its own perspective. When and where moving image "streams" will be replaced completely by 3-D computer generated scenes will depend not only on cultural acceptance of the computer scene's look but also on economics. A 3-D scene is much more functional than a film or video shot of the same scene, but, if it is to contain a similar level of detail, it may be much more expensive to generate.

The general evolution of all media types toward increased modularity, and the particular evolution of the moving image in the same direction, can be traced through the history of popular-media file formats. QuickTime developers early on specified that a single QuickTime movie may consist of a number of separate tracks, just as a still Photoshop image consists of a number of layers. QuickTime 4 format (1999) included eleven different track types, including video track, soundtrack, text track, and sprite track (graphic objects which can be moved independently of video).[2] By placing different media on different tracks that can be edited and exported independently, QuickTime encourages designers to think in modular terms. In addition, a movie may contain a number of video tracks that can act as layers in a digital composite. By using alpha channels (masks saved with video tracks) and different modes of track interaction (such as partial transparency), the QuickTime user can create complex compositing effects within a single QuickTime movie, without having to resort to any special compositing software. In effect, QuickTime architects embedded the practice of digital compositing in the media format itself. What previously required special software can now be done simply by using the features of the QuickTime format itself.

Another example of a media format evolving towards more and more data modularity is MPEG.[3] The early version of the format, MPEG-1 (1992), was defined as "the standard for storage and retrieval of moving pictures and audio on storage media." The format specified a compression scheme for video and/or audio data conceptualized in a traditional way. In contrast, MPEG-7 (to be approved in 2001) is defined as "the content representation standard for multimedia information search, filtering, management and processing." It is based on a different concept of media composition that consists of a number of media objects of various types, from video and audio to 3-D models and facial expressions, and information on how these objects are combined. MPEG-7 provides an abstract language to describe such a scene. The evolution of MPEG, thus, allows us to trace the conceptual evolution in how we understand new media—from a traditional "stream" to a modular composition, more similar in its logic to a structural computer program than a traditional image or film.

The Resistance to Montage

The connection between the aesthetics of postmodernism and the operation of selection also applies to compositing. Together, these two operations simultaneously reflect and enable the postmodern practice of pastiche and quotation. They work in tandem: One operation is used to select elements and styles from the "database of culture"; another is used to assemble them into new objects. Thus, along with selection, compositing is the key operation of postmodern, or computer-based, authorship.

At the same time, we should think of the aesthetic and the technological as aligned but ultimately separate layers, to use the metaphor of digital technology itself. The logic of the postmodern aesthetics of the 1980s and the logic of the computer-based compositing of the 1990s are not the same. In the postmodern aesthetics of the eighties, historical references and media quotes are maintained as distinct elements; boundaries between elements are well defined (the examples are David Salle's paintings, Barbara Kruger's montages, and various music videos). Interestingly, this aesthetic corresponds to the electronic and early digital tools of the period, such as video switchers, keyers, DVE, and computer graphics cards with limited colour resolution. These tools enabled hard-edge "copy and paste" operations but not smooth, multilayer composites. (A lot can be made of the fact that one of the key postmodern artists of the 1980s, Richard Prince, who became well known for his "appropriation" photographs, was operating one of the earliest computer-based photo editing systems in the late 1970s as part of his commercial job before he started making "appropriation" photographs.) Compositing in the 1990s supports a different aesthetic characterized by smoothness and continuity. Elements are now blended together, and boundaries erased rather than emphasized. This aesthetic of continuity can best be observed in television spots and special effects sequences of feature films that were actually put together through digital compositing (i.e., compositing in the narrow, technical sense). For instance, the computer-generated dinosaurs in *Jurassic Park* are made to blend perfectly with the landscape, just as the live actors, 3-D virtual actors, and computer-rendered ship are made to blend together in *Titanic* (James Cameron, special effects by Digital Domain, 1997). But the aesthetics of continuity can also be found in other areas of new media. Computer-generated morphs allow for a continuous transition between two images—an effect which before would be accomplished through a dissolve or cut.[4] Many computer games also obey the aesthetics of continuity in that, in cinematic terms, they are single takes. They have no cuts. From beginning to end, they present a single continuous trajectory through a 3-D space. This is particularly true of first-person shooters such as Quake. The lack of montage in these games fits in with the first-person point of view they employ. These games simulate the continuity of a human experience, guaranteed by the laws of physics. While modern telecommunication, from the telegraph, telephone, and television to telepresence and the worldwide web allowed us to suspend these laws, moving almost instantly from one virtual location to another with the toggle of a switch or press of a button, in real life we still obey physics: In order to move from one point to another, we have to pass through every point in between.

All these examples—smooth composites, morphing, uninterrupted navigation in games—have one thing in common: where old media relied on montage, new media substitutes the aesthetics of continuity. A film cut is replaced by a digital morph or digital composite. Similarly, the instant changes in time and space characteristic of modern narrative, both in literature and cinema, are replaced by the continuous non-interrupted first-person narrative of games and VR. Computer multimedia also does not use any montage. The desire to correlate different senses, or, to use new media lingo, different media tracks, which preoccupied many artists throughout the twentieth century, including Kandinsky, Skriabin, Eisenstein, and Godard, to mention just a few, is foreign to multimedia. Instead, it follows the principle of simple addition. Elements in different media are placed next to each other without any attempt to establish contrast, complementarity, or dissonance between them. This is best illustrated by websites of the 1990s that typically contain JPEG images, QuickTime clips, audio files, and other media elements, side by side.

We can also find strong anti-montage tendencies in the modern graphic user interface (GUI). In the middle of the 1980s Apple published guidelines for interface design for all Macintosh application software. According to these guidelines, an interface should communicate the same messages through more than one sense. For instance, an alert box appearing on the screen should be accompanied by a sound. This alignment of different senses can be compared to the naturalistic use of different media in traditional film language—a practice attacked by Eisenstein and other montage filmmakers. Another example of the anti-montage tendency in GUI is the peaceful coexistence of multiple information objects on the computer screen, exemplified by a number of simultaneously opened windows. Just as with media elements in a website, the user can add more and more windows without establishing any conceptual tension between them.

The aesthetics of continuity cannot be fully deduced from compositing technology, although in many cases it would not be possible without it. Similarly, the montage aesthetics that dominates much of modern art and media should not be thought of simply as the result of available tools, since these tools, with their possibilities and limitations, have also contributed to its development. For instance, a film camera enables one to shoot film footage of a certain limited length; to create a longer film, the separate pieces have to be put together. This is typical in editing, where the pieces are trimmed and then glued together. Not surprisingly, modern film language is built on discontinuities: short shots replace one another; point of view changes from shot to shot. The Russian montage school pushes such discontinuities to the extreme, but, with very few exceptions, such as Andy Warhol's early films and *Wavelength* (1967) by Michael Snow, all film schools are based on them.

In computer culture, montage is no longer the dominant aesthetic, as it was throughout the twentieth century, from the avant-garde of the 1920s up until the postmodernism of the 1980s. Digital compositing, in which different spaces are combined into a single seamless virtual space, is a good example of the alternative aesthetics of continuity; moreover, compositing in general can be understood as a counterpart to montage aesthetics. Montage aims to create visual, stylistic, semantic, and emotional dissonance between different elements. In contrast, compositing aims to blend them into a seamless whole, a single gestalt. Since I have already evoked the DJ as someone who exemplifies "authoring by selection," I will use this figure once again as an example of how the anti-montage aesthetics of continuity cuts across culture and is not limited to the creation of computer-generated still and moving images and spaces. The DJ's art is measured by his ability to go from one track to another seamlessly. A great DJ is thus a compositor and anti-montage artist par excellence. He is able to create a perfect temporal transition from very different musical layers; and he can do this in real time, in front of a dancing crowd.

In discussing selection from a menu, I pointed out that this operation is typical of both new media and culture at large. Similarly, the operation of compositing is not limited to new media. Consider, for instance, the frequent use of one or more layers of semi-transparent materials in contemporary packaging and architecture. The result is a visual composite, since a viewer can see both what is in front and what is behind the layer. It is interesting that one architectural project that explicitly refers to computer culture—"The Digital House" (Hariri and Hariri, project, 1988)—systematically employs such semitransparent layers throughout.[5] If in the famous glass house of Mies van der Rohe, the inhabitant looks out at nature through glass walls, the more complex plan of "The Digital House" creates the possibility of seeing through a number of interior spaces at once. Thus the inhabitant of the house is constantly faced with complex visual composites.

Having discussed compositing as a general operation of new media and as a counterpart of selection, I will now focus on a more particular case— compositing in the narrow sense, that is, the creation of a single moving image sequence from a number of separate sequences, and (optionally) stills, using special compositing software. Today, digital compositing is responsible for an increasing number of moving images—all special effects in cinema, computer games, virtual worlds, most television visuals, and even television news. Most often, the moving image constructed through compositing presents a fake 3-D world. I say "fake" because, regardless of whether a compositor creates a totally new 3-D space from different elements (*Cliffhanger*, for example), or only adds elements to live action footage (*Jurassic Park*, for example), the resulting moving image shows something that does not exist in reality. Digital compositing thus belongs together with other simulation techniques. These are the techniques used to create fake realities and thus, ultimately, to deceive the viewer—fashion and makeup, realist painting, dioramas, military decoys, and VR. Why has digital compositing acquired such prominence? If we are to create an archeology that will connect digital compositing with previous techniques of visual simulation, where should we locate the essential historical breaks? Or, to ask the question differently: What is the historical logic driving the evolution of these techniques? Shall we expect computer culture gradually to abandon pure lens-based imaging (still photography, film, video), replacing it instead with composited images and ultimately with 3-D computer-generated simulations?

Archeology of Compositing: Cinema

I will start my archeology of compositing with Potemkin's villages. According to the historical myth, at the end of the eighteenth century, Russian ruler Catherine the Great decided to travel around Russia to observe firsthand how the peasants lived. The first minister and Catherine's lover, Potemkin, ordered the construction of special fake villages along her projected route. Each village consisted of a row of pretty façades. The façades faced the road; at the same time, to conceal their artifice, they were positioned at a considerable distance. Since Catherine never left her carriage, she returned from her journey convinced that all peasants lived in happiness and prosperity.

This extraordinary arrangement can be seen as a metaphor for life in the Soviet Union where I grew up in the 1970s. There, the experience of all citizens was split between the ugly reality of their lives and the official shining façades of ideological pretense. However, the split took place not only on a metaphorical but also on a literal level, particularly in Moscow—the showcase Communist city. When prestigious foreign guests visited Moscow, they,

like Catherine the Great, were taken around in limousines that always followed a few special routes. Along these routes, every building was freshly
painted, shop windows displayed consumer goods, and drunks were absent,
having been picked up by the militia early in the morning. The monochrome,
rusty, half-broken, amorphous Soviet reality was carefully hidden from the
view of the passengers.

In turning selected streets into façades, Soviet rulers adopted the eighteenth-century technique of creating a fake reality. But the twentieth
century brought with it a much more effective technology for creating fake
realities—cinema. By replacing the window of a carriage or car with a
screen showing projected images, cinema opened up new possibilities for
simulation.

Fictional cinema, as we know it, is based upon lying to the viewer. A perfect example is the construction of a cinematic space. Traditional fiction film
transports us into a space—a room, a house, a city. Usually, none of these
exists in reality. What exist are a few fragments carefully constructed in a
studio. Out of these disjointed fragments, a film synthesizes the illusion of
a coherent space.

The development of techniques to accomplish this synthesis coincides
with the shift in American cinema between approximately 1907 and 1917
from a so-called primitive to a classical film style. Before the classical period, the space of film theatre and the screen space were clearly separated,
much like in theatre or vaudeville. Viewers were free to interact, come and
go, and maintain a psychological distance from the cinematic narrative.
Correspondingly, the early cinema's system of representation was *presentational*: Actors played to the audience, and the style was strictly frontal.[6]
The composition of shots also emphasized frontality.

In contrast, as I discussed earlier, classical Hollywood film positions each
viewer inside the fictional space of the narrative. The viewer is asked to
identify with the characters and to experience the story from their points of
view. Accordingly, the space no longer acts as a theatrical backdrop.
Instead, through new compositional principles, staging, set design, deep
focus cinematography, lighting, and camera movement, the viewer is situ-
ated at the optimum viewpoint of each shot. The viewer is "present" inside
a space that does not really exist.

In general, Hollywood cinema has always been careful to hide the artificial nature of its space, but there is one exception: the rear-screen
projection shots introduced in the 1930s. A typical shot shows actors sitting
inside a stationary vehicle; a film of a moving landscape is projected on the

screen behind the car's windows. The artificiality of rear-screen projection shots stands in striking contrast to the smooth fabric of Hollywood cinematic style in general.

The synthesis of a coherent space out of distinct fragments is only one example of how fictional cinema fakes reality. A film in general is comprised of separate image sequences. These sequences can come from different physical locations. Two consecutive shots of what looks like one room may correspond to two locations inside one studio. They can also correspond to locations in Moscow and Berlin, or Berlin and New York. The viewer will never know.

This is the key advantage of cinema over older fake-reality technologies, be they eighteenth-century Potemkin villages or nineteenth-century panoramas and dioramas. Before cinema, simulation was limited to the construction of a fake space inside a real space visible to the viewer. Examples include theatre decorations and military decoys. In the nineteenth century, the panorama offered a small improvement: By enclosing a viewer within a 360-degree view, the area of fake space was expanded. Louis Jacques Daguerre introduced another innovation by having viewers move from one set to another in his London diorama. As described by the historian Paul Johnson, its "amphitheatre, seating 200, pivoted through a 73-degree arc, from one 'picture' to another. Each picture was seen through a 2,800-square-foot-window."[7] But already in the eighteenth century, Potemkin had pushed this technique to its limit: He created a giant façade —a diorama stretching for hundreds of miles—along which the viewer (Catherine the Great) passed. In contrast, in cinema a viewer remains stationary: What moves is the film itself.

Therefore, if the older simulation technologies were limited by the materiality of a viewer's body, existing in a particular point in space and time, film overcomes this spatial and temporal limitation. It achieves this by substituting recorded images for unmediated human sight and by editing these images together. Through editing, images that could have been shot in different geographic locations or at different times create the illusion of a contiguous space and time.

Editing, or montage, is the key twentieth-century technology for creating fake realities. Theoreticians of cinema have distinguished between many kinds of montage, but for the purpose of sketching an archeology of the technologies of simulation that led to digital compositing I will distinguish between two basic techniques. The first technique is temporal montage: separate realities form consecutive moments in time. The second technique

is montage within a shot. It is the opposite of the first: Separate realities form contingent parts of a single image. The first technique of temporal montage is much more common; this is what we usually mean by "montage" in film. It defines the cinematic language as we know it. In contrast, montage within a shot is used more rarely throughout film history. An example of this technique is the dream sequence in *The Dream of the Rarebit Fiend*, by Edwin Porter in 1906, in which an image of a dream appears over a man's sleeping head. Other examples include split screens that, beginning in 1908, show the different interlocutors of a telephone conversation; the superimposition of images and multiple screens by avant-garde filmmakers in the 1920s (for instance, the superimposed images in Vertov's *Man with a Movie Camera* and the three-part screen in Abel Gance's 1927 *Napoleon*); rear-screen projection shots; and deep focus and special compositional strategies used to juxtapose close and faraway scenes (for instance, a character looking through a window, as in *Citizen Kane*, *Ivan the Terrible*, and *Rear Window*).[8]

In a fictional film, temporal montage serves a number of functions. As I have already pointed out, it creates a sense of presence in a virtual space. It is also utilized to change the meaning of individual shots (recall Kuleshov's effect) or, more precisely, to construct a meaning from separate pieces of pro-filmic reality. However, the use of temporal montage extends

still: Dziga Vertov's *Man with a Movie Camera* (1929)

beyond the construction of an artistic fiction. Montage also becomes a key technology for ideological manipulation, through its employment in propaganda films, documentaries, news, commercials, and so on. The pioneer of the ideological montage is, once again, Vertov. In 1923, Vertov analyzed how he put together episodes of his news program *Kino-Pravda* ("Cinema-Truth") from shots filmed in different locations and at different times. Here is one example of his montage: "the bodies of the people's heroes are being lowered into the graves (filmed in Astrakhan in 1918); the graves are being covered with earth (Kronstadt, 1921); gun salute (Petrograd, 1920); eternal memory, people take off their hats (Moscow, 1922)." Here is another example: "montage of the greetings by the crowd and montage of the greetings by the machines to the comrade Lenin, filmed at different times."[9] As theorized by Vertov, film can overcome its indexical nature through montage, by presenting a viewer with objects that never existed in reality.

Archeology of Compositing: Video

Outside cinema, montage within a shot becomes a standard technique of modern photography and design (the photomontages of Alexander Rodchenko, El Lissitzky, Hannah Höch, John Heartfield, and countless other lesser-known twentieth-century designers). However, in the realm of the moving image, temporal montage dominates. Temporal montage is cinema's main operation for creating fake realities.

After World War II, a gradual shift takes place from film-based to electronic image recording and editing. This shift brings with it a new technique —keying. One of the most basic techniques used today in any video and television production, keying refers to combining two different image sources. Any area of uniform colour in one video image can be cut out and substituted with another source. Significantly, this new source can be a live video camera positioned somewhere, a prerecorded tape, or computer generated graphics. The possibilities for creating fake realities are multiplied once again.

When electronic keying became part of standard television practice in the 1970s, the construction not only of still but also moving images finally began routinely to rely on montage within a shot. In fact, rear projection and other special effects shots, which had occupied a marginal place in classical film, became the norm: the weatherman in front of weather map, announcer in front of news footage, singer in front of animation in a music video.

An image created through keying presents a hybrid reality, composed of two different spaces. Television normally relates these spaces semantical-

ly but not visually. To take a typical example, we may be shown an image of an announcer sitting in a studio; behind her, in a cutout, we see news footage of a city street. The two spaces are connected through their meanings (the announcer discusses events shown in the cutout), but visually they are disjointed, as they share neither the same scale nor the same perspective. If classical cinematic montage creates the illusion of a coherent space and hides its work, electronic montage openly presents the viewer with an apparent visual clash of different spaces.

What will happen if the two spaces seamlessly merge? This operation forms the basis of the remarkable video *Steps*, directed by Polish-born filmmaker Zbigniew Rybczynski in 1987. *Steps* is shot on videotape and uses keying; it also utilizes film footage and makes inadvertent reference to virtual reality. In this way, Rybczynski connects three generations of fake reality technologies: analog, electronic, and digital. He also reminds us that it was the 1920s Soviet filmmakers who first fully realized the possibilities of montage, possibilities that continue to be expanded by electronic and digital media.

In the video, a group of American tourists is invited into a sophisticated video studio to participate in a kind of virtual reality/time machine experiment. The group is positioned in front of a blue screen. Next, the tourists find themselves literally inside the famous Odessa steps sequence from Sergei Eisenstein's *Potemkin* (1925). Rybczynski skillfully keys the shots of the people in the studio into the shots from *Potemkin*, creating a single coherent space. At the same time, he emphasizes the artificiality of this space by contrasting the colour video images of the tourists with Eisenstein's original grainy black-and-white footage. The tourists walk up and down the steps, snap pictures of the attacking soldiers, play with a baby in a crib. Gradually, the two realities begin to interact and mix: Some Americans fall down the steps after being shot by soldiers from Eisenstein's sequence; a tourist drops an apple that is picked up by a soldier.

The Odessa steps sequence, already a famous example of cinematic montage, becomes just one element in a new ironic remix by Rybczynski. The original shots, already edited by Eisenstein, are now edited again with video images of the tourists, using both temporal montage and montage

still: Zbigniew Rybczynski's *Steps* (1987)

within a shot, the latter done through video keying. A "film look" is juxtaposed with a "video look," colour is juxtaposed with black and white, the "presentness" of video is juxtaposed with the "always already" of film.

In *Steps*, Eisenstein's sequence becomes a generator for numerous kinds of juxtapositions, superimpositions, mixes, and remixes. But Rybczynski treats this sequence not only as a single element of his own montage but also as a singular, physically existing space. In other words, the Odessa steps sequence is read as a single shot corresponding to a real space, a space that could be visited like any other tourist attraction.

Along with Rybczynski, another filmmaker who systematically experimented with the possibilities of electronic montage within a shot is Jean-Luc Godard. While in the 1960s, Godard was actively exploring new possibilities of temporal montage such as jump cuts, in later video works such as *Scénario du film "Passion"* (1982) and *Histoire(s) du cinéma* (1989-) he developed a unique aesthetics of continuity that relies on electronically mixing a number of images together within a single shot. If Rybczynski's aesthetics is based on the operation of video keying, Godard's aesthetics similarly relies on a single operation available to any video editor—mixing. Godard uses the electronic mixer to create very slow cross-dissolves between images, cross-dissolves that seem never to resolve in a singular image, ultimately becoming the film itself. In *Histoire(s) du cinéma*, Godard mixes together two, three, or more images; images gradually fade in and out, but never disappear completely, staying on the screen for a few minutes at a time. This technique can be interpreted as the representation of ideas or mental images floating around in our minds, coming in and out of mental focus. Another variation of the same technique used by Godard is to move from one image to another by oscillating between the two. The images flicker back and forth over and over, until the second image finally replaces the first. This technique can be also interpreted as an attempt to represent the mind's movement from one concept, mental image, or memory to another—the attempt, in other words, to represent what, according to Locke and other associationist philosophers, is the basis of our mental life—forming associations.

Godard wrote: "There are no more simple images.... The whole world is too much for an image. You need several of them, a chain of images...."[10] Accordingly, Godard always uses multiple images, images cross-dissolved together, coming together and separating. The electronic mixing that replaces both temporal montage and montage within the shot becomes for Godard an appropriate technique to visualize this "vague and complicated system that the whole world is continually entering and watching."[11]

Digital Compositing

The next generation in simulation technologies is digital compositing. On first glance, computers do not bring any conceptually new techniques for creating fake realities. They simply expand the possibilities of joining together different images within one shot. Rather than keying together images from two video sources, we can now composite an unlimited number of image layers. A shot may consist of dozens, hundreds, or thousands of image layers. These images may all have different origins—film shot on location ("live plates"), computer-generated sets or virtual actors, digital matte paintings, archival footage, and so on. Following the success of *Terminator 2* and *Jurassic Park*, most Hollywood films began to utilize digital compositing to create a least some of their shots.

Thus, historically, a digitally composed image, like an electronically keyed image, can be seen as a continuation of montage within a shot. But while electronic keying creates disjointed spaces that remind us of the avant-garde collages of Rodchenko or Moholy-Nagy from the 1920s, digital composing brings back the nineteenth-century techniques of creating smooth "combination prints" like those of Henry Peach Robinson and Oscar G. Reijlander.

But this historical continuity is deceptive. Digital compositing does represent a qualitatively new step in the history of visual simulation because it allows the creation of *moving* images of nonexistent worlds. Computer-generated characters can move within real landscapes; conversely, real actors can move and act within synthetic environments. In contrast to nineteenth century "combination prints," which emulated academic painting, digital composites simulate the established language of cinema and television. Regardless of the particular combination of live-action elements and computer-generated elements that make up the composited shot, the camera can pan, zoom, and dolly through it. Interactions between the elements of a virtual world over time (for instance, the dinosaur attacking the car), along with the ability to look at this world from different viewpoints, become the guarantee of its authenticity.

The new ability to create a virtual world that moves—and that can be moved through—comes at a price. Although compositing fake news footage takes place in real time in *Wag the Dog*, aligning numerous elements to create a convincing composite is, in reality, a time-consuming task. For instance, the forty-second sequence in *Titanic* in which the camera flies over the computer-generated ship, populated by computer-generated characters, took many months to produce and its total cost was $1.1 million.[12] In contrast, although images of such complexity are out of reach for video keying, it is possible to combine three image sources in realtime. (This tradeoff between image-construction time and its complexity is similar to another trade-off I have already noted—that between image-construction time and its functionality; that is, images created with 3-D computer graphics are more functional than image streams recorded by film or video cameras, but in most cases, they are much more time-consuming to generate.)

If a compositor restricts the composite to just a few images, as was done with electronic keying, compositing can also be created in real time. The resulting illusion of a seamless space is stronger than what was possible with electronic keying. An example of real-time compositing is Virtual Sets technology, which was first introduced in the early 1990s and since then has been making its way into television studios around the world. This technology allows compositing video-image and computer-generated 3-D elements on the fly. (Actually, because the generation of computer elements is computation-intensive, the final image transmitted to the audience may be seconds behind the original image picked up by the television camera.) A typical application of Virtual Sets involves compositing an image of an actor over a computer-generated set. The computer reads the position of the video camera and uses this information to render the image of the set in proper perspective. The illusion is made more convincing by generating shadows and/or reflections of the actor and integrating them into the composite. Because of the relatively low resolution of analog television, the resulting effect is quite convincing. A particularly interesting application of Virtual Sets is the replacement and insertion of arena-tied advertising messages during live TV broadcasts of sports and entertainment events. Computer-synthesized advertising messages can be inserted into the playing field or other empty areas of the arena in the proper perspective, as though they were actually present in physical reality.[13]

Digital compositing represents a fundamental break with previous techniques for visual deception in another way. Throughout the history of representation, artists and designers have focused on the problem of creating a convincing illusion within a single image, whether a painting, film frame, or a view seen by Catherine the Great through the window of her carriage. Set making, one-point perspective, chiaroscuro, trick photography, and other cinematography techniques were all developed to solve this problem. Film montage introduced a new paradigm—creating an effect of presence in a virtual world by joining different images over time. Temporal montage became the dominant paradigm for the visual simulation of non-existent spaces.

As the examples of digital compositing for film and Virtual Sets applications for television demonstrate, the computer era introduces a different paradigm. This paradigm is concerned not with time but with space. It can be seen as the next step in the development of techniques for creating a single convincing image of nonexistent spaces—painting, photography, cinematography. Having mastered this task, the culture came to focus on how to join seamlessly a number of such images into one coherent whole (electronic keying, digital compositing). Whether compositing a live video of a newscaster with a 3-D computer-generated set or compositing thousands of elements to create the images of *Titanic, the problem is no longer how to generate convincing individual images but how to blend them together.* Consequently, what is important now is what happens on the edges where different images are joined. The borders where different realities come together is the new arena where the Potemkins of our era try to outdo one another.

Compositing and New Types of Montage

In the beginning of this section, I pointed out that the use of digital compositing to create continuous spaces out of different elements can be seen as an example of the larger anti-montage aesthetics of computer culture. Indeed, if at the beginning of the twentieth century, cinema discovered that it could simulate a single space through temporal montage—a time-based mosaic of different shots—by the end of the century, it had arrived at a technique to accomplish a similar result without montage. In digital compositing, the elements are not juxtaposed but blended, their boundaries erased rather than foregrounded.

At the same time, by relating digital compositing to the theory and practice of film montage, we can better understand how this new key technique of assembling moving images redefines our concept of a moving image. While traditional film montage privileges temporal montage over montage within a shot—technically the latter was much more difficult to achieve—compositing makes them equal. More precisely, it erases the strict conceptual and technical separation between the two. Consider, for instance, the interface layout typical of many programs for computer-based editing and digital compositing, such as Adobe Premiere 4.2, a popular editing program, and Alias|Wavefront Composer 4.0, a professional compositing program. In this interface, the horizontal dimension represents time, while the vertical dimension represents the spatial order of the different image layers making up each image. A moving image sequence appears as a number of blocks staggered vertically, with each block standing for a particular image layer. Thus, if Pudovkin, one of the theorists and practitioners of the Russian montage movement the 1920s, conceived of montage as a one-dimensional line of bricks, now it becomes a 2-D brick wall. This interface makes montage in time and montage within a shot equal in importance.

If the Premiere interface conceptualizes editing as an operation in 2-D dimensions, the interface of one of the most popular compositing programs, After Effects 4.0, adds a third dimension. Following the conventions of traditional film and video editing, Premiere assumes that all image sequences are the same size and proportion; in fact, it makes working with images that do not conform to the standard three-by-four frame ratio rather difficult. In contrast, the user of After Effects places image sequences of arbitrary sizes and proportions within the larger frame. Breaking with the conventions of old moving image media, the interface of After Effects assumes that the individual elements making up a moving image can freely move, rotate, and change proportions over time.

Sergei Eisenstein already used the metaphor of many-dimensional space in his writings on montage, naming one of his articles *Kino cheturekh izmereneii* ("The Filmic Fourth Dimension").[14] However, his theories of montage ultimately focused on one dimension—time. Eisenstein formulated a number of principles, such as counterpoint, that can be used to coordinate changes in different visual dimensions over time. The examples of visual dimensions he considered are graphic directions, volumes, masses, space, and contrast.[15] When the sound film became a possibility, Eisenstein extended these principles to handle what, in computer language, can be called "synchronization" of visual and audio tracks; and later he added the dimension of colour.[16] Eisenstein also developed a different set of principles ("methods of montage") according to which different shots can be edited together to form a longer sequence. The examples of "methods of montage" include metric montage, which uses absolute lengths of shots to establish a "beat," and rhythmic montage, which is based on pattern of movement within the shots. These methods can be used by themselves to structure a sequence of shots, but they also can be combined within a single sequence.

The new logic of a digital moving image contained in the operation of compositing runs against Eisenstein's aesthetics with its focus on time.

Digital compositing makes the dimensions of space (3-D fake space being created by a composite and 2-1/2-D space of all the layers being composited) and frame (separate images moving in 2-D within the frame) as important as time. In addition, the possibility of embedding hyperlinks within a moving sequence introduced in QuickTime 3 and other digital formats adds yet another spatial dimension.[17] The typical use of hyperlinking in digital movies is to link elements of a movie with information displayed outside of it. For instance, when a particular frame is displayed, a specific web page can be loaded in another window. This practice "spatializes" a moving image: no longer completely filling the screen, it is now just one window among many.

In summary, if film technology, film practice, and film theory privilege the temporal development of a moving image, computer technology privileges spatial dimensions. The new spatial dimensions can be defined as follows:

1. Spatial order of layers in a composite (21/2-D space)
2. Virtual space constructed through compositing (3-D space)
3. 2-D movement of layers in relation to the image frame (2-D space)
4. Relationship between the moving image and linked information in the adjustment windows (2-D space)

These dimensions should be added to the list of visual and sound dimensions of the moving image elaborated by Eisenstein and other filmmakers. Their use opens new possibilities for cinema as well as poses a new challenge for film theory. *No longer just a subset of audio-visual culture, the digital moving image becomes a part of audio-visual-spatial culture.*

Of course, simple use of these dimensions in and of itself does not result in montage. Most images and spaces of contemporary culture are juxtapositions of different elements; calling any such juxtaposition "montage" renders the term meaningless. Media critic and historian Erkki Hutamo suggests that we should reserve the use of the term "montage" for "strong" cases, and I will follow his suggestion here.[18] Thus, to qualify as an example of montage, a new media object should fulfill two conditions: juxtapositions of elements should follow a particular system, and these juxtapositions should play a key role in how the work establishes its meaning, and its emotional and aesthetic effects. These conditions would also apply to the particular case of new spatial dimensions of digital moving images. By establishing a logic that controls the changes and the correlation of values on these dimensions, digital filmmakers can create what I will call *spatial montage.*

Although digital compositing is usually used to create a seamless virtual space, this does not have to be its only goal. Borders between different worlds do not have to be erased; different spaces do not have to be matched in perspective, scale, and lighting; individual layers can retain their separate identities rather than being merged into a single space; different worlds can clash semantically rather than form a single universe. I will conclude this section by invoking a few more works, which, together with videos by Rybczynski and Godard, point to the new aesthetic possibilities of digital compositing if it is not used in the service of traditional realism. Although all these works were created before digital compositing became available, they explore its aesthetic logic—for compositing is, first and foremost, a conceptual, not only a technological operation. I will use these works to introduce two other montage methods based on compositing: *ontological montage* and *stylistic montage*.

Rybczynski's film *Tango* (1982), made when he was still living in Poland, uses layering as a metaphor for the particular overcrowding characteristic of socialist countries in the second half of the twentieth century, and for human cohabitation in general. A number of people perform various actions moving in loops through the same small room, apparently unaware of each other. Rybczynski offsets the loops in such a way that even though his characters keep moving through the same points in space, they never run into one another.

Compositing, achieved in *Tango* through optical printing, allows the filmmaker to superimpose a number of elements, or whole worlds, within a single space. (In this film, each person moving through the room can be said to form a separate world.) As in *Steps*, these worlds are matched in perspective and scale—and yet the viewer knows that the scene being shown could not occur in normal human experience at all given the laws of physics, or is highly unlikely to occur given the conventions of human life. In the case of *Tango*, the depicted scene could have occurred physically, but the probability of such an occurrence is close to zero. Works such as *Tango* and *Steps* develop what I will call an *ontological montage*: the coexistence of ontologically incompatible elements within the same time and space.

The films of Czech filmmaker Konrad Zeman exemplify another montage method based on compositing, which I will call *stylistic montage*. In a career spanning from the 1940s to the 1980s, Zeman used a variety of special effect techniques to create juxtapositions of stylistically diverse images in different media. He juxtaposes different media in time, cutting from a live-action shot to a shot of a model or documentary footage, as well as within the same shot. For example, a shot may combine filmed human figures, an old engraving used for background, and a model. Of course, such artists as Picasso, Braque, Picabia, and Max Ernst were creating similar juxtaposition of elements in different media in still images already before World War II. However, in the realm of the moving image, stylistic montage only came to the surface in the 1990s when the computer became the meeting ground for different generations of media formats used in the twentieth century—35mm and 8mm film, amateur and professional video, and early digital film formats. While previously filmmakers usually worked with a single format throughout the whole film, the accelerated replacement of different analog and digital formats since the 1970s made the coexistence of stylistically diverse elements a norm rather than the exception for new media objects. Compositing can be used to hide this diversity—or it can be used to foreground it, creating it artificially if necessary. For instance, the film *Forrest Gump* (1994) emphasizes stylistic differences between various shots; this simulation of different film and video artifacts is an important aspect of its narrative system.

In Zeman's films such as *Baron Prásil* (*Baron Munchhausen*, 1961) and *Na komete* (*On the Comet*, 1970), live-action footage, etchings, miniatures, and other elements are layered together in a self-conscious and ironic way. Like Rybczynski, Zeman keeps a coherent perspectival space in his films while making us aware that it is constructed. One of his devices is to superimpose filmed actors over an old etching used as a background. In Zeman's aesthetics, neither graphic nor cinematographic elements dominate; the two are blended together in equal proportion, creating a unique visual style. At the same time, Zeman subordinates the logic of feature filmmaking to the logic of animation; that is, the shots in his films that combine live-action footage with graphic elements position all elements on parallel planes; the elements move parallel to the screen. This is the logic of an animation stand, where the stack of images is arranged parallel to each other, rather than live-action cinema, where the camera typically moves through 3-D space. This subordination of live action to animation is the logic of digital cinema in general.

St. Petersburg artist Olga Tobreluts, who uses digital compositing, also respects the illusion of a coherent perspectival space, while continuously playing tricks with it. In *Gore ot Uma* (1994, directed by Olga Komarova), a video work based on a famous play written by the nineteenth-century Russian writer Aleksandr Griboedov, Tobreluts overlays images representing radically different realities (a close-up of plants; animals in the zoo) on the windows and walls of various interior spaces. In one shot, two characters converse in front of a window behind which we see a flock of soaring birds taken from Alfred Hitchcock's *The Birds*; in another, a delicate computer-rendered design keeps morphing on the wall behind a dancing couple. In these and similar shots, Tobreluts aligns the two realities in perspective but not in scale. The result is an ontological montage—and also a new kind of montage within a shot. Which is to say, if the avant-garde of the 1920s, and MTV in its wake, juxtaposed radically different realities within a single image, and if Hollywood digital artists use computer compositing to glue different images into a seamless illusionistic space, Zeman, Rybczynski, and Tobreluts explore the creative space between these two extremes. The space between modernist collage and Hollywood cinematic realism is new terrain for cinema, ready for exploration with the help of digital compositing.

Endnotes

1. Thomas Porter and Tom Duff, "Compositing Digital Images," *Computer Graphics* 18, no. 3 (July 1984), 253-259.

2. www.apple.com/quicktime/resources/qt4/us/help/QuickTime%20Help.htm

3. www.drogo.cset.it/mpeg

4. For an excellent theoretical analysis of morphing, see Vivian Sobchack, "'At the Still Point of the Turning World': Meta-Morphing and Meta-Stasis," in Sobchack, ed., *Meta-Morphing* (Minneapolis: University of Minnesota Press, 2000).

5. Terence Riley, *The Un-private House* (New York: Museum of Modern Art, 1999).

6. On the presentational system of early cinema, see Charles Musser, *The Emergence of Cinema*, (Berkeley: University of California Press, 1994), 3.

7. Paul Johnson, *The Birth of the Modern: World Society*, 1815-1830 (London: Orion House, 1992), 156.

8. The examples of *Citizen Kane* and *Ivan the Terrible* are taken from Jacques Aumont et al., *Aesthetics of Film*, (Austin: University of Texas Press, 1992), 41.

9. Dziga Vertov, "Kinoki: Perevorot" ("Kinoki: A revolution"), *LEF 3* (1923), 140.

10. Jean-Luc Godard, *Son + Image*, ed. Raymond Bellour (New York: Museum of Modern Art, 1992),171.

11. Ibid.

12. See Paula Parisi, "Lunch on the Deck of the Titanic," *Wired 6.02* (February 1998)
<www.wired.com/wired/archive/6.02/cameron.html>.

13. *IMadGibe: Virtual Advertising for Live Sport Events*, (a promotional flyer by ORAD, P.O. Box 2177, Far Saab 44425, Israel, 1998).

14. Sergei Eisenstein, "The Filmic Fourth Dimension," in *Film Form*, trans. Jay Leyda (New York: Harcourt Brace and Company, 1949).

15. Eisenstein, "A Dialectical Approach to Film Form," in *Film Form*, trans. Jay Leyda (New York: Harcourt Brace and Company, 1949).

16. Eisenstein, "Statement" and "Synchronization of Senses," in *Film Sense*, trans. Jay Leyda (New York: Harcourt Brace and Company, 1942).

17. For an excellent theoretical analysis of QuickTime and digital moving images in general, see Vivian Sobchack's "Nostalgia for a Digital Object," *Millenium Film Journal* 35 (Fall 1999), 4-23.

18. Private communication, Helsinki, October 4, 1999.

An Ersatz of Life: The Dream Life of Technology

Zoe Beloff

I work with moving images: film; stereoscopic projection performance; installations; and interactive cinema on CD-ROM and websites. My ongoing project is an exploration of what could be described as "the dream life of technology" (not what technology is or was, but what people believed or desired it to be).

In the last century, there existed a multiplicity of cinematic apparatuses. My dream is to open up the moving image once again to new languages of vision. The cinemas I imagine are marginal, fragile, sometimes coalescing only momentarily in the act of projection. They create parallel universes, calling into question corporate visions of progress with their digital utopias. I wish to reawaken the psychic charge that was unleashed by the birth of photography, film, and audio recording. At the same time, I have no desire to turn back the clock; rather, I wish to explore critically the deep assumptions built into the machines through which we understand our world.

Cinema Incognito

I am inspired by the writings of a great cinematic alchemist, Raul Ruiz, specifically this short passage from his book *Poetics of Cinema*:

> I will recount the life of cinema past, present and future, as though it had never existed, or had never been anything more than sheer conjecture. I will try to lay out some of the philosophical problems that this vanished art proposed, and I will seek to explain its journey incognito through the grammatical city known for the moment as virtual reality.[1]

What sets fire to my imagination is just this conjecture, the possibility of a reinvention of cinema that moves us imaginatively from the past into the future.

still: Zoe Beloff's *Beyond* (1997)

A Chance Encounter Between a Quick Cam and a Film Found at the Flea Market

In the summer of 1995, with no money to shoot film and no place to show my work, I began my first digital project in the form of QuickTime movies. The computer was simply something I had around the house. Challenging myself to make one movie a week, I opened my own cinema on the web. It was the beginning of *Beyond* in serial form. Early motion picture serials and toy projection devices inspired me. The computer is today's home movie projector. I liked the idea of cinema trickling down the phone lines into people's homes.

Philosophical Toys

What I make could be described quite simply as "philosophical toys," heirs to nineteenth-century devices such as magic lanterns, zoetropes, and hand-cranked projectors. I often describe this apparatus as forming the secret history of QuickTime movies, producing images that are tiny, unstable, and, most importantly, interactive. They remind us that interactivity, far from being a new phenomenon, was integral to the production of the nineteenth-century moving image.

I've deliberately stuck with the word "toy" to describe my CD-ROMs because to my mind, the cinematic toy is not simply a machine in miniature; it has an extra expenditure of energy invested in play, in the pleasure of the moment. "Machine" suggests something altogether too functional, too goal- oriented. In the conventional cinematic apparatus, a film is put on the projector and the machine is switched on for a certain duration until the film runs out. However, most philosophical toys are constructed around loops, which remove us from linear time into an altogether more hypnotic state. Classical cinema knows only "next," the philosophical toy, only "now" and "again."[2]

Intimacy

In its classical form, cinema signifies the creation of an illusionistic world that exists apart from us, governed by its own temporal laws, its own spatial laws, and above all oblivious to us, a great machine that effaces all traces of its production. And if we are to enter into it, we must leave our corporeal selves behind. Capturing us in its glare, it holds us still and obliterates us in the dark. In contrast, my CD-ROMs are designed specifically for an audience of one. An intimate dialogue is created.

An Interface

The CDs are constructed by linking QuickTime movies and QuickTime VR panoramas to create the illusion of a world that invites the viewer to explore a new kind of mental geography. They find themselves travelling through time and space, encountering my virtual alter ego, which, as a medium that interfaces between the living and the dead, leads the viewer on a journey that is as mysterious as it is unpredictable. Very simply, QuickTime VR panoramas are virtual 360-degree spaces that one can explore by dragging the mouse around the space. They are constructed by "stitching" together in the computer twelve still photographs taken in rotation. The viewer can zoom in and out and, by clicking on "hotspots," access the short movies. *Beyond* contains twenty panoramas and eighty QuickTime movies.

The location is an actual abandoned asylum, dating back to the nineteenth century. It stands in for many places, both real and fictional (from Charcot's clinic at the Salpêtrière, to Roussel's fictional world of *Locus Solus*, to the destroyed buildings of the two World Wars, to the Paris Arcades of the Second Empire, to the ruins of the great world expositions).

A Phantasmagoria of Progress

In practice, digital technologies are the most fleeting of media, as hardware and software mutations bring in their wake ever-faster obsolescence: a faster way of forgetting. Walter Benjamin wrote about the beginnings of this phenomenon in his *Arcades Project*, seeing nineteenth-century capitalism as a hellish time in its endless promotion of the new:

> The dreaming collective knows no history. Events pass before it as always identical and always new. The sensation of the newest and most modern is, in fact, just as much a dream formation of events as the eternal return of the same.[3]

As I began working on *Beyond*, I felt that these issues should urgently be addressed. Benjamin wished, through examining the past, to make the

mechanisms of our own delusions, our own dream state, clear to us. He aimed to do this, not through examining the big events of history, but through examining its scraps and remains: images, objects, buildings, the landscape of the everyday that has been discarded. He spoke of, not life-remembered, but life-forgotten; illuminated at the very moment of its disappearance. It is just this debris, washed up at the flea market, that I hope in my own way to make speak again, but differently—to illuminate the present through the past.

I was not interested in being literal or illustrative, but instead in letting the past breathe through small discarded objects. For example, in *Beyond*, the "dead" are represented by fragments of home movies from 1920 to 1940 found at flea markets, as well as early film footage from the Library of Congress Paper Print collection. Long outdated forms resurfacing anew in the digital realm fascinated me. Such are panoramas. Actual panoramas painted around specially constructed circular rooms were a popular form of entertainment in the nineteenth century. Long since forgotten, they now reappear on the computer.

Mental Geography

The possibilities opened up by interactivity allowed me to realize ideas of mental geography that previously could only be described rather than actually experienced in art. A geography described in the words of Baudelaire as "A city full of dreams where ghosts accost the passers-by in broad daylight."[4]

Unlike film or video, my CDs are designed to be experienced more than once. Each time the viewer enters *Beyond*, they can choose a different route. There are no maps, because, to me it is a city of the mind, a city of metaphor; it is a virtual city, in which the ordinary laws of geography do not apply.

Ideas, in the form of movies, cluster around particular rooms or spaces. There are two methods of travel: literally (on foot), or a filmed simulation of walking from place to place. Panoramas are also linked by narrative

stills: Zoe Beloff's *Beyond* (1997)

movies, thus trains of thought connect the viewer from one place to another. Baudelaire became a key figure in *Beyond*, perhaps because he was the first great writer of the modern city, the first Modernist. It was he who first defined this idea of "mental geography" as a state of mind: the city shot-through by allegory. My QuickTime movie based on his prose poem "Symptoms of Ruin" could serve very well as an introduction. Here, by describing his dream of a fantastic endless and impossible building, which only he knows is on the verge of collapse, he is perhaps actually describing his mental state and his own body. A body slowly dying, exteriorized in the form of a "building attacked by some hidden disease."[5] He was the archetypal *flâneur*, while my work might also be considered as an exercise in digital *flânerie*.

Spectacular Symptoms

What fascinates me is that the birth of mechanical reproduction opened up almost limitless possibilities in the mind of the nineteenth-century viewer. Was it simply that people were just more gullible and that now hard science has dispelled their fantasies? I don't know. One could argue equally the converse: that because something was conceivable, then it became, perhaps, possible. My thesis is that if something (which we now take for granted) like photography was experienced as an uncanny phenomenon (which seems to me to undermine the unique identity of objects), creating a parallel world of phantasmal doubles, then the possibility of the production of, for example, *Spirit Photographs* was not nearly as implausible as it might be today. In *Beyond*, I felt these were important issues to address, that with the onrush of today's technology, our capacity for wonder, to dream through our machines, was closing down.

Virtual Machines

All technologies are also mental constructs: we think through them, but at the same time they define the boundaries of our thoughts. My CDs are very much about these mental constructions, cinemas of the mind. I see them as twins. As philosophical toys. *Beyond* is a dualist machine. *Where Where There There Where* is a logical and materialist machine. The key figure for me here was Raymond Roussel, the first great constructor of fantastic machines in the twentieth century. It is Roussel's madness, in the form of his novel *Locus Solus*, that is at the heart of *Beyond*. Here we are confronted with a symptomatic work, symptoms of fact, symptoms of fiction, symptoms of an age, each I believe illuminating the other. Written in 1914,

Locus Solus simply recounts a tour of the estate of a famous inventor, Martial Canterel (who was modeled on Edison). One by one, bizarre mechanical inventions are described in a style at once dry and fantastic.

What I began to discover was that a work of fiction, written by a so-called madman, or at least, in the words of his doctor, Pierre Janet, "a singular neuropath," was not nearly as bizarre as it appeared on first reading. Instead, this book might better be regarded as a strange mirror reflecting back symptomatically and with almost uncanny clarity the crossroads of media technology and psychology at this time. Roussel's explanatory mania always goes beyond the fantastically detailed mechanical descriptions of moving parts, cogs, and wheels, to become, as it were, case histories. The resulting machines can be seen as the outcome of some kind of psychological disturbance on the part of his characters. These machines are the externalization of the mind at work.

Re-Animation

Most resonant for me was Roussel's description of the Ice House. It reveals a series of dioramas that are open to public viewing behind glass. Within each little stage, an actor performs the same melodramatic set piece over and over again with uncanny exactitude. These scenes become truly strange when we discover that all the so-called "actors" are dead. Through electricity, Martial Canterel has mechanically re-animated these dead people. They are not conscious, but instead, once revived, repeat unconsciously (with unvarying motions) the most traumatic moments of their lives, in a suitably chilled environment: hence the Ice House.

Vitalium

At last, after a great deal of trial and error with corpses submitted to the

still: Zoe Beloff's *Beyond* (1997)

required degree of cold, Professor Canterel prepared on the one hand Vitalium and on the other Ressurrectine. The latter was injected as a liquid into the skull of some defunct person from a laterally pierced opening, solidifying of its own accord around the brain. It is then only necessary to put some point of the internal envelope into contact with Vitalium, for the two new substances, each of them inactive without the other, to release a powerful current of electricity, which penetrating the brain and overcoming its cadaveric rigidity, thus endows the corpse with an impressive artificial life.[6]

What are we to make of this grotesque scene? In my view, a little research reveals that it was at the time, perhaps, much less strange than it appears to be now. Here it is very interesting to note, as has been pointed out in an essay by Vanessa Schwartz, that up until the turn of the century, the Paris Morgue was an extremely popular place of public entertainment.[7] Schwartz connects this spectacle with panoramas and the wax museum as pre-cinematic entertainments that this new technology more or less killed off. And in a sense this is a turning point that we discover in Roussel's writing. For the dead in his Ice House are not unlike those frozen figures that would mechanically come to life in the earliest movies.

Remember that the first films were initially shown with a still frame up on the screen that would then suddenly come to life as the projectionist cranked the projector. At the same time these films, less than a minute long, were often shown as loops so that the same gestures were repeated with uncanny precision over and over again.

An Ersatz of Life

In his book *Life to those Shadows*, Noël Burch wrote:

> Edison's wish to link his phonograph to an apparatus capable of reproducing pictures is not just the ambition of an astute captain of industry; it is also the pursuit of the fantasy of a class become the fantasy of a culture: to extend "the conquest of nature" by triumphing over death through an ersatz of life itself.[8]

Central to my work is this theme of death and artificial resurrection. The machine mediating between these two states. I believe that this legacy, so often forgotten, of the suppression of death, continues to haunt the creation of virtual reality.

An Electric Brain

Again in my next CD-ROM, *Where Where There There Where*, I came back to the Ice House as a kind of guiding metaphor. To just stop and explain for a moment, in 1996 I was approached by the Wooster Group Theater Company and asked to do something in relation to a new work that they were rehearsing. The work is called *House/Lights* and is related in a very idiosyncratic way to Gertrude Stein's play *Doctor Faustus Lights the Lights*. In no sense was my work to be a document of the play itself. Rather, one might describe it as a satellite work. It exists purely in the virtual realm. Here, Roussel's description of the dead body as electrical automata insensibly acting out the most traumatic moments of its life became in my mind the Steinian figure caught in a loop of language. Her Doctor Faustus sold his soul to the devil for the secret of electric light, only to discover he had no soul to sell. Only then, in anguish, he discovers that he cannot die, for without a soul he is in essence already dead, or like any machine, neither alive nor dead.

stills: Zoe Beloff's *Where Where There There Where* (1998)

A Window or a Door

Ultimately the computer is simply one apparatus of many that I use in my work. My QuickTime movies allowed me to sketch out ideas that I am currently fleshing out through resurrecting lost or forgotten technologies, particularly 3D projection, to explore the histories of (what we think of as) virtual reality. In my CDs, I attempted to evoke an imaginary landscape beyond or behind the screen of the computer. More and more, I am fascinated by conjuring up phantoms that come out to greet us, that invade our own three-dimensional space. My recent stereoscopic film *Shadow Land, or Light from the Other Side* is based on the 1897 autobiography of Elizabeth d'Espérance, a materializing medium, who could produce full-body apparitions. It suggests how one might think of a medium as a kind of "mental projector," and the phantoms as representations of her psychic reality. Visually the film explores the origins of what we think of as the virtual. While twentieth-century cinema can be described as a "window into another world," the nineteenth century conceived of spectres that could cross over into our world. Currently I am working on an installation, *The Influencing Machine of Miss Natalija A.*, that uses stereoscopic diagrams and interactive video to conjure up the hallucinations of a schizophrenic.

stills: Zoe Beloff's *The Influencing Machine of Miss Natalija A.* (2001)

Time Machines

As I have tried to demonstrate, all media technologies could be said to be shot through with this idea of artificial resurrection, with time and death. They are time machines. Cinema is a time machine of movement. Stereo photography brings about the artificial reconstitution of space, congealed now like waxworks or the dead frozen behind glass in the morgue. Is it then so strange that people believed in the literal possibility of travel in time? I end *Beyond* with a quote from Pierre Janet, who actually believed in the possibility of time travel: "The past exists and endures in a place we do not know and cannot go."[9]

This is a slightly abridged version of an essay that first appeared in *The New Screen Media: Cinema/Art/Narrative*, edited by Martin Rieser and Andrea Zapp (London: British Film Institute, 2002); it is reprinted here by permission of the author.

Endnotes

1. Raul Ruiz, *Poetics of Cinema* (Paris: Editions Dis Voir, 1995), 107.
2. My website *Illusions*, an exploration of the relationship between digital media and cinematic toys, can be found at www.turbulence.org/Works/illusions/index.html.
3. Walter Benjamin, *The Arcades Project* (Cambridge/London: The Belknap Press, 1999), 546.
4. Charles Baudelaire, "Les Sept Vieillards," in *Les Fleurs du Mal*, trans. Francis Scarfe (London: Anvil Press Poetry, 1986), 177.
5. Charles Baudelaire, "Symptômes de Ruine," in *The Poems in Prose*, trans. Francis Scarfe (London: Anvil Press Poetry, 1989), 206.
6. Raymond Roussel, *Locus Solus*, trans. R. C. Cunningham (London: John Calder, 1983), 118.
7. Vanessa R. Schwartz, "Cinematic Spectatorship Before the Apparatus: The Public Taste for Reality. Fin-de-Siècle Paris," in Linda Williams, ed., *Viewing Positions* (New Jersey: Rutgers University, 1994).
8. Noël Burch, *Life to those Shadows*, trans. Ben Brewster (Berkeley: University of California Press, 1990), 7.
9. Quoted in Henri F. Ellenberger, *The Discovery of the Unconscious: The History and Evolution of Dynamic Psychiatry* (New York: Basic Books, 1970), 354.

The Pain of Ordinariness: The Art of Tabaimo

Morishita Akihiko   translated by Narushima Miya

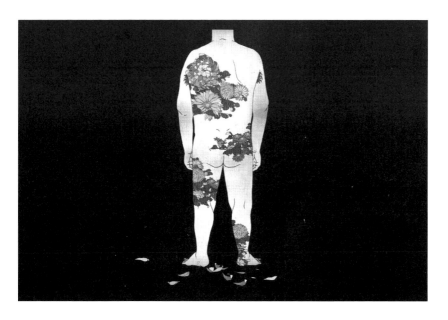

1. Introduction

In the spring of 1999, I encountered the work of Tabaimo (1975-) for the first time, specifically her installation *Nippon no Daidokoro* (*Japanese Kitchen*, 1999), which was exhibited in the Graduation Work Exhibition of the Kyoto University of Art and Design at the Kyoto Municipal Museum of Art. She was still a student then, using her real name, Tabata Ayako, a clear indication that she had not yet developed a strong self-consciousness as an artist. Nevertheless, her work was carefully completed and of very high quality—it hardly looked like a student's work. (She showed the same work in her first private exhibition at a rented gallery in Kyoto shortly after her graduation. She named the exhibition *Tabaimo Show* at that time). This piece earned the Chancellor's Award and turned out to be her breakthrough work. Yet, it was when this piece won first prize at the "Kirin Contemporary Awards 1999" that her career was really launched. In 2000, she held a large-scale exhibition in Osaka celebrating the victory, including several new works. Since then, she has attracted growing attention, which has led to invitations to exhibitions not only in Japan but abroad as well. In short, she became the darling of the art world in a flash.

Parenthetically, I should say a little bit about my professional relationship with Tabaimo, although it slightly disrupts the time sequence. Around April

still: detail from Tabaimo's video installation *hanabi-ra* (2003) ©Tabaimo/Courtesy of Gallery Koyanagi

1999, I asked Tabaimo to submit her work to a group exhibition, *Kobe Art Annual '99 'I⇄ ,'* which is regarded as a gateway to success for young artists in the Kansai region (Kobe, Kyoto, Osaka). When she showed me the portfolio she had brought along, I was at a loss for words. It was a big heavy file about A1-size and filled to bulging with the fruits of her past work, from school projects to pieces done for exhibitions. I was impressed not only by the amount of her work, but also by its wide range and quality. I was amazed by the fact that an art student had managed to produce such quantity during her school years (including even before her college days).

Tabaimo introduced her new work, *Japanese Zebra Crossing* (1999) in the Kobe Art Annual '99. Although I will later describe this piece in detail, what should be mentioned here is the written statement that Tabaimo contributed to the exhibition catalogue. (This passage was cited on several later occasions, and is also available in English translation.[1]) She writes that during her childhood, she had considered herself special. As she made no effort during her middle and high school days, however, she eventually fell behind others. Painfully, she came to realize that she was just "the most ordinary of the ordinary" (*futsuu no naka no futsuu*).[2] In short, what she wrote about was her rediscovery of herself through the experience of setbacks: i.e. the disclosure of the negative aspects of her character. At the same time, however, she also showed her self-confidence, since it was upon this experience of tasting the bitterness of being no more than an ordinary person that she established the solid basis of her creativity. "Being honest with myself (i.e. the absurd, dirty, and superficial me)"[3] is the point of self-awareness on which she stands.

This life history combined with the specific education she obtained through the Information Design Course, which has a comprehensive curriculum that stretches across the fields of design and art, to establish her artistic character. It is possible to imagine that Tabaimo would not have become the artist she is today, the master of a variety of media and techniques, had she studied at an educational institution specializing only in animation or experimental film. In addition, the influence of Tanaami Keiichi (1936-), Tabaimo's teacher, should not be overlooked. Tanaami, a creator of experimental films and animations, is active as a graphic designer in the business world. His art is characterized by its multi-directionality: impressively lurid simplified illustrations (e.g., goldfish, pine trees, and people); drawings of his daily dreams; and three-dimensional works. Tanaami's orientation must have provided Tabaimo with no small stimulation, and, following his example, she has been working in a wide range of media, including graphic design and bookbinding, while producing plastic arts at the same time.

I would like to take a quick glance at one piece of media art contained in Tabaimo's 1999 portfolio. It was her proposal for a simple interactive installation using a computer and a video projector, which she had entered in The 4th Fukui International Youth Media Art Festival (where it received an Honorable Mention).[4] In this work, an image of a human abdomen opens to reveal the internal organs. When a viewer selects an organ, the head and four limbs turn into cartoons which delineate other people's adversities. For example, one figure inadvertently cuts off his finger and puts it back into his nostrils in a mad panic, or thousands of cockroaches swarm in to fill a kitchen, and so on. The images were designed for audiences to experience the enjoyment of someone else's unhappiness as "your own happiness." We can perceive the germ of Tabaimo's later work in this concept, developed even before her professional debut.

2. Form: Illustration and Animation

It would be impossible, in the art world, to make any conclusive comments about a young artist who, though already famous, has been pursuing her career for only five years. I will therefore quickly review her progress as of this moment and point to several original characteristics of her art. Of course, some of these characteristics will continue thriving, and some will decay as she develops as an artist.

First, I will examine Tabaimo's work from the perspective of artistic form. Her approach to the moving image employs not photographic live-action films but animations, through which she can make use of her strong illustration skills. Although she uses computers as a device, she outlines her drawings by hand in pen, deliberately blurring the lines and making the movement of her animations clumsy. Her animations are the opposite of fluid motion, as represented by Disney's animation, being closer to the line of "limited animation" seen in series such as UPA's *Mister Magoo* cartoons, and also common in Japanese commercial animation. Another related technique is to intentionally make her work look unskillful, which is particularly evident in her handwritten characters. Being *heta-uma* used to be a dominant trend in the art and design world in Japan. This word, still in occasional use today, means that a work is actually well-made, even though it looks unskilled at first glance. As for colours, Tabaimo sometimes borrows from the *ukiyoe* (woodblock prints) of Katsushika Hokusai (1760-1849), for example, and applies his colour schemes to her work. This is exemplified in her usage of some monochromes and, in particular, gradations from yellow to blue or red.

These lines, movement, colours, and shadowing are distinctive characteristics of Tabaimo's work. Besides these elements, she uses *hanafuda* (Japanese playing cards) as a motif, and in some cases refers to Hokusai's famous print *Aka-Fuji* (*Red Mt. Fuji*). For these reasons, one can easily identify a conscious connection between Tabaimo's work and traditional Japanese visual representations such as *ukiyoe* and *kusazoshi* (woodblock-illustrated novels published during the Edo and Meiji periods). (In addition to those examples, there are others: The clouds floating in the sky in the backgrounds of her work remind us of shapes particular to Japanese paintings of the Heian Period, and so on.) Tabaimo's art is a sort of contemporary version, created by image media, of those inexpensive popular printed materials common folk were able to buy during the Edo Period. As well, the affinity between Tabaimo's art and *manga* comics emerges when her work is compared to that of Ohtomo Katsuhiro (1954-), famous for the *Akira* series (published in magazine form between 1982 and 1990, and as a series of books between 1984 and 1993).

We can clearly see "the inevitability of things being as they should be" (*so araneba naranu hitsuzensei*) behind Tabaimo's animations. What is less clear, however, is whether she will keep using animation as her primary means of expression. It would not be a surprise if she became a director of movie dramas, given a chance in the future. But drawing pictures and animating them makes it possible for Tabaimo to freely express her ideas, allowing her to construct, without practical limitations, an unrealistic and delusional world that could never occur in an everyday setting. Tabaimo's unique visual world is different from either the voluptuous lines of Aihara Nobuhiro (1944-), a prominent Japanese independent animator, or the skillfulness of Yamamura Koji (1964-). The reality of Tabaimo's world, however, cannot be described fully through a mere analysis of her artistic form. I will therefore set this topic aside for now, and return to it towards the end of the essay, after I examine the thematic elements of her work.

3. Form: Integration

A key feature of Tabaimo's work is her skill in mixing and integrating media. Of course, many artists recently have been expanding their work using media such as video, but these works are often mere projections in galleries or museums. By contrast, Tabaimo's work is characterized by its elaborately conceived and finished architectural installations, which are never just appendages of her visual images. In her installations, the integration of time and space is beautifully accomplished in various ways. This had already happened in *Japanese Kitchen*. When one opened the *shoji*, or Japanese paper sliding doors, there extended before one a tiny *tatami*-matted room, in which one could see three different images projected in a small alcove. Later this was developed into the space which almost encircled the audience in *Nippon no Tsukin Kaisoku* (*Japanese Commuter Train*, 2001). (What is interesting in this piece is that the images appear in a nested structure, so that they look as if they could be continued *ad infinitum*, like an infinite regress.) In addition, the images slowly shift from screen to screen as if the room were rotating—a panoramic technique she first used in the *Nippon no Yuya—Otokoyu* (*Japanese Bathhouse—Gents*, 2000). Another strategy for integrating the audience into the architectural space of her works can be found in *Nippon no Odanhodo* (*Japanese Zebra Crossing*). In that work, the audience was forced to stand uncomfortably on a steeply angled floor in the darkness. By contrast, in the more recent *Obake Yashiki* (*Haunted House*, 2003), the inside of the semicircular space becomes a screen, and fragmented images appear one after another, moving to the right and left, reminding us of a searchlight or a lighthouse. However, the audience can only see these images through a peephole. In her hypertext-like interactive piece *Nippon no Onuchi* (*Japanese Interior*, 2002), such panoramic space is expanded from real space to virtual space through a computer.

Still, her works make it clear that even infinite space, in the end, only occurs within a certain frame or limit. These could be the paper sliding doors in the kitchen, the door of the bathhouse, or the peephole. In short, they address a symbolized infinity, the endless desire for a horrifying illusionary found in either the creator or the audience. Even a storm in a glass, if transposed, can place one in a vast and boundless cosmos, a different dimension. We cannot, however, settle forever in that space; we are always pulled back into real space where we live. To be the object of a work as well as the subject who looks at it—it is this dual nature within ourselves that Tabaimo always endeavours to bring into the consciousness of the viewer.

This is because Tabaimo's work is focused not only on Japanese social conditions as an object, but also on the attitudes—in particular, the indifference—of the Japanese people (including Tabaimo herself and me), who accommodate and passively accept the conditions of their daily lives. I will return to this point in the next section.

4. Thematic: "Nippon"

When we look at Tabaimo's works from the aspect of artistic form, or the ways she creates her animations, we find elements that give us the impression that her work can be related to visual expressions peculiar to Japan, including traditional paintings and prints, and contemporary comics. Indeed, things like *hanafuda* and *ukiyoe* are used as motifs in some of her pieces. Yet, beyond all of these rather trivial details, the main theme of her work is the everyday lives of contemporary Japanese people, an irrational and half-delusional unreality lurking beneath a reality that is alluring at first glance. In *Japanese Kitchen*, a "salary-man," or white-collar worker, literally has his head cut off on a cutting board ("having one's head cut off" also means "being fired" in Japanese), and a high school student throws himself to his death the moment a middle-aged housewife cracks an egg. A group of middle-aged women break into the men's section of the public bathhouse in *Japanese Bathhouse—Gents*. The menstrual blood of a female student is discharged in the shape of the Rising Sun, Japan's national flag in *Japanese Zebra Crossing*. Interestingly, all these expressions are subtly related to certain body sensations or the senses of our internal organs (including our appetite) and skin. In response to such works, people uphold Tabaimo as an artist who can frankly describe the negative and dark

still: detail from Tabaimo's video installation *Haunted House* (2003) ©Tabaimo/Courtey of Gallery Koyanagi aspects of Japanese life—to them, her work is cruel and humorous.

At the beginning of this article, I quoted from a passage written by Tabaimo in 1999 (at almost the same time as her debut exhibition), and remarked that Tabaimo calls for "being honest with myself (i.e. the absurd, dirty, and superficial me)." This could be directly applied to the *Nippon* that she deals with in her works. In other words, Tabaimo tries to reveal the "honest (absurd, dirty, and superficial) aspects of Japan," disclosing those parts which, if not shameful, we would prefer to avoid or ignore as if they don't exist. (Of course, these ingredients are not presented as they are, but rather cooked Tabaimo-style.) The fact that she uses the word *Nippon* (Japan) in the titles of her major works implies that she is not dealing with the official prim and proper surface of Japan, but is empathizing with the reality of the society. This can be connected to the fact that we Japanese shout "Nippon!" when we cheer for our national team in international soccer tournaments and so forth. (Thus the emotional nuance of this word is lost if we simply translate it as "Japan.")

5. Conclusion: Criticism in Tabaimo's work

Where should I locate Tabaimo's work in the context of art in Japan and in the world at large, even if only provisionally? A large-scale exhibition tracing the history of modern Japanese paintings was held some time ago, where a certain trend of art from the nineteen-fifties through the sixties and eighties was categorized as "Japan Pop" in the light of its popular appeal.[5] Although great artists such as Fukuda Miran (1963-) and Morimura Yasumasa (1951-) were included among the exhibitors in the section on the nineteen-eighties, some works from the earlier period (fifties and sixties) captured my attention. In particular, I found some connections between Tabaimo's works and paintings like Yamashita Kikuji's (1919-86) *Akebono-mura Monogatari* (*A Tale of Akebono Village*, 1953) and Nakamura Hiroshi's (1932-) *Enkan Ressha A (Boenkyo Ressha)* (*Circular Train A [Telescope Train]*, (1968)). These depicted, with surrealistic maneuverings, real aspects of Japanese society (especially abhorrent and dark events) during the postwar reconstruction period. The coexistence of pop and surrealism found in Yamashita and Nakamura's paintings can be regarded as a distant progenitor of Tabaimo's work.

Even if I genealogize Tabaimo's work in this way, however, there remains an essential but unresolved question relating to Tabaimo's point of view. In the aforementioned short passage from 1999, Tabaimo wrote that she regards herself as "the most ordinary of the ordinary." In other words,

Tabaimo is aware of herself as an ordinary person, and it is from this view-point that she tries to depict the everyday life of ordinary *Nippon-jin* (Japanese people) in her own way. In fact, however, there are many layers of complex inflections that point to a troublesome paradox on this point.

Regarding herself as an "ordinary" person, Tabaimo argued that people appearing in her works should be representatives. "What I am searching for," she says in an interview with an art critic, "are prototypes; for example, a man whom everyone can easily imagine or a situation which everyone acknowledges as a normal consequence in a certain situation. I don't want to insert my own messages in my art."[6]

Later in this passage, she mentions that she had judged it impossible to pass on *information* to audiences during the short duration of an animated artwork, using characters no one could imagine. The thought lying behind this judgment is Tabaimo's belief that there is "another way to make the story understood when audiences open their bureau drawers and pull out their own information."[7] Thus, Tabaimo further normalizes normality. In other words, she relies on the ordinariness of ordinary people, or cleverly takes advantage of it.

In our daily lives, what we see and think is, so to speak, clouded or blurred by our customs and culture, which makes it difficult for us to reach the truth of things. We tend to push whatever we are not interested in away from our consciousness. Things that actually exist are made transparent and invisible. This is why we cannot perceive ordinary things as they are. One can call it a filter surrounding our mind—an internalized filter. Or, in the way we view things, multiple layers of membranes sticking like moss. Therefore, ordinariness can never be seen as a natural, *a priori* category. Rather, it is something that we set up and construct as if it is "ordinary" to us. We don't notice this stage management and accept it as "ordinariness." Although innocent ordinariness never exists anywhere, we continue to assume that it exists.

Art has the power to peel away these membranes adhering to things, scrape off the filth, and disclose the truth of things. Naked truth. It is the zero degree of meaning (*imi no zerodo no jokyo*)—yet it is quite rare that such a state occurs, and it is an extremely lucky situation when it happens. Then, at that moment when the hidden truth becomes evident, it is banished again from our sight by the pressure of concealment, which is widespread even in the art world. Nevertheless, we keep trying to improve ourselves every day so that we can appreciate such manifestations of truth for even a moment. Artists polish their keen sense through their creative work, and so do audiences through their enjoyment of that which is created.

In short, art is the world where being ordinary is not permitted; the artist's version would have to be a dressed-up pretense of ordinariness. Therefore, the ordinariness that Tabaimo advocates is a consciously produced "ordinariness." The effusion of "truth" may come to be realized by expounding our views on ordinariness among the ordinary, or by disclosing the abnormality that is latent in normality. How, we may wonder, does Tabaimo view this situation? The strategy she uses is to try to conquer the ordinariness of the ordinary by transforming it into a pop and surreal form. In short, she reverses that which she picked up from daily life into something that initially appears unrealistic, cruel, and immoral. (For example, cutting off the head of a "salary-man" to make sushi and eating it up, menstrual blood that becomes a flag of the Rising Sun, and so forth.) She seems to be attempting to break down the ordinary of the ordinaries by transforming it into something that could not exist but can be imagined in art.

Such a surreal flourish, however, cannot help but betray its ordinariness somewhere. It is much like the concept of "horror": Something we might see as horrible falls apart all too easily once a horror movie goes too far beyond the threshold of an audience's imagination, and the structure which supports that consciousness is taken away. Nor is the surreal necessarily the only style to break down ordinariness. For example, it might be enough if one would slide ordinariness a short distance from its natural state. Although it is beyond the capacity of this article to go into further detail, I expect possibilities for other kinds of ordinariness to emerge through Tabaimo's work in the future.

There is one more point that needs to be argued: doesn't the cause of the problem lie in the ordinary people's image of themselves as ordinary? As I mentioned it before, the main theme of Tabaimo is not only the social conditions of "*Nippon*," but also Japanese people's indifference, including her own. Although we become familiar with various accidents and problems through TV and newspapers, we cannot see these problems as our own without taking some sort of action. Tabaimo describes herself in the following way: "As for the events daily reported in the media—I just passively accept them as mere information without any sense of reality. They don't drive me to try and solve the problems confronting Japan."[8] All these incidents are problems to someone else, and she is nothing but an indifferent onlooker. Therefore, she continues, "Unless I was actually involved in a traffic accident, I would not be able to feel the pain."[9] This comment is not necessarily relevant only to her.

To link this point to the ordinariness and the truth that I mentioned before, pain is the cost one must to pay in order to disclose the truth. Just like the ancient scientist who lost his eyesight when he looked at the sun, to a lesser extent, we all have to pay a reasonable cost. In our everyday world, our indifference makes us incapable of feeling pain, or we turn our attention to something else to avoid it. In the world of art, however, we must face pain. This special role is the *raison d'être* of art.

In Tabaimo's case, she has expressed her pain, not because she got involved in a traffic accident, but because she got involved with art by having felt herself deeply as "an ordinary among the ordinary." As a result, she probably came to feel pain for the first time. This must account in some way for the great success she has experienced in the short period since she appeared in the world of art. I hope that she will deepen and develop her pain, namely "the pain of ordinary people" in her future works. Indeed, this hope should be directed not only to Tabaimo, but to Japanese in general (including me). Tabaimo's work encompasses various meanings and values. The most important message contained in her work—what I wish to emphasize at the end of this article—is: Please feel pain as pain. This is a difficult but extremely urgent wish as well as a problem.[10] That is also why the message emerging from Tabaimo's work needs to be disseminated, not just to the Japanese, but to all people.

still: detail from Tabaimo's video installation *hanabi-ra* (2003) ©Tabaimo/Courtey of Gallery Koyanagi

Endnotes

1. Tabaimo, untitled text, in *Kobe Art Annual '99 'I⇄,'* (Kobe: Kobe Art Village Centre, 1999), unpaginated. The English version, albeit a loose translation, was published as an "Artist Statement" in *Mame-imo*, a catalogue for the *Tabaimo Exhibition* at the Kirin Plaza Osaka, 2000. The two citations quoted in this article are not included in the English version of the "Artist Statement," and have been translated here for the first time.

2. Ibid.

3. Ibid.

4. Tabata Ayako, "The other's unhappiness = My happiness," in the catalogue of *The 4th Fukui International Youth Media Art Festival* (Fukui: Fukui Media-City Forum, 1996) pg. 20.

5. *Saiko Kindai Nihon no Kaiga: Biishiki no Keisei to Tenkai* (*Remaking Modernism in Japan 1900-2000*), exhibition catalogue (Tokyo:The University Art Museum—Tokyo National University of Fine Arts and Music and Museum of Contemporary Art, 2004) pg. 240-251.

6. Okabe Aomi, "Ato to Josei to Eizo—Gurokaru Wuman," (*Art, Femininity and Image—Glocal Women*) (*Saiki-Sha*, 2003) pg. 222.

7. Tabaimo, *Nippon no Odanhodo* (*Kobe Art Annual '99 'I⇄,'*), (*Kobe: Kobe Art Village Centre*, 2000) unpaginated.

8. Ibid.

9. Ibid.

10. While the author was writing this article, an event which greatly shocked all Japanese people resurfaced in the news. A psychiatric test showed that an 11-year-old girl who had stabbed her classmate to death "did not have any condition that could be classified as 'aberrant.'" The morning headlines read, "Problems that lurk behind 'the ordinary'" (*The Asahi Shinbun*, Sept. 16, 2004, morning edition, pg.1). This incident demonstrates how deep problems related to "ordinariness" can run.

"The Rock": William Kentridge's
Drawings for Projection

Rosalind Krauss

1.

If it is true that Kentridge's *Monument* is, as we are told, "loosely based" on Beckett's *Catastrophe*, how are we to understand this relationship between film and play? Does it occur at the most manifest level, that of the utter subjugation of one man by another, the first turning the second into stone?

The bit of business, after all, that makes up *Catastrophe* concerns a stage director and his assistant as they "dress" a totally motionless figure for the play's final moment, its—to use the theatrical term—catastrophe. Raised on a pedestal, the object of this attention, initially clad in black, is gradually divested of his hat and coat to reveal his bald head and grey pajamas. The piecemeal adjustments demanded by the director then involve rolling up the pants and whitening the exposed areas of skin—the face, the skull, the partially bared chest, the legs. Monochrome and immobile, the figure is then ready for the final tableau in which a single spotlight isolates him from a now darkened stage and then slowly constricts itself to pick out the face alone. The director, viewing the effect from the audience, expresses his satisfaction. "Great!" he says, "We've got our catastrophe." Appreciation. Applause.

still: William Kentridge's *Felix in Exile* (1994), courtesy of Marian Goodman Gallery

Is this the core around which Kentridge imagined his own "catastrophe" —South Africa's catastrophe? For in *Monument*, the mine owner Soho Eckstein is seen performing as civic benefactor as, with a flourish of media attention and to the applause of the crowd, he unveils the apparition of a dispossessed labourer whom we had seen walking at the outset of the film, now standing immobilized on the pedestal, his load still on his back. That it is the live man and not his representation is assured to us by a detail almost certainly drawn from the Beckett. As the final shot irises in on the face of the monument—in a parallel with Beckett's spotlight—the "statue" lifts its head and opens its eyes; the sound of its breathing continues over the blackened field of the credits. This had been the final moment—post-cata-strophic, so to speak—of *Catastrophe*, as the figure, in defiance of the director, also raises his head and fixes the audience with his stare.

For Beckett, this last gesture is fully ambiguous. Slipping the bonds of total control, the figure's ultimate act of will would seem to open a chink of light onto a world beyond this walled-off stage, in order to allow a sign of freedom or redemption to enter, like the bird that arrives in *Endgame*. But if indeed there is nothing beyond this grip and its boundaries, nothing out-side the totalizing system of the "director," then it would follow that this very act of voluntarism and the thought that propels it is the catastrophe.[1]

Kentridge has spoken about the danger for him, as for any South African artist, of addressing the catastrophe of apartheid head-on, of making a work either fixated on its record of dehumanization or invested in the image of a possible redemption. He calls apartheid "the rock"; and it is a rock on which art itself must always founder. Writing in 1990, the same year as *Monument*, he says:

> These two elements—our history and the moral imperative arising from that—are the factors for making that personal beacon rise into the immov-able rock of apartheid. To escape this rock is the job of the artist. These two constitute the tyranny of our history. And escape is necessary, for as I stated, the rock is possessive, and inimical to good work. I am not saying that apartheid, or indeed, redemption, are not worthy of representation, descrip-tion, or exploration, I am saying that the scale and weight with which this rock presents itself is inimical to that task.[2]

But if the dehumanizing petrification represented in *Monument* clearly derives from "the rock," the indirect address to the problem urged by Kentridge—"you cannot face the rock head on; the rock always wins"—sug-gests that his attachment to Beckett's play might in fact have reached under the specifics of theme to find itself attracted to something else, something more formal in kind.

Most of *Catastrophe* is focused not on the immobile figure but on the space between it and the director, a space which is articulated by the constant movement of the assistant who, notebook in hand and pencil at the ready, jots down the director's modifications even as she shuttles back and forth from the side of the stage to its centre in order to carry out his commands on the body of the figure. It is she who removes the hat, who takes the hands out of the pockets, who whitens the skull, who rolls up the pants, each time moving back to the side of the director to join him in regarding their creation and to light his cigar and to note down his instructions on her pad. It is her traffic between the two points, that of command and that of execution, that makes up the business of the play or, as Gogo and Didi say to each other in *Waiting for Godot*, that makes the time pass.

Now it is just this walking back and forth, this constant shuttling between the movie camera on one side of the studio and the drawing tacked to the wall on the other, that constitutes the field of Kentridge's own operation. The drawing on which he works is at all times complete and at all times in flux since, once he has recorded it from his station at his Bolex, he moves across the floor to make an infinitesimal modification in its surface, only then to retreat once more to the camera.[3] This is what he calls "the rather dumb physical activity of stalking the drawing, or walking backwards and forwards between the camera and drawing; raising, shifting, adapting the image." (WK 93) Working with no overall plan in mind, without the filmmaker's scenario or the animator's storyboard, he is instead dependent on this strange space of back-and-forth, at once mechanical and meditational, for the conception of his work: the individual images, their development, their interconnection which becomes, in the end, the "plot." It is a space which, as we have seen, is technical, dictated by an "animation" process in which a single drawing is gradually transformed through a combination of additions and erasures, each occurring a few millimetres at a time and each change recorded by exposing a single frame of film. The result is that an eight-minute film might be made through the modification of only twenty drawings. As opposed to the endless proliferation of drawings dictated by traditional animation, with each change of bodily position calling for a new rendering, and thus a separate graphic object, this is a technique of extreme parsimony and of endless round trips.

But that the technical should open onto the conceptual leads Kentridge to associate a different notion of the wheel to this treadmill, one he calls "fortuna." Caught up within the quasi-automatism of the process, he is strangely enough left free to improvise and to do this in the grip of agencies he characterizes as "something other than cold statistical chance, and something too, outside the range of rational control" (WK 68). The analogy he makes is to the way ordinary language, deploying itself in the course of conversation, is for the most part guided by habit, by learned patterns of speech, by rote formulations, by gambits and clichés. Thus, though we embark on our discourse knowing generally what we want to say, much of the activity of choosing the words and forming the sentences is pre-programmed, semi-mechanical, a form of automatism.

But this very fact also allows a kind of free association to what we are saying, as we are saying it, to occur. In mid-course, our remarks might, therefore, take off in an entirely unforeseen direction, one we could not have meant at the outset. In this sense, as Kentridge puts it, "in the very activity of speaking, generated by the act itself, new connections and thoughts emerge." (WK 69) And this new sense of automatism—the upsurge from the unconscious of the unanticipated, the unexpected—a sense that is the very opposite of the first, with its idea of the routinized and the programmed, is nonetheless folded together with it in the concept of *fortuna*.

Kentridge has given three examples of the operation of *fortuna* from the opening stages of the conception of *Mine* (1991), the third of the series of works he calls Drawings for Projection—a rubric that holds open the possibility that there might be a problem, one to which we will return, in simply naming these works "animated films." The first example was the effort just to make an opening dent in the long process of conceiving the film, which in this case meant organizing an image whose changes would be wholly automatic, programmed from the outset, so that after a day's work at least something—several seconds of footage—would result. Accordingly he drew a geological section of the black earth riven by the mine shaft within which the lift's slow ascension towards the top could be more or less mechanically shot and, bit by bit, erased and redrawn.

With the lift at the face of the earth, the emergence of a crowd of workers came next, the crowd itself another "automatism" of Kentridge's process. "With this charcoal technique," he says, "each person is rendered with a single mark on the paper. As more marks are added, so the crowd emerges. It is far easier to draw a crowd of thousands than to show a flicker of doubt passing over one person's face" (WK 67). Having decided that this teeming landscape would acknowledge its own "possession" by the mine owner, Soho Eckstein, an "earthquake" then transformed this field into Soho's bed covers, as he rolls over in awakening from sleep. This meant that the plot

now contained Soho, in bed, on the one hand, and the mine with its workers on the other. The visual—and conceptual—link between the two was the next gift from *fortuna*.

While trying to figure out how to get Soho out of bed and into his office, from which he directs his industrial empire in the other films, Kentridge played for time by letting Soho have breakfast. The smoke from his cigar having transformed itself into a bell, the bell in turn was ready to metamorphose into a coffee pot so that the meal could commence. The kind of coffee pot Kentridge put in Soho's hand, however, was simply the accident of what happened to be in his studio that day, namely a cafetière: a glass cylinder with a metal plunger that compresses the grains of coffee within the pot.[4] "It was only when the plunger was half way down, in the activity of drawing, erasing it, repositioning it a few millimetres lower each time," Kentridge recounts, "that I saw, I knew, I realized (I cannot pin an exact word on it) that it would go through the tray, through the bed, and become the mine shaft" (WK 68). And in this becoming, the whole of the film opened up for him: the meaning of the relationship between the mine and the bed, in which Soho will be seen "excavating from the earth an entire social and eco history. Atlantic slave ships, Ife royal heads, and finally a miniature rhinoceros, are dragged up through the miners embedded in the rocks to Soho having his

still: William Kentridge's *Mine* (1991), courtesy of Marian Goodman Gallery morning coffee." (*WK* 60)

In characterizing this aspect of *fortuna*, Kentridge goes on: "The sensation was more of discovery than invention. There was no feeling of what a good idea I had had, rather, relief at not having overlooked what was in front of me." And he stresses the improvisational character of his discovery, along with the fact that he came upon it on the prowl: "What was going on while I was in the kitchen preparing something to drink? Was there some part of me saying 'Not the tea, there, you fool, the coffee, not espresso, the cafetière, you daft... Trust me. I know what I'm doing.' If I'd had tea that morning, would the impasse of Soho in bed have continued?" (*WK* 68) That his prowl through the kitchen forms a parallel for him with his very process of "stalking the drawing," echoes in his remark: "It is only when physically engaged on a drawing that ideas start to emerge. There is a combination between drawing and seeing, between making and assessing that provokes a part of my mind that otherwise is closed off."(*WK* 68)

The generosity with which Kentridge opens his process, in all its minutia, to his listener—these comments come from a 1993 lecture called "'Fortuna': Neither Program nor Chance in the Making of Images"—would seem to be motivated by the desire to displace the focus on the general field of his activity from "the rock" and its ideological imperatives to the work and its routines. It is for this reason that the link between *Monument* and *Catastrophe* needs to be held in suspension between the thematics of outrage and the choreography of process, neither given dominance, and with the possible understanding that the artist's leverage on the former is best exercised through the latter.

2.

Let us then pursue that half of the connection that focuses on *fortuna*, with its stress on the automatic and automatism. It is related, as Kentridge himself admits, to the singularity of his process. Because that process arose from the graphic medium and Kentridge's desire to track the course of his drawings as they evolved, it didn't begin with the problem of filmic animation; animation here—the run-on projection of the frames recording successive phases of the drawing which thereby generates the sense of a single work in motion—is a kind of derivative of drawing. This is why the first of his films announced itself as Drawings for Projection before appending, as a subtitle, *Johannesburg, 2nd Greatest City after Paris* (1989). And this is why Kentridge has maintained the same master title for the developing series as a whole. And why it is important for him to hang on to the context of art—museum or gallery—as the place of exhibition for the films, insisting as well that they be screened alongside their constitutive drawings. This has annoyed certain commentators who, otherwise admiring Kentridge's work, don't see why he shouldn't just show them as animation films, entering them into the space of cinema and its particular theatres of display and competition. They find his resistance to this strangely arty, a tic.[5]

What these critics miss, however, is the uniqueness of Kentridge's medium and, with this, his desire to stress its specificity. Though they freely acknowledge the strangeness, even the perversity, of making animation not by addition but, so to speak, by subtraction, this peculiarity nevertheless remains for them a special case within that subset of film called animation. They do not see that for Kentridge animation is merely a technical support, like the slide-tape James Coleman exploits. As such it brings along with it not only a set of material conditions, but also a dense layering of economic and social history that ranges from, on the one hand, its particular modes of commercialization and thus the need for industrialized production and mass dissemination, to the forms of serial repetition of its narratives and characters, on the other, as though it were the modern day inheritor of the *commedia dell'arte* and the Grand Guignol only now played entirely by animals.

But in Kentridge's practice filmic animation is a support or ground for what takes place within or on top of it, namely a type of drawing that is extremely reflexive about its own condition, that savours the graininess of the clouds of charcoal or pastel as they are blown onto paper, that luxuriates in the luminous tracks of the eraser that open onto Turneresque fogs, that examines the particular form of the palimpsest as a graphically specific signifier, that delimits the frame within which the drawing's marks will appear and within that, ever smaller frames—drawing placing its own defining characteristic as contour *en abyme*. It is this very density and weight of the drawing, this way it has of producing the hiccup of a momentary stillness and thus dragging against the flow of the film, that opens up the gap between Kentridge's medium and that of film itself, a divide which produces the specificity of the thing that, like Coleman, he is "inventing."[6]

The connection between the specificity of a medium and something like Kentridge's *fortuna* has been wrought in a not-unrelated context through the philosopher Stanley Cavell's decision to choose the word *automatism* to explore the very condition of mediums themselves. Arguing that the problem now posed by modernism is that the job its artists are asked to undertake "is no longer to produce another instance of an art but a new medium within it," Cavell alternatively describes this concern as "the task of establishing a new automatism."[7] In locating the idea of *automatism* in relation to what in traditional art might have been called the "broad genres or forms in which an art organizes itself (the fugue, the dance forms, blues) and those local events or topoi around which a genre precipitates itself (e.g. modulations, inversions, cadences)," Cavell clarifies: "In calling such things automatisms, I do not mean that they automatically ensure artistic success or depth, but that in mastering a tradition one masters a range of automatisms upon which the tradition maintains itself, and in deploying them one's work is assured of a place in that tradition." (*WV* 104)

The peculiarity of this verbal substitution—"automatism" for "medium"—is explained perhaps by the importance within an earlier discussion by Cavell of the concept of musical improvisation, which because it is undertaken against the backdrop—or rather with the support—of ready-made formulae, is a peculiar blend of the kind of liberating release of spontaneity that we associate with, for example, the Surrealists' invocation of the word *automatism* (as in psychic automatism) and the set of learned, more or less rote conventions (*automatisms*) contained within the traditional media that not only make it conceivable to improvise—as when Bach could improvise a single voice into the extraordinary complexity of a five-part fugue—but make it possible to test the validity of a given improvisation: the success or failure of a pianist's invention of the final cadenza for which a composer has called, for example. Arguing that one can imagine all music up to Beethoven as being, to a certain extent, improvised, Cavell says:

> Reliance on formula seems to allow the fullest release of spontaneity.… The context in which we can hear music as improvisatory is one in which the language it employs, its conventions, are familiar or obvious enough that at no point are we or the performer in doubt about our location or goal.[8]

Now, if Cavell is driven to discuss improvisation, this is because post-war music appears to him to have produced the same dilemma to which Kentridge refers in his "Fortuna" lecture, namely the choice between two equally impossible alternatives, either the absolute mechanization of chance (John Cage) or the utter submission to total organization (Ernst Krenek's electronic programming). In either one of these options, the results are not only cut loose from a subject who can neither be said to have "intended" them nor be held responsible for them, but they are deprived of any way of being tested; there is neither any goal contained within the musical outcome against which it might be judged or appreciated nor is there any condition within which chance itself might be seen to count. But that the taking and seizing of chance—which is another way of naming the capacity to improvise—now imposes itself as both the expression of the withdrawal of the traditional media and the alternative to that withdrawal, means that both improvisation and automatism take on a special weight within this argument. Improvisation now names both the freedom and the isolation of the artist operating without the guarantees of tradition.

In turning his attention from the tensions of modern music to the problem of modernism in film, Cavell adds a new layer to his use of *automatism*. The photographic basis of cinema, he says, means that a certain automatism is naturally guaranteed to film. This is not just because the camera is a machine and thus its recording of the world, bracketing human agency, is produced "automatically," but because it mechanically assures that as spectators our presence to that world will be suspended: "In viewing a movie, my helplessness is mechanically assured: I am present not at something happening, which I must confirm, but at something that has happened, which I absorb (like a memory)." (WV 26) It is this idea of the automatic conditions built into the medium's physical basis that issues into Cavell's global definition of film as "a succession of automatic world projections."

But the mechanical nature of film's guarantee of absence, and thus its automatic suspension of the modern problems of individuality and isolation, is not enough to raise this form of absence to the level of art. For if "film is a candidate for art through its natural relation to its traditions of automatism," then Cavell argues: "The lapse of conviction in its traditional uses of its automatism forces it into modernism; its potentiality for acknowledging that lapse in ways that will redeem its power makes modernism an option for it." (WV 103)

And it is here that the two automatisms layer over one another, the material basis on the one hand and the task of creating a new medium on the other, since as Cavell adds: "What gives significance to features of this physical basis are artistic discoveries of form and genre and type and technique, which I have begun calling automatisms" (WV 105). If it seems perverse to use the same term for film's material support and the conventions generated by it as a medium, this is necessitated in part by what he calls "the fate of modernist art generally—that its awareness and responsibility for the physical basis of its art compel it at once to assert and deny the control of its art by that basis." But then, standing at that crossroads imposed by the formalist implosion to which I have repeatedly referred,[9] Cavell goes on: "This is also why, although I am trying to free the idea of a medium from its confinement in referring to the physical bases of various arts, I go on using the same word to name those bases as well as to characterize modes of achievement within the arts." (WV 105)

The formalist implosion, through which in the 1960s mediums were understood as "essentialized" around a material condition—painting now read as having stripped away all superfluous conventions to reduce itself to the defining bedrock of its physical flatness—is thus resisted by Cavell. And the concept of automatism is the mode of this resistance. An artistic automatism is the discovery of a form—call it a convention—that will generate a continuing set of new instances, spinning them out the way a language does;[10] further, it recognizes the need to take chances in the face of a medium now cut free from the guarantees of artistic tradition; finally it implies the way in which the work so created is "autonomous," liberated from its maker.

Much of all of this is acknowledged in Kentridge's invocation of *fortuna*. The automatism he has discovered—"drawings for projection"—works itself out in a continuing series. Whatever else that series focuses on—apartheid, capitalist greed, eros, memory—the automatism of his process places procedure before meaning, or rather trusts to the fact that his new medium—his new automatism—will induce meaning: "The hope is that without directly plunging a surgeon's knife, the arcane process of obsessively walking between the camera and the drawing-board will pull to the surface, intimations of the interior." (WK 112)

3.

If Cavell's automatism is revealing about what is at stake for Kentridge's aspirations for a medium—in all its invented specificity—the term also harbours a deep reservation about the possibility of that medium's seriousness. For Cavell is particularly unforgiving about the idea of animation, a reservation he expresses by insisting on referring to it as "cartoons." In being drawn, or in any event, in avoiding photography as its basis, animation is excluded from both the automatic (or mechanical) and the world (or realistic) parts of his definition of film as "a succession of automatic world projections." Indeed, one index of animation's specific release from the conditions of this definition is marked by the fact that cartoons are primarily inhabited by talking animals.[11]

This animistic world, Cavell argues, is essentially a child's world:

The difference between [it] and the world we inhabit is not that the world of animation is governed by physical laws or satisfies metaphysical limits which are just different from those which condition us; its laws are often quite similar. The difference is that we are uncertain when or to what extent our laws and limits do and do not apply (which suggests that [within the world of animation] there are no real *laws* at all). (*WV* 170)

In this freedom from law, it is weightlessness and thus an eccentric relation to gravity that obtain; there, too, the conditions of both physical identity and physical destruction are suspended; indeed, the fact that the bodies of cartoon characters never seem to get in their way, makes them almost immortal. "Beasts which are pure spirits," Cavell says of these creatures,

> they avoid or deny *the* metaphysical fact of human beings, that they are condemned to both souls and bodies. A world whose creatures are incorporeal is a world devoid of sex and death. Its creatures elicit from us a painful tenderness. (*WV* 171)

And the conclusion he draws from all of this is that, since what he sees as defining for film's development into the various movie genres is its opening onto a world we recognize as the one we inhabit, then "cartoons are not movies." (*WV* 168)

It could be objected that for Kentridge's purposes it is quite irrelevant whether or not animated cartoons qualify as "movies," and thus as a medium for film in Cavell's sense. For Kentridge is not pursuing film as such but is, rather, building a new medium on the technical support of a widespread and mostly mass-cultural cinematic practice, welcoming its condition as a popular rather than a high art the way Barthes had turned to photo-novels and comic books as forms of support for what he was calling the "third meaning."[12] Further, Kentridge is patently interested in the conventions cartoon animation developed, conventions that involve the serialized exploits of stock characters on the one hand and the possibility of physical metamorphosis on the other. Thus he found himself not only generating a repertory of personae whose actions would be tracked within a continuing series of works but confronting the fact of how resistant such a set is to random expansion (Kentridge tells us how, in the case of *Mine*, he imagined introducing another character—Liberty Eckstein—to the company he had developed, at that point consisting of Soho Eckstein, Mrs. Eckstein, and Felix Teitlebaum—introduced in *Johannesburg, 2nd Greatest City* and brought back as a group for *Sobriety, Obesity, & Growing Old* [1991]—but was unable to do so, the principle of repetition that governs stock repertories such as the *commedia dell'arte* or animated cartoons applying equally to him). And further, this rigidity of the cast finds its equal but opposite principle in the amazing elasticity of the forms.

This latter, of course, had been what most struck and excited Sergei Eisenstein as he theorized the phenomenon of Disney cartoons. Calling this "plasmaticness," he compared the freedom with which animated figures change identities—the mobility of their shapes, their endless metamorphic potential—to the phenomenon of fire. The universal fascination with fire, the libidinal energy associated with its formal flux, and the parallel to this presented by animation go part of the way to explain the grip cartoons exert. Another part, he suggests, is produced by a kind of ontogenetic memory, the unconscious trace of the evolutionary transformations through which the human species itself developed; for a Disney figure presents its viewers with the sense of a being which "behaves like the primal protoplasm . . . skipping along the rungs of the evolutionary ladder."[13]

This elasticity of shape which, like the fascination with fire, he finds cross-culturally—in Carroll's *Alice in Wonderland*, in the illustrator Trier, in eighteenth-century Japanese etchings—leads him to explain the power of this phenomenon as stemming from the desire for "a rejection of once-and-forever allotted form, freedom from ossification, the ability to dynamically assume any form." One example he gives to demonstrate how any part of the body might be submitted to this "plasmatic" principle focuses on Mickey Mouse's white-gloved hands:

> How easily and gracefully these four fingers on both of Mickey's hands, playing a Hawaiian guitar, suddenly dissolve into . . . two pairs of extremities. The two middle fingers become little legs, the two outer fingers—little hands. The second hand becomes its partner. And suddenly there are no longer two hands, but two funny, little white people, elegantly dancing together along the strings of the Hawaiian guitar.[14]

But the most compelling explanation Eisenstein has for the attraction exerted by Disney, is a socio-economic one: given modernity's "mercilessly standardized and mechanically measured existence," Disney offers a "triumph over the fetters of form," his spectacle of perpetual change is a revolt against the greyness of what Eisenstein names as both Fordism and "partitioning." He draws a parallel between Disney and the eighteenth-century protest the animal population of La Fontaine's fables could be seen as staging against seventeenth-century rationalization and mechanization. "The heartless geometrizing and metaphysics [in Descartes]," he writes, "here give rise to a kind of antithesis, an unexpected rebirth of universal animism."[15]

Is there not a sense, however, in which Disney's "triumph," along with that of the other Hollywood cartoonists, is not a revolt against the rationalization of the human body, but its cast shadow, its dialectical underside now made to surface as comic? The legs of little Jerry trying to escape from Tom transformed into frantically turning wheels are not only a picture of the human body endlessly available to mechanization, but fully opened to subdivision according to the requirements labour imposes on human motion, a Taylorist subdivision ("partitioning") that turns parts of the body into independent organisms of movement, like Mickey's fingers become a tiny couple, waltzing along the strings of his ukulele. Disney's "plasmaticness" may thus be not a twentieth-century version of the phenomenon of fire or the primitive idea of animism but, instead, an analogue of the principle of universal equivalence that reigns at the heart of capital. And if this is true there is no real opposition in the end between Eisenstein's vision of Mickey Mouse (even Eisenstein cannot avoid saying of Disney's works "because of the fleeting ephemerality of their existence, you can't reproach them for their mindlessness") and Cavell's condemnation of the weightlessness of cartoons.[16] The abstract condition of the general equivalent, the fluidity of its circulation and exchange, the sense of its endlessly transformative power, make the cartoon figure and money peculiarly apt mirrors of one another.[17]

Now it is precisely *weight* that is a continuing concern for Kentridge. It

still: William Kentridge's *WEIGHING and WANTING* (1998), courtesy of Marian Goodman Gallery appears in the very names of his works—*WEIGHING and WANTING* (1998), *Sobriety, Obesity, & Growing Old*—as in the words he uses to name moral responsibility (with regard to *The History of the Main Complaint* (1996), he says: "here's a person who's in a coma because of the weight of what he's seen" (WK 179)). We find it in what he obviously intends for the physical character of his drawing, as captured by a critic's acknowledgement: "Unlike Daumier and Grosz, Kentridge is not a caricaturist, yet his drawings contain the same authority of line, the same contour and weight...." (WK 178) But specifically concerning the "plasmaticness" inherent in animation, weight makes its appearance through his sense that this transformative power needs to have a certain drag placed on it, a certain resistance or pressure exerted against its weightless fluidity, hence the report of another critic who ends by quoting him: "[Kentridge] is wary of the threat of arbitrariness and guards against an underground series of chance images in which 'anything changes into anything else too easily, in which anything is possible without any pressure.'" (WK 182)

This does not mean that Kentridge's films totally avoid the principle of universal equivalence; in a world inhabited by mine owners and bankers this would be peculiar. General equivalence is one of the conditions of the universe Kentridge is addressing. Hence the cafetière becoming a mine shaft (*Mine*), the cigarette smoke becoming a typewriter (*Johannesburg*), the stethoscope becoming a telephone (*History of the Main Complaint*), the camera's tripod becoming helicopter blades or its lens a machine gun (*Ubu Tells the Truth*), and even more to the point, columns of numbers becoming office buildings or derricks (*Stereoscope*). But another condition that equally reigns within these films operates against the principle of anything changing into anything else, or at least works to dilate the time within which the change occurs and to underscore the impossibility of predicting the form it will take, thus investing that change with a kind of weight (emotional? moral? mnemonic?), as when in *Sobriety, Obesity, & Growing Old*, Soho pets the cat which lies in bed next to him in the absent Mrs. Eckstein's place, and the cat, leaping onto his face as though to comfort him, transforms itself into a gas mask, grotesque and terrifying.

If transformation is built into the very weft of animation—because they are drawn, the successive images can not only render the variations in a moving figure's posture but by the same token can change the very nature of the figure, impossibly stretching or shrinking parts of its body or giving it a new identity altogether—pressure exerted against effortless transformation could also signal pressure exerted against animation itself, which is to say, animation's very illusion of movement. In this case the momentary stillness interleaved between the frames so to speak, the sense of a kind of rictus that brakes the forward motion, reinstating the stillness of a single drawing, would alter the conditions of Kentridge's support.

In theorizing the flow of cinematic illusion, which he calls the movement-image, Deleuze opposes two types of photography: time-exposure (*pose*) and snapshot (*instantané*). The former, which derives from the tradition of painting, strives after an idealization of its subject, the construction of a single posture replete with meaning. This possibility is not open to the latter, which merely nets what Deleuze calls "any-instant-whatever." In its address to themes of movement, painting had always tried to precipitate out the pose that would constellate its idea, but in so doing, motion which (as Zeno had long ago told us) occurs *in between* the possible postures would always have escaped. For any given minute, however, the movie camera, in its total arbitrariness, captures twenty-four any-instants-whatever, none of them infected with the fatal stillness of the pose, each of them capable of ceding its place to its successor in the relay that constitutes the in-between of a motion that is never *in* the moving subject but in the relay itself, in the space between two "nows," one appearing and one disappearing.

Given the importance of the mechanical—photographic—capture of these any-instants-whatever, Deleuze's theory would seem to make animation problematic for his definition of film, although in an entirely different way from Cavell's, since for him the drawn image would not be too light but too heavy for cinema. Deleuze, however, explicitly makes a place for animation:

> If the cartoon film belongs fully to the cinema, this is because the drawing no longer constitutes a pose or a completed figure, but the description of a figure which is always in the process of being formed or dissolving through the movement of lines and points taken at any-instant-whatevers of their course. The cartoon film is related not to a Euclidean, but to a Cartesian geometry. It does not give us a figure described in a unique moment, but the continuity of the movement which describes the figure.[18]

Indeed, to test his drawings for this continuity, the traditional cartoon animator had recourse to the flip book or flicker book as a tool with which to guard against the *pose*:

> When an animator sketches out the scene in his flicker book, what is being expressed in the constant alternation between drawing and how it is seen as the book is flicked through is just this simultaneity of the pose and motion. Though the animator is only able to work from one to the other, what must

nevertheless be captured in the flicker book, separated only by the thickness of the page or support itself, is the simultaneity of the pose and motion, the simultaneity—at once the same and different—of two poses.[19]

However technically primitive, then, the flicker book already projects the framework of film's mechanization of movement as it also already implies the proliferation of images needed to construct it. If at nothing but the crudest, material notion of a medium's support, then, Kentridge's technical alternative, his eschewal of the flip book, sets his medium—his "drawings for projection"—at an angle to animation, one that seems "below" it, which is to say even less technologically invested than the flicker book itself.

One way of characterizing this quality of being "lower" or more regressed than the flicker book would be historical. One could say that in the sense one has in his work of finished drawings substituting themselves for one another, Kentridge is invoking an earlier moment within the prehistory of animation, seeking among the optical toys through which a primitive version of the filmic was glimpsed for something even less apparatus-like than the whirling drum of the zoetrope, or the spinning wheel of the phenakistoscope. It is as though something even more primitively handcrafted is being appropriated as a model, something as moronically simple as the thaumatrope—that type of little disc whose sashes one twiddled between one's fingers so that as it spun, the image on the disc's back would optically marry itself to the image on its front, the bareback rider jumping thereby onto the galloping horse or the pictured canary finding itself within the image of its cage.

Alternatively, the idea of "lower" could be a matter of retrogression from what the Frankfurt School termed the "second nature" of technology, which film invokes through the mechanism of its apparatus, to the "first nature" not just of the handcrafted but of the bodily condition of the human subject. There is a sense in which the body's rhythms have penetrated Kentridge's support, to slow it down, to thicken it, to give it density. This is not just in the breathing that is thematized in so many of the works: the "statue's" laboured breath at the end of *Monument*; the rise and fall of the chests of the workers asleep in their terrible bunks in *Mine*; Soho's troubled wheezing through the gas mask of *Sobriety, Obesity, & Growing Old*; the open-mouthed rasping of the comatose Soho in *The History of the Main Complaint*. It occurs at a deeper level of representation in which the hesitations in the continuity of the movement seem the registration within the film's visual field of Kentridge's body "stalking the drawing," of his own movement both tracking and slowing that of the image.

Both these senses of "below"—as something more primitive that invests the procedures of animation which serve as Kentridge's technical support —converge in the relationship this very crudeness bears to the primary matrix of the drawing itself. For the most striking character of the line generated by Kentridge's "altered" form of animation is that it exists as palimpsest. As the charcoal contours of one stage of the drawing are erased they remain as ghosts through the next stage and the stage following that, to be joined by other ghosts and still others. So that the density of these pale tracks shadows the formation of each new drawing, like a leaf stuck to one's shoe.

4.

Critics have not failed to describe the experience of Kentridge's work in terms of the palimpsest. The sense of the removal and redrawing of the line, the feeling of watching something having been peeled away or lightened while at another, almost contiguous spot something weighty has abruptly been added, the pale pseudo-cast-shadows that seem to underwrite the appearance of any line, each produced as the correction of a former one, all this has led to titles like "The Art of Erasure" for reviews of Kentridge's exhibitions. Indeed, since the early days of Abstract Expressionism, when an almost obsessional layering of contours, of the partial scraping away of undercoats and the addition of ever new versions of the same figuration—particularly obvious in the work of De Kooning and Kline—never has the paradigm of the palimpsest so made its way into the discourse on modes of contemporary drawing. This most ancient of graphic phenomena—the residue of primitive markers on the walls of caves where, as at Ruffignac with its visual braid of overlaid bison and mammoths not so much cancelling each other out as providing an ever fresh ground for the formation of a new figure—is thus implausibly joined to the "second nature" of modern technology. The powdered pigment blown by the paleolithic artist onto the stone surface is now reprised by the equally powdery substance of charcoal, but this now hovers above the luminous ground of either projection screen or backlit monitor like a dense cover of black fog, sometimes greasily opaque, sometimes brokenly grainy, at other times a radiant mist.

It is this *form* of the drawing that one needs to hold at some distance from Kentridge's graphic style. As in Hjemslev's structuralist system in which both the content and expression of a given sign are each subdivided into form and (material) substance, Kentridge's style of drawing, with its multiple art-historical references—to Max Beckmann, to Grosz, to Daumier, to Goya—belongs to the level of the works' content.[20] The semiologists would call these stylistic decisions "the form of the content," and indeed they project a set of concerns at the thematic level: the association with a lineage of political draftsmen; a type of strongly black-and-white rendering meant to hook into even earlier forms of popular protest such as woodcut broadsides or posters.

If these references are a manifestation of content, however, the palimpsest is a function of the support for that content, its "expression." And on this level, in which the substance of the expression is charcoal, constantly modified by the application of the eraser, the form of the expression is the palimpsest. Which means that once again there is a gap in Kentridge's work between content and form—as was the case between the two types of "catastrophe" in *Monument*: that of the dehumanization of its depicted African subject; and that of the interminable shuttle set up by the act of "stalking the drawing." Yet once again this gap is not opened for the purpose of choosing, say, the formal over the political, but rather of seeing how the formal might indeed be invested by the political and how this in turn might reorganize one's sense of the political field itself.

As a "form of expression," the palimpsest could be usefully joined to the typology set up by Benjamin Buchloh for the analysis of graphic paradigms since the onset of Modernism. Dividing the full range of drawing into two basic types, matrix and grapheme, Buchloh sees each of these as the condensed and abstracted rendering of the form of the "object" on the one hand and that of the "subject" on the other.[21] Whether grid or concentric structure, the matrix serves not only as the emblematic residue of those systems of projection, such as perspective, through which the objective world of three-dimensions was formerly traced, but doubles and thereby manifests the infrastructure of the aesthetic object itself (the weave of the canvas, the armature of the sculpture). As for the grapheme, it is the precipitate of the universe of subjectively expressive marks now reduced to the pure trace of either the neuro-motor or psychological-libidinal manifestations of a curiously voided subject. As examples of his dichotomy, Buchloh gives Johns and Twombly, the first as the master of the matrix, the second the producer of the grapheme.

But the palimpsest, graphically distinct from both grapheme and matrix, belongs neither to the world of the subject nor to that of the object. As an abstract form, it simply implies residue. As the possible deposit of many

markers, it so disperses the field of the subject as utterly to depersonalize and thus denature it. And as the trace of a series of events, it eats away at the substance of anything we might call an object. The palimpsest, we could say, is the emblematic form of the temporal and as such it is the abstraction of narrative, of history, of biography—the latter implying a subject seen not from its own point of view but from that of a third, objectivised viewer, an outsider.

Buchloh's own typology was produced from the retrospective position necessitated by the efflorescence of drawing at the hands of Raymond Pettibon. For it is Pettibon, he argues, who forces onto this neat aesthetic distinction the disturbances wrought by mass-cultural incursions that have transformed both the world of the "object" and that of the "subject." If Pop art had already challenged the matrix's presumption to access—in no matter how abstracted a form—to the objective world, by demonstrating how that very world has been permeated by the image-system of media and thereby already reproduced as spectacle, Pettibon in turn challenges Pop art's supposed objectivity with regard to spectacle itself. For in opposition to the sinuous elegance of late Pop drawings (Warhol, Lichtenstein), with their "placid acceptance of the cartooned forms of social interaction and articulation, Pettibon reinscribes the compulsive, fractured immediacy of notation made under duress."[22] But equally, lest the authority of subjective

expressiveness be allowed to resurrect itself on the basis of this felt pressure, Buchloh adds: "At the same time, the purely corporeal grapheme of a draftsman like Twombly is recharged with a mass-cultural concreteness and circumstantial specificity that purges the corporeal notation of even its last remnants of bodily *jouissance*." In the grip of this dialectical intersection in which grapheme and matrix infect one another, the world of Pettibon is thus a choreography of "the entwining of public and private spheres" both, now, mass-culturally reorganized as "delusional systems."[23]

The joint presence of Pettibon and Kentridge within the art practice of the 1990s demonstrates the unlooked-for recrudescence of drawing, which is to say, the upsurge of the autographic, the hand-wrought, in an age of the mechanization and technologizing of the image via either photography or digital imaging. The extent to which each must acknowledge the penetration of drawing by technology and thus of the individual hand of the draftsman by mass-culture is registered, however, by Buchloh's withering account of the shrunken domain left to Pettibon.

As I pointed out, Buchloh's bipartition of the graphic terrain omits the third term of the palimpsest, with all that it implies of the encoding of the temporal and thus its access to a kind of historical narrative otherwise left no place in a mass-culturally invested world of "delusional systems." But if Kentridge has recourse to the palimpsest, his practice—no less than Pettibon's—is cognizant of the ubiquitous force of mass-culture and thus the precariousness of a narrative subject's claim to the position of historical reckoning. Indeed, it is this recognition that tends to be omitted by the unquestioning embrace of Kentridge's work as "about" memory and forgetting, "about" history and responsibility—a typical statement: "Kentridge's art stresses the importance of remembering and takes a stance against the risk of lapsing into amnesia and disavowal of historical memory, as well as of psychic removal, characteristic of society after traumatic events" (WK 31) —as though access to these things has not become incredibly complex. If

stills: William Kentridge's *History of the Main Complaint* (1996), courtesy of Marian Goodman Gallery

Kentridge himself cautions "You cannot face the rock head on; the rock always wins," this is because in the age of spectacle, it is impossible for the memory of apartheid not to be itself spectacularized—as in the sessions of the Truth and Reconciliation Commission broadcast nightly on South African television.[24] As we are learning from the Holocaust, it is extremely hard for the business of memory not to be exploited to the point of becoming itself a business.

Hence the importance of admitting the penetration of the technological into the palimpsest, the invasion of a "first nature" by the "second." The technical support—animation—of Kentridge's medium might be alienated from itself by an incursion of the bodily, yet in an equal but opposite way, his graphic construction—the palimpsest—is infected by the mechanical.

This occurs at the most basic level of production since Kentridge's reinvented version of the palimpsest depends for its very visibility on the intervention of the camera and the stop-shoot process. But the mechanistic also finds its way into the image field, as when the perceived erasures of a given contour move the experience of the palimpsest away from the reference to the caves and into the embrace of an entirely different primitivism, that of the early technology of movement. Thus when we see the laborer at the beginning of *Monument* walking in a close-up in which each of his feet seems to be dragging a train of ghostly contours behind it, or when in *History of the Main Complaint* we watch the windshield wipers of Soho's car leave a sputter of spoke-like effigies in their path, we feel ourselves in the presence of Jules-Etienne Marey's photographic motion studies, with each figure generating its trail of linear traces. And this permeability of the drawn palimpsest by the history of photographic technologies is echoed by the parallel Kentridge sets up in *History of the Main Complaint* between the handcrafted palimpsest, with its smudges and cloudiness, and the look of high-tech medical imaging such as CAT scans, sonar, MRI scans, and even X-rays. As he says, "there is a great affinity between the velvety grey tones of an X-ray and the softness of charcoal dust brushed onto paper." (*WK* 112)

In the one film that is directly "about" drawing—*Felix in Exile*, in which Felix Teitlebaum in his hotel room in Paris looks at the corpses scattered over the veld via the drawings made by the African woman Nandi which he carries with him—the narrative desubjectivizes this drawing by mechanizing it. Nandi is a surveyor and her graphic instrument is a theodolite. Furthermore, in addition to registering the theodolite's cross-hairs, the only lines we see her making belong to the world of impersonal traces, the forensic contours drawn around bodies at the scenes of crime.

This infiltration of the graphic by the technological occurs as well at that level in which the expressive medium of drawing is taken as the stand-in for the subject him—or herself. For when in *History of the Main Complaint*, for example, the exploration of Soho's bedridden, comatose body through the sophisticated imaging that will render it transparent yields up a succession of ticker-tape machines, telephones, hole-punches, typewriters, as the equipment of his consciousness, subjectivity itself is now portrayed as infected by "second nature." Or at the end of *Mine*, when Soho's state of intense satisfaction is signaled by his sweeping all his other possessions off his bed in order to play with the tiny rhinoceros just delivered to him through the mine shaft, the spontaneity of this "emotion" is already compromised by the degree to which this miniaturized animal resonates with associations not to Africa but to Disney.

5.

To a degree equal to their attention to the presence of the palimpsest, Kentridge's critics have been struck by his recourse to the outmoded. The ringing of the Bakelite telephones, the clacking of the ribbon typewriters, the clanging of the trolley cars that drive a rift through the massing crowds, all call to us from the horizon of the 1940s. The political stage of these films may be choreographed by the chronological present of apartheid—its exceedingly recent dismantling and the painful national reconstruction it now necessitates—but its decor is that of the past.

The parameters of this pastness vary somewhat. Sometimes it is located in the decades of interwar Modernism with its social-utopian cast, whether this be in the importation of Bauhaus architecture (Soho's International Style house in *WEIGHING and WANTING*) or in the associations Kentridge's drawing style more generally makes to Weimar. Often it speaks from the late forties and early fifties, that ambiguous moment just after World War II where, as the Bauhaus had predicted, technology had thoroughly reconceived the "furniture" of one's life—the telephones, the typewriters, the picture windows, the industrially designed china—but where the utopian frame that was to inform this reconstruction had all but receded, supplanted as it was by an ethos of consumption. At other times this reference to the past is shifted back to the late teens and early twenties and the history of silent film, such as the use of vignetting in D. W. Griffith (as in the iris-in at the end of *Monument* or the irises-in and -out that punctuate *Johannesburg, 2nd Greatest City*), and the more general deployment of intertitles. In this latter case the associations are to the progressive implications of mass-culture as it was received by the Surrealists, for example, or by Walter Benjamin.

Indeed animation, the technical support for Kentridge's "drawings for projection," had itself been at stake in the argument Benjamin makes in "The Work of Art in the Age of Mechanical Reproduction," the thirteenth section of which—the one treating the optical unconscious—had originally been titled "Micky-Maus." That Disney's character was the product of animation meant on the one hand that he was not open to being reinfected by the "aura" that could regather around the human film actor become "star"; and on the other, that in Mickey's "plasmaticness" (to use Eisenstein's term), he offered the possibility of a release of subjectivity from its confinement to the human shape, rupturing as Benjamin said, "the hierarchy of creatures predicated on the human being." (OMD 47)

In this latter idea, which he also called "the cracking of natural teleology," is contained part of the utopian possibilities Benjamin imputed to film in general, which he saw as preparing the human subject for a necessary and ultimately liberating integration with technology. Not only was film to release men and women from the confines of their private spaces and into a collective realm—"Then came film and exploded this prison-world with the dynamite of one-tenth seconds, so that now, in the midst of its far-flung ruins and debris, we calmly embark on adventurous travels"[25]—but it was to infiltrate and restructure subjectivity itself, changing damaged individual experience into energized collective perception. And in this idea of a newly organized psychological collective, the animating figure was Mickey Mouse. "Film has launched an attack against the old Heraclitean truth that in waking we share a world while sleeping we are each in separate worlds," Benjamin wrote in the first draft of the Artwork essay. "It has done so, less with representations of dreams, than with the creation of figures of the collective dream such as the globe-orbiting Mickey Mouse." (OMD 35)

Specifically, Benjamin's recourse to Mickey Mouse revolved around the effects of collective laughter, which he saw as the antidote to the deadening of individual experience under the assaults of modern technology. To the individual anaesthetized by the shocks of contemporary life, this laughter would serve as a kind of countershock, a form of the same assault only now converted into "a therapeutic detonation of the unconscious." In this sense sufferers from the effects of technology could be protected by that same technology.

And this physiological conversion could also have a cognitive function. For

Benjamin spoke of the "possibility of psychic inoculation by means of certain films in which a forced articulation of sadistic fantasies or masochistic delusion can prevent their natural and dangerous ripening in the masses. The collective laughter signifies a premature and therapeutic eruption of such mass psychoses." (OMD 31-32) Imagining this as a process of transference by which individual alienation makes a leap into a form of collective, public recognition, Benjamin thus sees both the physiological and cognitive value of this laughter. It is in this sense that film becomes a case of technology itself providing a homeopathic shock experience that would allow for a collective adaptation of and to technology. As Miriam Hansen puts it, Benjamin saw film as "a perceptual training ground for an industrially transformed physis." For as he writes: "To make the vast technical apparatus of our time an object of human innervation [i.e. stimulation]—this is the historical task in whose service film has its true meaning." (OMD 38)

If Mickey Mouse vanished from the Artwork essay in its later versions, this was because Benjamin soon began to take seriously the note he had included in the first draft warning of the "usability of the Disney method for Fascism." (OMD 52) He now began to side with the opinion Adorno expressed in his letter responding to the Artwork essay in which he warns that "The laughter of the audience at a cinema ... is anything but good and revolutionary; instead, it is full of the worst bourgeois sadism."[26] Calling this laughter the "iron bath of fun" administered by the culture industry, Adorno saw it as persuading mutilated subjects to identify masochistically with the forces of social authority. And indeed, as Miriam Hansen points out in her treatment of the Benjamin/Adorno debate, the present-day variations on Benjamin's idea of "play versions of second nature," as in video games for example, "have become a major site for naturalizing violence, destruction, and oppression." (OMD 54)

With this reference to video games, however, we find ourselves in a very different technological field from that of Disney and cel animation.[27] For video games, with their insertion of the computer chip into the field of action, heralded a wholesale shift in the visual media themselves. Animation, having now become a matter of computer programming and digital imaging, has lost the kind of handcraft that had still survived even in its late forms of industrialization—something Chuck Jones, the animator of Bugs Bunny and Daffy Duck, underscored by saying, "The only thing all of us had in common was that we all could draw. We all could draw the human figure";[28] or Benjamin maintained in his belief that in Disney technology doesn't altogether permeate the characters' bodies, rendering them literalized figures of mechanization, but instead remains a "hidden figure," still permitting the sense of an imbrication of technology with natural beings out of which the transformations of the body seem to be improvised. (OMD 42)

And at the same time that the computer has rendered cel animation utterly outmoded, it has also overtaken photographically based cinema, the kind of film that had declared its indexical connection to the contingencies of time and presence, the kind Cavell had called "automatic world projections." The digitizing of film means precisely that Cavell's distinction between "movies" and "cartoons" has utterly collapsed, so that just as animation increasingly penetrates photographically filmed material—not only in special effects, but in the integration of animated characters with live actors—the adult world of film invests the child's world of cartoons, projecting into the new breed of full-length animation the pornography and blood that Cavell had assumed this world could not support.[29] And for Benjamin's analysis this implosion means that far from being a medium to "master the interplay between human beings and nature," the "leap into the apparatus" facilitated by film now constructs the subject as no more than one element "in a loop that processes information and sensory signals."[30]

The death knell that currently rings on all sides, as film is either infiltrated or replaced by digital technologies, signals its ever rapid slide into obsolescence. "This is why," Miriam Hansen warns, "taking Benjamin's imperative to 'actuality' seriously today means recognizing that the cinema, once celebrated for articulating the secret affinities among things in an age of accelerated obsolescence, may itself have become a thing of the past."[31]

Techno-teleologists such as Friedrich Kittler or Norbert Bolz greet this rising cybernetic tide, in which all previous forms of media are now engulfed by digitization, as the inevitable course of progress, itself encoded within the logic of electronic systems.[32] In their eyes Benjamin's technological pessimism from the late thirties and his reinvestment in forms of subjectivity utterly threatened by technology render his own reflections on film no more than "beautiful ruins in the philosophical landscape."[33]

But in the matter of art Benjamin was very canny on the subject of ruins, for they allowed him to think an "outside" to the increasingly totalized system of "second nature." Thus his late considerations on photography leap over the 1935 Artwork essay to cycle back to his thoughts from the opening of the decade and to reconsider the advantages of obsolescence.[34] Reflecting on the life cycles of technologies—the hopes with which they are born and the ignominious fates to which they are consigned at the moment of their obsolescence, moments which come with increasing speed as the pace of technology grows exponentially—he wondered whether photography had, like other technologies before it, released a fleeting image of the utopian promise it might contain at the moment when it was still an amateur past-time, still the medium of exchange between friends, the moment that is before it became commercialized and hardened into a commodity. Further, it was Benjamin's thought that at the point when a technology is suddenly eclipsed by its own obsolescence, its armouring breaks down and it releases the memory of this promise. And here, he hoped, through the outmoded's creation of a chink in the armour, one could glimpse an outside to the totality of technologized space.[35]

The mediums that are now being "invented" are lodging themselves precisely in this space where obsolescence brackets technological determinism long enough for us to think our way back down the path of "progress" to the earlier, stranger forms of expressiveness primitive technologies contained and to imagine mining these as just that source of "automatism" or *fortuna* that will yield the conventions necessary to a medium. If this has been true for Coleman's regression not just to the outmoded slide-tape but to its ancestor, the magic lantern, it is true as well for Kentridge's insistence on the most primitive imaginable animation in the face of digital imaging. Kentridge's technical support is already obsolescent through and through, even before he renders it internally riven—self-different, self-differing—by the hesitations and contradictions encoded by the palimpsest.

Kentridge's recourse to the outmoded at the level of content—the old-fashioned telephones, typewriters, styles of architecture—is, then, like his recourse to the graphic styles of Weimar or of earlier political art. It operates on the form of the content of his work. To have it there at all runs a certain kind of risk. For the danger Kentridge courts in these references is one of "nostalgia," a kind of retro-fashionableness that produces the historical itself as a form of spectacle.[36] Kentridge is aware of this: "Of course the rough monochromatic drawings refer back to early black-and-white movie making. I am not blind to the nostalgia inherent in this." (WK 64-5) And acknowledging that this nostalgia might be "for a period in which political image-making seemed so much less fraught," he also understands that he has "to take responsibility" for such a choice.

But like the issue of the palimpsest in the matter of drawing, Kentridge's concern for outmodedness at the level of the support—his animation technique, which flaunts the hand-drawn in the very teeth of digital imaging, thus siding with the now obsolescent cel production, in comparison to which it itself is also conspicuously more primitive—operates below the content. Instead it lodges itself in the domain of expression, becoming an aspect of the form of the expression: its imposition of stasis in the midst of movement; its investment of the traces of bodily production in the midst of the apparatus. Addressing itself to the specificity of the expressive level of the support (animation) in its historical dimension, this formal engagement is far from "nostalgic." It is, we could say, what attempts to undermine a certain kind of spectacularization of memory.

Endnotes

1. Written in 1982 as a direct response to the persecution of Vaclav Havel, to whom it is dedicated, *Catastrophe* uses the protagonist's appearance—the whitened face and gray pajamas—to call up the image of concentration camp inmates, as it mobilizes the atmosphere of total control to refer to Stalinism. When critics described the meaning of the protagonist's final gesture as ambiguous Beckett complained in response; "There's no ambiguity there at all. He's saying 'you bastards, you haven't finished me yet'."

2. Carolyn Christov-Bakatgiev, *William Kentridge* (Brussels: Palais des Beaux-Arts, 1998), 75; hereafter cited in the text as *WK*.

3. Although Kentridge speaks of using a Bolex (*WK* 61), he now employs a slightly more sophisticated version of the same kind of 16mm camera, an Ariflex. He has explained that he does not embrace this by-now primitive film equipment in the same spirit as he depicts the outmoded telephones and teletype machines in his films. Rather, these simple cameras make it far easier to shoot one, or perhaps two, frames at a time than any more technologically complex camera, whether 35mm or video.

4. I am retaining Kentridge's name for this plunger type of coffee pot. A French *cafetiére* is, on the other hand, a pot for making coffee by the drip method.

5. For example, Elisabeth Lebovici, "Kentridge, l'art de la gomme," *Libération*, July 20, 1999, 25.

6. For my discussion of James Coleman's "invention" of a medium, see "'... And Then Turn Away?' An Essay on James Coleman," *October, no. 18* (Summer, 1997) and "Reinventing the Medium," *Critical Enquiry, 25* (Winter, 1999).

7. Stanley Cavell, *The World Viewed, Enlarged Edition* (Cambridge, Mass: Harvard University Press, 1979), p 104; hereafter cited in the text as *WV*.

8. Stanley Cavell, "Music Discomposed," in *Must We Mean What We Say?* (New York: Schribner's, 1969), 201.

9. See, "Reinventing the Medium," op. cit., and *A Voyage on the North Sea: Art in the Age of the Post-Medium Condition* (London: Thames & Hudson, 1999).

10. Both Cavell and Kentridge have recourse to the example of language's dependence on habit and unconscious reflexes to ballast their concepts of automatism and *fortuna*. Kentridge's references to language have been cited above; Cavell's can be found in a remark such as "[A medium] provides, one might say, particular ways to get through to someone, to make sense; in art, they are forms, like forms of speech" (*WV* 32).

11. Cavell wrote about cartoons in 1974 in the essay added to the "expanded edition" of his book that addressed his critics. He was thus framing his ideas about animation in terms of his own innocence about the radical restructuring of the technique with the advent of video and computers. Thus while his remarks about traditional cel animation, as practiced by Hollywood studios and received by mass audiences well into the 1960s, are entirely relevant to the issues of animation as a medium, they don't address the historical fate of the medium that was even then appearing on the horizon. See section 6, below.

12. Roland Barthes, "The Third Meaning," *Image/Music/Text*, trans. Stephen Heath (New York: Hill & Wang, 1977). For the relationship between Barthes's third meaning and Coleman's use of the photo-novel for his own medium, see "'... And Then Turn Away?'" op. cit., 12-13, 20-23.

13. *Eisenstein on Disney*, ed. Jay Leyda (Calcutta: Seagull Books, 1986), 21.

14. Ibid., 39.

15. Ibid., 35.

16. Walter Benjamin also took note of the weightlessness of the Disney figures: "There appears as a redemption [from the endless complications of the everyday] an existence which at every turn is self-sufficient in the most simple and simultaneously most comfortable way, in which a car does not weigh more than a straw-hat and the fruit on the tree grows round as fast as a hot-air balloon" (as cited in Miriam Hansen, "Of Mice and Ducks: Benjamin and Adorno on Disney," *South Atlantic Quarterly*, Vol. 92 (January 1993), 42; hereafter cited in the text as "*OMD.*")

17. In "The Illusion of Illusion," Keith Broadfoot and Rex Butler make this very point: "But the attempt at an ideological reading and an understanding of animation as a reified reflection of consumer society ultimately collapses for Eisenstein. This is because with animation it is impossible for the spectator to achieve the necessary distance required for critique, or inversely, for ideology, to operate. There can be no critique of the representation of capital in animation for the simple reason that animation itself is the presentation of capital." They broaden this to Deleuze's theorization of film: "With regard to cinema, Deleuze proposes that money is the obverse side of the time-image, but in animation money is the

image itself. This perhaps explains why cartoon characters are the true Icons of the twentieth century ... for in a certain sense any cartoon character is the incarnation of the ethereal spirit of the media" (in *The Illusion of Life: Essays on Animation*, ed. Alan Cholodenko [Sydney: Power Institute of Fine Arts, 1991], 272).

18. Gilles Deleuze, *Cinema 1: The Movement-Image*, trans. Hugh Tomlinson and Barbara Habberjam (Minneapolis: University of Minnesota Press, 1986), 5.

19. Bradfoot, "Illusion of Illusion," 286.

20. Louis Hjelmslev, *Prolegomena to a Theory of Language*, trans. Francis Whitfield (Madison and Milwaukee: University of Wisconsin Press, 1969).

21. Benjamin Buchloh, "Raymond Pettibon: Return to Disorder and Disfiguration," in *Raymond Pettibon: A Reader*, ed. Ann Temkin and Hamza Walker (Philadelphia: the Philadelphia Museum of Art, 1998), 230.

22. Ibid., 231.

23. Ibid., 232.

24. The complexity becomes clear as one listens to different accounts of the Truth and Reconciliation Commission's organization of personal memory into testimony. Kentridge himself reports: "One by one witnesses come and have their half hour to tell their story, pause, weep, be comforted by professional comforters who sit at the table with them. The stories are harrowing, spellbinding. The audience sits at the edge of their seats listening to every word. This is exemplary civic theater" (*WK* 125-26). Okwui Enwezor, on the other hand, applauding Kentridge's film *Ubu Tells the Truth*, dismisses these performances before the TRC as the "farcical and lengthy process of testimonies" (*WK* 189).

25. Walter Benjamin, "The Work of Art in the Age of Mechanical Reproduction," in *Illuminations*, trans. Harry Zohn (New York: Schocken Books, 1969), 236.

26. Theodor Adorno, letter of March 18, 1936, in *Aesthetics and Politics* (London: New Left Books, 1977), 123.

27. In the 1920s and 30s, Hollywood animators worked on transparent layers of celluloid, hence the term "cel animation." This allowed the minute changes in a character's posture to be registered without the need to redraw the entirety of the background each time. It was, one could say, a primitive form of digital graphics.

28. Chuck Jones, "What's Up, Down Under? Chuck Jones Talks at The Illusion of Life Conference," in *The Illusion of Life*, ed. Alan Cholodenko (Sydney: Power Publications, 1991), 64.

29. In his discussion of the weightless, disembodied condition of cartoons, Cavell adds, "In cartoons, sexuality is apt to be either epicene [either intersexual or asexual] or caricatured. I suppose this is because cartoons, being fleshless, do not veer toward the pornographic, although given a chance, they may naturally veer toward the obscene." In "More of the World Viewed," *The World Viewed*, op. cit, 172.

30. Miriam Hansen, "Benjamin and Cinema: Not a One-Way Street," *Critical Inquiry, 25* (Winter 1999)., 325.

31. Ibid., 343.

32. Friedrich Kittler, *Discourse Networks 1800/1900*, trans. Michael Metteer (Stanford: Stanford University Press, 1990); and Norbert Bolz, *Theorie der neuen Medien* (Munich, 1990).

33. Norbert Bolz, "Die Zukunft der Zeichen: Invasion des Digitalen in die Bilderwelt des Films," in *Im Spiegelkabinett der Illusionen*, ed. Ernst Karpf, Doron Kiesel, and Karste Visarius (Marburg, 1996), 57, as cited in Miriam Hansen, "Benjamin and Cinema," ibid., 343.

34. The relevant texts are Walter Benjamin, "A Small History of Photography," in *One Way Street and Other Writings*, trans. Edmund Jephcott and Kingsley Shorter (London: New Left Books, 1979); and Walter Benjamin, "Lettre parisienne (no. 2): Peinture et photographie," in *Sur l'art et la photographie*, ed. Christophe Jouanlanne (Paris: 1997), 79.

35. See my "Reinventing the Medium," op. cit., 289-305. Susan Buck-Morss develops this issue importantly in *The Dialectics of Seeing: Walter Benjamin and the Arcades Project* (Cambridge, Mass: MIT Press, 1989), for example 245 and 293.

36. Arguing, in relation to the contemporary predilection for nostalgia forms that the historical past is beyond anything but aesthetic retrieval, Fredric Jameson says "the attempt to appropriate a missing past is now refracted through fashion change." But he argues that a postmodernist "nostalgia" art language is incompatible with genuine historicity. Adding that in these filmic tropes, "The past is offered up mythically" through style (in Roland Barthes' use of the notion of myth) a given film will thus be redolent with fifties-ness or forties-ness. Furthermore, he adds, "This mesmerizing new esthetic mode is a

symptom of the waning of our historicity, of our lived possibility of experiencing history in some active way." Fredric Jameson, "The Cultural Logic of Late Capitalism," in *Postmodernism* (Durham, Duke University Press, 1984), 19-21.

Institute Benjamenta: An Olfactory View

Laura U. Marks

In liquid slow motion, a bullet moves through a dense pine forest, curving impossibly through the syrupy air, until it finally lodges in a pinecone. In a flea's-eye-view, a gigantic length of thread snakes through the tiny needle hole in a nightshirt, producing a sort of disciplinary garment whose neat column of thimbles will prevent the sleeper from lying on his back. A group of seven men, attending at the door of their ailing mistress, sways as one in a luminous swath of light, which dances and swirls about them.

These are three images from *Institute Benjamenta, or, This Dream People Call Human Life* (1995), the first feature-length film by the Brothers Quay. They convey some of the sense in which non-sentient life seems to take precedence over human life in the film, but perhaps they do not convey the film's sense of *smell*. How does a film leave a viewer with an overwhelming impression of fragrance, as though she has been inhaling it as intensely as seeing it?

The Quay brothers, Timothy and Stephen, have developed a style in which a film, which is of course an audiovisual medium, offers itself as richly to the senses of smell and touch as it does to vision and hearing. *Institute Benjamenta* takes smell, and the knowledge afforded by smell, as a theme, and it employs the Quays' trademark uses of miniature photography and haptic imagery to convey the sense of smell to viewers. Not coincidentally,

still: The Brothers Quay's *Institute Benjamenta* (1995), courtesy of Atelier Koninck/Zeitgeist Films the film appeals to a subjectivity that is not human, or not only human; it lingers on the lives of inanimate objects and unseen things, dispersing the subjectivity usually reserved for human characters over the entire image. What connects the film's sense of smell with its dispersion of the subject is aura, or the animate force of objects organic and inorganic, human and filmic. The novel on which the film is based charts its characters' gradual loss of selfhood. The Quays do this as well, but they counter this deathful path with a tide of non-human life. While the characters seem to sleepwalk, the objects and the space among which they move are endowed with a vibrating, tactile life.

The Quays are known for their exquisitely detailed animations, in works such as *The Cabinet of Jan Svankmajer* (1984), *Street of Crocodiles* (1986), *The Comb (From the Museums of Sleep)* (1991), and *In Absentia* (2000). With *Institute Benjamenta*, the Quays bring their obsessive abilities with animation to the world of live action. *Institute Benjamenta* is a sort of fairy tale based upon a novel, *Jakob von Gunten* (1909), by the eccentric Swiss writer Robert Walser. The Institute is a school for servants run by siblings Lisa Benjamenta (played by Alice Krige) and Johannes Benjamenta (Gottfried John). When Jakob von Gunten (Mark Rylance) enrolls in the school, he disrupts its somnambulistic rhythm, like the prince in *Sleeping Beauty* awakening the sleeping princess, and brings the castle into rusty motion. The plot is slim: The seven male students endlessly go through the motions of servanthood. The head student Krauss (Daniel Smith) keeps a watchful eye on his mistress as she begins to lose her composure. Both sister and brother fall in love with the new student. Jakob narrates the process of losing his identity in this machine for producing human machines, the school for servants. Lisa dies from repressed longing. Herr Benjamenta dissolves the Institute, and in the penultimate scene he and Jakob are walking away from the school, strangely giddy, snow whirling around them as though inside a glass snow-globe.

Quay films are produced by Atelier Koninck, which comprises Stephen and Timothy Quay and producer Keith Griffiths. The film's score, by Lech Jankowski, uses jazz, orchestral, and antique instruments in brilliant, spare combinations. Like other experimental feature films, *Institute Benjamenta* was difficult to fund and ultimately found international co-production. Past Quay films have been funded by the British Film Institute and the BBC's Channel Four. The first financial support for *Institute Benjamenta* came from Image Forum, the Tokyo-based centre for avant-garde cinema; then Channel Four offered major sponsorship, together with British Screen, and finally the German-based Pandora Film kicked in. The Quays support their more experimental work by producing cultural documentaries and "graphic interludes" for commercial television, and design theatre and opera productions for director Richard Jones.

Criticism of *Institute Benjamenta* has tended to represent it as a chilly, inhuman film, a parable of alienation, alienated labour, and sexual repression.[1] Critics may be forgiven for being anthropocentric, but I would argue that the Quays' works are not so much inhuman as *unheimlich* in their attention to non-human and non-organic life. In this filmic space teeming with life, humans, the Quays say, are just "no more important than anything else."[2] In this the Quays share much with Walser, whose attitude toward objects was not so much fetishistic as animistic. That is, objects in his writings have a life of their own not by virtue of their contact with humans, but for their own sake. In stories like "An Address to a Button" [1915] and "A Cigarette" [1925], Walser addresses lowly objects with respect and even envy. To the button he says, "You, why you are capable of living in such a way that nobody has the slightest recollection you exist. You are happy; for modesty is its own reward, and fidelity feels comfortable within itself."[3] This attention to the most negligible of objects animates the Quays' films as well, with their herds of tiny rolling screws, their twanging comb-teeth, their lively heaps of dust.

The Institute Benjamenta is a school for training servants. Servants, in Walser's writings, aspire to a state of nothingness. The writer himself enrolled in a school for servants and briefly worked as a house servant in a castle in Upper Silesia.[4] In *Jakob von Gunten*, the head servant Krauss inspires this speech in Lisa Benjamenta:

> There isn't a single person alive who understands that there is some delicate meaning behind this nameless, inconspicuous, monosyllabic Krauss. No one will ever be grateful to him, nor is gratitude necessary. Krauss will never go to ruin because there will always be great and loveless difficulties confronting him. I think that I am perhaps the only person who realizes what we have in Krauss.

Certainly one could say that the novel, and the film, are about alienated labour, the sort of work that demeans people and strips them of their humanity. Yet this slightly misses the point, for in Walser's writing this self-abnegation is perversely and knowingly desired. Like Jakob, all the students have "no high hopes in life"; yet even so their education seems sure to teach them little. Lisa walks the seven apprentices through absurd, repetitive exercises: folding napkins, arranging spoons in perfect circles, shifting their weight from one foot to the other. (Jakob, still too zealous, disrupts the class by chanting phrases such as "Be careful Viscount, the steeple, it is wobbling!") The seven men move together in leaden synchrony, each doing his best to abandon any trace of individuality. When Herr Benjamenta sees a bite mark on the new student's hand, evidence of his self-repressive struggle, he smiles approvingly.

The task of a servant is to efface himself or herself, to become part of the engine of a house. The film's human characters are at work to still their senses and silence their will. But the living building surrounds them with its fragrant traces. Time in the film is organized around what the Quays call the "masturbatory ritual" of feeding a fish that swims in a globe-shaped bowl in the house's inner sanctum. The magnetic force that flows through the house seems to be channeled by its only female inhabitant, Lisa Benjamenta, who lies in her room perspiring and breathing heavily in a sort of sexual catatonia. In the room above hers, Krauss sluices bucketfuls of water on the floor so that it will run down the walls and cool her. The entire building is an erotic machine, of which the people are only parts.

Although the film is inspired by a novel, the Quays are quick to say that "it was always conceived from the camera's point of view; not an adaptation from a novel but always as images first, closer to the domain of the silent film."[5] Like a silent film, *Institute Benjamenta* relies on the expressiveness of gesture, camerawork, and editing to convey meaning, and the few words uttered by its characters hang in the air, I am tempted to say, like perfume. The magic of *Institute Benjamenta* is the way it uses film to evoke a possessed, animistic world. The dark quality of Czech, Polish, and Russian animation influences the Quays' manipulation of objects. In Nic Knowland's cinematography, the light too has a life of its own: The black-and-white film is full of exquisite images where light pours in one side of the frame or (when a tram passes outside) speeds across the walls in tracery patterns while the rest of the space is submerged in velvety darkness.

The Quays describe animation as "an experiment with what the camera can do choreographically." Their animations work with small-scale models populated by small objects. Focal length and lens choice create a sense of space in which the most interesting events do not occur in human scale. The camera moves delicately among these tiny theatres, creating a point of view that seems to belong to one of the objects or something even smaller and more ambient—the point of view of dust, or of the air. In *Institute Benjamenta*, it is interesting to see these animation sets worked into live

action scenarios. Rather than acting as objects for the human characters, the miniature sets create the point of view for the entire film. The live-action sequences play into the tactile space established by the Quays' animations, reversing the usual anthropocentric hierarchy of scales. The animation sequences create a densely populated miniature world, of which the bulky humans seem only obscurely aware.

In one scene Jakob has been shown to his bedroom at the Institute by Lisa Benjamenta. Jakob is already overcome by the conflict between his desire for his teacher and his stated wish to nullify himself by becoming a servant. In the room, he finds a table piled with pinecones, which we see close-up like a miniature forest. Kneeling, he takes one in his mouth; still holding it, he pours a glass of liquor, and the camera moves in for one of those impossible close-ups of the bottle's label (it is the pine-scented schnapps that Walser liked). The combined gigantism and miniaturism of the scene make Jakob's act almost unbearably erotic, in the eroticism of an "unsuitable" match. What can the pinecone have that Jakob wants? Perhaps he is using the pinecone as a gag; perhaps it is a substitute for some human part. But his tentative, interested approach makes it seem not as though he were simply using the pinecone, but as though he suspects the pinecone knows more than he does.

How does the eroticism of this hard and fragrant object replace the better-known eroticism of human bodies? The film, like the novel, is powered

still: The Brothers Quay's *Institute Benjamenta* (1995). courtesy of Atelier Koninck/Zeitgeist Films by thwarted sexual desire. Yet *Institute Benjamenta* is not simply a film about sexual repression. Sexuality is abundantly expressed in the film, if not in the usual human ways. The pinecone scene is only one of several in which sexual expression is displaced onto plants and animals. The characters seem to be fumbling with erotic codes well known to other creatures but only dimly, clumsily remembered by humans. One of these codes is smell.

Haptic and Olfactory Space

How does film express the sense of smell? What sort of image invites olfactory perception? For one thing, a haptic image may. The work of the Brothers Quay provides an example of film that is haptic not because the image is blurred or hard to see but the converse, by virtue of pulling the viewer into a richly textured space-or perhaps it is better to say, pushing texture out to meet the viewer. In works such as *The Comb* (1991) and *Anamorphosis* (1991), as well as *Institute Benjamenta*, their elaborate, miniaturist sets create a world richly populated with inanimate objects-dolls, cutlery, a comb, pinecones. This overwhelming presence of detail invites the sort of look that would travel along textures of detail.[6] All the surfaces in Quay films have a heavy patina of tarnish and decay, so that even floors and furniture have a sense of aura, that is, the marks of a long-gone, living presence. These richly textured, miniature scenes compel a viewer to move close, yet at the same time they multiply the points of contact all over the screen.

I've argued that haptic images have the effect of overwhelming vision and spilling into other sense perceptions. This is in part because they do not provide enough visual information on their own to allow the viewer to apprehend the object, thus making the viewer more dependent on sound and other sense perceptions. This shift of sensory focus may be physical, or, as in film, through associating the available audiovisual information with other, remembered sense experiences. Film cannot stimulate a memory of smell: Only the presence of the same smell can call up its memory associations.[7] Yet a haptic image asks memory to call on other associations by refusing the visual plenitude of the optical image. In addition, because haptic images locate vision in the body, they make vision behave more like a contact sense, such as touch or smell. Thus haptic images invite a multisensory, intimate, and embodied perception, even when the perceptions to which they appeal are vision and hearing alone.

The Quays' films have always played with the haptic dimension of vision, by drawing vision into a miniature scale in which the image is filled with small, lively things, all competing for attention. With *Institute Benjamenta*, this tactile vision expands to encompass the sense of smell. They do this not only by using smell as a narrative element but also by inviting the embodied, haptic vision I have described. Smell, another sense based on contact, is the basic animating force in the film. Interestingly, the Quays decided to locate Walser's Institute in a former perfume factory, which still contains exhibits of the deer whose musk was used as an ingredient. Deer haunt the Institute (in another addition to the book), their antlers protruding from the walls, an anamorphic painting of rutting deer on the wall of an interior garden. In one hidden room there is a bell jar containing powdered stag ejaculate, labeled "Please Sniff." In *Institute Benjamenta*, deer are magic creatures because their sexuality is contained in their smell—something that most contemporary humans disdain, for our being is defined by our verbal, visual, and intentional activity in the world.

Smell, Sexuality, and Chemical Communication

The filmmakers appear to have been quite obsessed with certain smells as they were making the film. In an interview with Thyrza Nichols Goodeve, there is a fascinating discussion (in a bit of a detour from the interviewer's concerns) of the connection between deer, deer testicles, and perfume.[8] Male Himalayan deer secrete musk in a sac located behind the testicles; they must be slaughtered in order to extract it. It is well known that musk and a very few other animal sexual/excretory fluids (or their synthetic analogues) are used as the base notes in many perfumes. Top notes of perfumes, those that the nose first receives, are usually floral; middle notes may be heavier florals or resins (such as myrrh and benzoin); base notes come from resins and animal products. Tom Robbins' delightful 1984 novel *Jitterbug Perfume*, a romp through the centuries in search for the base note of a legendary perfume, peaks when the scent is discovered to be—not to spoil it for you—a common but quite unexpected sexual odour. And of course the scandalous *Perfume* by Patrick Süskind turns around the theft of the body odours of beautiful and nubile women, supposedly the essence of human sexual desirability. As Tasmanian zoologist D. Michael Stoddart puts it, "The perceiver's attention is drawn to the more volatile and active floral notes much as one is drawn to a newspaper by its headlines. The real message is in the fine print."[9] Top notes are extracted from the sex organs of flowers; the middle notes often have odours similar to sex steroids; the base notes, which have a urinous or fecal odour, are chemically similar or identical to human sex steroids. In other words, we tend to wear perfumes that communicate on an unconscious level the same smells that we consciously wash away. (This practice is not universal: for example, Dassanetch men in Ethiopia traditionally bathe their hands in cow urine and rub their bodies with cow manure, which connotes prosperity and fertility for this cattle-raising people.[10]) There is debate among psychologists and neurologists about the role of the unconscious in human smell: some assert that smell is an entirely plastic, "soft-wired" sense; i.e., we learn which smells are pleasant or unpleasant through association.[11] How much of this association is unconscious, and thus might be connected with infantile attraction to body odors, for example, is not clear. It is different for humans than for other animals, since in humans, odour sensation connects to both cognitive and precognitive areas in the brain, while for animals the connections are only precognitive.[12] Yet since for millennia perfumes have been manufactured to evoke those odours, it is probable that some of the pleasant associations with bodily smells are learned and maintained at an unconscious level.

The Quays compare the light surrounding Lisa Benjamenta to "liquid myrrh."[13] The metaphor not only captures the feel of a viscous, golden afternoon light but also literalizes the atmosphere of sexuality, and indeed the sense of religious sublimation, that surround her. For millennia, myrrh has been an ingredient in incense, used for religious purposes by ancient Egyptians, Greeks, Jews, and (after some debate over whether the Divine, being incorporeal, had a sense of smell) Christians.[14] Like other resins used in incense, its chemical composition is very similar to that of animal steroids that contribute to human body odor.[15] By pushing the references to smell, the Quays are appealing to a sense that makes a sublime connection between the human, the animal, and the divine. The rich sensory lives of animals and plants appear in the film not as a primitive existence that human evolution has overcome, but an as alternative way of being in the world, forking away from the vision-centred and humanistic modern cogito. *Institute Benjamenta* willfully reinvents the possibilities of human nature by turning decisively away from it. Hence the erotic lesson Jakob might learn from a pinecone (whose odour, incidentally, is shared by some male sex steroids).

After the encounter with the pinecone, Jakob murmurs, in sentences from Walser's book, "Perhaps I shall never put out roots and branches. One day I shall put out fragrance, and I will flower. I will be dead. Not really dead, but in a certain way—dead." Jakob's wish to disappear becomes an aspiration to sainthood, to emit the odour of sanctity. As though only by losing his individuality could he become part of something larger, something mediated by smell.

Although psychoanalysis explains why humans tend not to wear perfumes whose top notes denote sexual/excretory smells, instead communicating these smells at a subconscious level, we need not rush to psychoanalysis to explain why these odours should be attractive at all. Chemical communication is the most ancient form of communication. It is also a form of communication based on contact: contact between chemicals and receptor cells, such as those in our noses. In us higher mammals, our main form of chemical communication with the outside world occurs through the sense of smell. Yet the chemicals that carry all this information are remarkably few, since these communicative systems have not evolved much at all.[16] Thus, what attracts insects to flowers is chemically almost identical to what attracts does to stags and humans to humans. What I hope to demonstrate in this digression into olfactory evolution is that a sense based on (chemical) contact is also a sense that we humans share with all other living creatures. Research is young on the chemical communication systems of plants; but we can speak of the sense of smell of maple trees, which can, for example, release hormones warning other maples of predators or signaling insects that they are ready to be pollinated. Smell, then, is a fundamental leveller, a warning system, delight, and physical contact shared by all living beings.

In one scene in the failed romance between Lisa Benjamenta and Jakob, she blindfolds him and takes him to the forest (saying, "It is so beautiful here, Jakob. If only you could see it"). Telling Jakob to "try to find the warmth," Lisa turns her body upside down, so that he can be guided to her by the warmth and smell of her sex (clad in thick woolen tights). Since in most cultures humans apparently find the smell of women's genitals unpleasant,[17] Lisa's appeal to Jakob is metaphoric, a willful appeal to the sense memory of other animals. She bypasses the usual visual and auditory cues in an attempt to communicate to him the way the deer memorialized on the garden murals communicated to each other. Lisa's act reverses the famous evolutionary act of standing upright that, in Freud's famous overstatement, displaced human sexual attraction from the olfactory to the visual.[18]

Extra-human Subjectivity

The reaction to Quay films is often a sort of morbid fascination, a paranoia that the world of things has taken on a life of its own. Even the dust is alive. Quay films are full of ghosts, life in things that ought to be dead: this is both disquieting and, in a certain way, reassuring. Earlier films surprise the viewer with a pocketwatch that, assaulted by little screws, springs open to

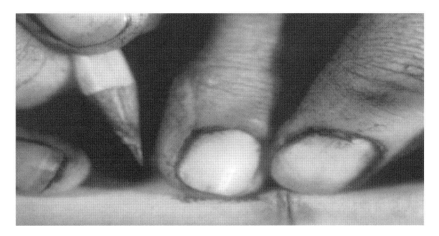

reveal wet, pink flesh (*Street of Crocodiles*), or walls that suddenly leak blood (*Rehearsals for Extinct Anatomies*, 1988). These images suggest that life is everywhere—not a benign life force but myriad, peculiar, sensible lives. Many viewers find these films unbearably disturbing, perhaps because the Quays' films threaten the preeminence of the human (and perhaps, especially male) body by endowing inanimate objects with the ability to suffer.[19] But Quay films only inspire paranoia if one finds non-organic life threatening. And what is animation but to make animate—to impart life, or to divine the interior life of objects? In other words, animation acknowledges the aura of things, the life they contain whether imparted by humans or somehow inherent.

Late twentieth-century critics turned nervously away from the notion that objects and works of art might have aura. This was in part a necessary rejection of the irrational, of the idea that power might reside in non-human entities. Benjamin's famous essay was decisive in this regard. Yet the German writer was also reluctant to completely abandon the mystical notion that the non-human and non-organic world is also alive and somehow operating, indeed acting, in synchrony.[20] As we begin to perceive the annihilating capacity of the simulacral image in a world whose objects are increasingly produced by mechanical reproduction, there seems to be a new urgency to rediscover aura. Can this be achieved without an automatic regression to the fascist and religious mystification that Benjamin rightly feared? I cannot tell whether the aura with which the Quays endow non-human life is a warning against hubris or a kind of game with annihilation. However, I do think their films provoke because they redefine subjectivity and who is allowed to have it.

still: The Brothers Quay's *In Absentia*, (2000), courtesy of Atelier Koninck/Zeitgeist Films

When subjectivity is so thoroughly decentred from human characters and onto animals, plants, inorganic beings, and air and light themselves, it seems necessary to ask how one identifies with such a film. Identification is certainly possible if one gives up some degree of anthropocentrism and seeks to feel a sympathy, born of respect, with these other objects. Yet, as with Walser's servants, this respect implies a reduction of the human to a zero: the film's second subtitle is "The Beatification of Zero." Identification with *Institute Benjamenta* involves a decision whether to identify with the humans who are in the process of dissolution, an exercise in self-erasure; or to move beyond anthropocentrism and find common subjectivity with animals, plants, and even less visible and organic "life" forms.

The willingness to pull away from individual human subjectivity that is a theme of the film may well have to do with the constitution of the Quays themselves. Reviews of the Quays' films tend to take a prurient fascination in the fact that they are identical twins. It is true they finish each other's sentences, dress similarly, sign their beautifully hand-written letters "Quays," and exhibit other twin-like eccentricities. Yet talking with them, I had the impression that their bicephalic identity was not a willful public hoax but a sincere lifelong experiment in the meaning of subjectivity. Using the willfully antiquarian term "atelier" for their production company connotes a devotion to anonymous craft rather than authorship. This explains in part the filmmakers' unwillingness to be examined as auteurs, let alone analyzed as identical twins. Certainly, when each director knows instinctively what the other has in mind, the production process becomes organic: this may explain the intimacy between the camera and its world in Quay films. Other things could be inferred about the nature of authorship when the author is two people. Yet simply, the brothers seem to practice in life what they seek to do in their films; namely, distribute subjectivity. Why must a subject be contained in one individual? Why not shared between two, the way electrons jump orbits from one atom to another? For that matter, why can't a whole space have a personality, like the interconnected miniature passages and breath-filled rooms of a Quay animation. Quay films remind us that we biological creatures are surrounded by non-organic life. The reaction to this may be fear; or it may be a sort of animistic humility that attributes subjectivity and will to pinecones and motes of dust.

Endnotes

1. Leslie Felperin, review of *Institute Benjamenta, Sight and Sound* 5, no. 12 (Winter 1995) 46; Jonathan Romney, "Life's a Dream," *Sight and Sound* 5:8 (August 1995) 12-13; Thyrza Nichols Goodeve, "Dream Team: An Interview with the Brothers Quay," *Artforum* (April 1996) 82-85, 118, 126.

2. Quays, in Goodeve, 84.

3. Robert Walser, "An Address to a Button," trans. Mark Harman, in *Robert Walser Rediscovered: Stories, Fairy-Tales, and Critical Responses*, ed. Mark Harman (Hanover and London: University Press of New England, 1985), 28.

4. Mark Harman, "Introduction: A Reluctant Modern," in *Robert Walser Rediscovered*, 4.

5. Unless otherwise noted, this and other quotes from the Quays are from interviews with me on September 13, 1995 and May 21, 1996.

6. The sort of gaze to which such a detailed look appeals is discussed in, for example, Svetlana Alpers, *The Art of Describing: Dutch Art in the Seventeenth Century* (Chicago: University of Chicago Press, 1983) and Naomi Schor, *Reading in Detail: Aesthetics and the Feminine* (New York and London: Methuen, 1987). The great-uncle of tactile visuality is art historian Alois Riegl; see *Late Roman Art Industry*, trans. Rolf Winkes (Rome: Giorgio Bretschneider Editore, 1985; originally published 1927).

7. Trygg Engen, *Odor Sensation and Memory* (New York, Westport, CT, and London: Praeger, 1991), 5.

8. Quays, in Goodeve, 84-86 passim.

9. D. Michael Stoddart, *The Scented Ape: The Biology and Culture of Human Odour* (Cambridge: Cambridge University Press, 1990), 163. Other material in this paragraph is drawn from 161-163.

10. Constance Classen, David Howes, and Anthony Synnott, *Aroma: The Cultural History of Smell* (London and New York: Routledge, 1994), 124.

11. Engen, 2-3, 115-117; Rachel S. Herz and Trygg Engen, "Odor memory: Review and analysis," *Psychonomic Bulletin & Review 3* (3) (1996), 307.

12. Stoddart, 33-35.

13. Quays, in Goodeve, 85.

14. Stoddart, 171-180.

15. Ibid., 196-97.

16. Ibid., 12-13.

17. Ibid., 96-97. I suspect that this aversion to women's genital odours is strongest in dualist, patriarchal cultures. Stoddart notes, however, the tradition of "love magic" in some Melanesian cultures, based on the "fishy smell" of some women's vaginas. A male suitor uses a small red ground cherry to catch a fish. If it catches a fish, it should also be able to attract the vagina of his beloved! (91)

18. Freud wrote to his colleague Wilhelm Fleiss: "I have often suspected that something organic played a part in repression.... In my case the notion was linked to the changed part played by sensations of smell: upright carriage adopted, nose raised from the ground, at the same time a number of formerly interesting sensations attached to the earth becoming repulsive—by a process still unknown to me. (He turns up his nose—he regards himself as something particularly noble.)" In *The Complete Letters of Sigmund Freud to Wilhelm Fleiss*, 1887-1904, ed. and trans. Jeffrey Moussaieff Masson (Cambridge, MA, and London: Belknap Press of Harvard UP, 1985), 279. Thanks to Akira Mizuta Lippitt for pointing out this reference to me.

19. When I screened *Street of Crocodiles* in a second-year film course, the class internet newsgroup exploded in a virtual riot. One student wrote, "I would rather have my left testicle severed with a dull butter knife than ever sit through a film like that again"; others made equally creative and graphic, as well as occasionally thoughtful, rejoinders. This was the same newsgroup that requested we see more violent movies in class.

20. Miriam Hansen shows how reluctantly Benjamin expunged cabalistic, astrological, and other non-scientific ideas from earlier drafts of the "Artwork" essay. Hansen, "Benjamin, Cinema, and Experience: 'The Blue Flower in the Land of Technology," *New German Critique,* 40 (Winter 1987) 179-224.

The Discrete Charm of the Digital Image:
Animation and New Media
David Clark

A Year and a Day

Although it is explained clearly to us in the titles before the film starts, we find it astonishing all the same: There he is, Tehching Hsieh, aging before our eyes. His body jerks and convulses. Hair sprouts from his head. His face betrays the strain of interrupted sleep. The film, entitled *One Year Performance: 1980-1981* (commonly known as *Time Piece*), is documentation of a performance that condenses a year of his life into about six minutes of film. A frame of the 16mm film showing the artist dressed in simple overalls standing beside a punch clock was taken every hour on the hour from 7 p.m. on April 11, 1980 until 6 p.m. on April 11, 1981. A camera has been given control over a man's life and the result shows us the fact that time passes and we age. I can think of no other film that shows us this naked truth about time so succinctly. Life is short and brutish when it is seen at one second a day.

Peter Osborne points out "film is, famously, the technology of representation most closely associated with philosophical insight into the mutual and paradoxical constitution of time and self."[1] The indexical qualities of film, the insistence on the *this was*, is very pronounced in Hsieh's work. The film devoutly records what happens to Hsieh for a year and yet I have the sinking feeling that time isn't like this. He has been cheated of the time between each frame. I have the same feeling when I can't remember my dreams—when the moment I wake seems like the very same moment after I fell asleep. Although intellectually we know that this film represents a year, the audience lives this film in the present. And here we get to the philosophical problem embodied by film: although film is indexical—we are at a remove from the moment that is being represented—we experience film in the present, in our present, the only present that exists. Animation and "live action" construct these presents differently. Live action is recorded continuously in time whereas in animation the image is usually recorded discontinuously. Hsieh's film is a paradox then. Is it a live-action film recorded at a very slow frame rate—twenty-four frames a day—or is it an animation, an index of discrete moments contrived to give us the impression of time passing continuously?

In his 1993 video installation *24 Hour Psycho*, Scottish artist Douglas Gordon took the entire Hitchcock film *Psycho* (1960) and slowed it down so that it took twenty-four hours to play—about two frames a minute or thirty seconds a frame (which is, by the way, longer than the statistics say the

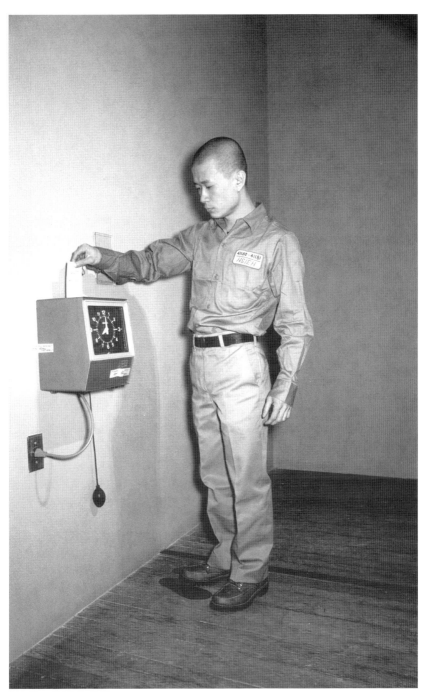

still: Tehching Hsieh's *One Year Performance: 1980-1981 (Time Piece)* (1981)

average viewer considers a painting in a gallery). The film has been trans-ported from the cinema, where we sit immobile and let images flow over us, to the gallery, where we are accustomed to go to contemplate static images. We see frames from the film as if they are photographs demonstrating Lev Manovich's point that "behind even the most stylized cinematic images we can discern the bluntness, the sterility, the banality of early nineteenth-century photographs."[2] And although we know they describe time passing, in the gallery these frames take on an air of timelessness. They have been returned to their immortal roots as photographs. This work exposes what Gilles Deleuze calls the great paradox of cinema: that time is represented by the quick succession of discrete images one after another.

Time Frames and Frames of Mind

The American video artist Phyllis Baldino takes a different tack in consider-ing the discrete properties of cinematic image. In her video *In the Present*, she looks for the basic psychological unit of cinema. The video consists of a series of strange performative vignettes, each seven to twelve seconds—the length of time that an image stays in short-term memory before being com-mitted to long-term memory. Each fragment is separated by a long pause as the screen goes white. This white screen functions to erase the short vignette from our mind, thus disabling our capacity to sequence it through memory. We take in each scene with only the part of the mind that exam-ines sensation. By keeping us in the present, the video gives us a glimpse of a strange world free from the effects of long-term memory. This work seeks to disrupt the effect of continuity created by the cinematic image. It is a work that wants to deny the effect that animation relies on. And it is here that we see that animation engages a different psychology than the indexi-cal qualities of live film. Animation enacts what Freud termed the uncanny, that category of aesthetic feeling that accompanies our uncertainty about what is alive and dead. And so perhaps we could contrast the category of "live action" film and with what should perhaps be called "dead action" film or perhaps even "undead" cinema—the haunted realm of the animated film that produces the effect of time without an index.

This uncanny effect is exposed in the work of Viennese filmmaker Martin Arnold. He applies frame by frame animation techniques to pre-existing Hollywood films. He does not alter individual frames, but animates by repeating and reversing sequences. This was originally done with meticu-lous optical printing, but Arnold now employs the microscopic precision of non-linear digital editing systems. Arnold's work includes thousands of edits where before there had been only a single continuous shot. In his 1998 film *Alone. Life Wastes Andy Hardy*, Martin Arnold uses this technique to examine, amplify, and distort subtle motions and gestures he finds in the actors' gestures in an Andy Hardy film. By repeating, scrubbing, and elongating individual frames, he reanimates the motion and sound of individual scenes to create what seem like monstrous puppets spewing emphatic utterances. Judy Garland, in one sequence of Arnold's film, comically and hauntingly calls out "Alone, Alone, Alone." When Andy Hardy (played by Mickey Rooney) plants an innocent kiss on the neck of his mother, Arnold is able to transform this scene into a terrifying Oedipal attack. While this work has a certain resemblance to scratch video, where these techniques are deployed to create an ironic distance from the original material, this work amplifies the micro-narratives and disturbing psychology that can be drawn out of the seemingly innocent world of the 1940s family drama. Arnold's work is animation's zombie revenge on live cinema.

The Mark of Zeno

The ancient Greek philosopher Zeno attempted to prove that when an arrow flies, it is actually at rest. This famous paradox asks us to accept that at each moment in the arrow's flight, it must occupy the space equal to its own length and therefore, in that discrete moment, it must be still. Film, as an accumulation of still photographs, enforces this picture of time as a series of instances. Unlike live film, with animation we don't expect that each image was created simultaneously with the moment it represents. The image is constructed, not captured. Animation presents us with a different model of thinking about the problem of time. Animations are constructed out of quite obviously discrete frames and yet, are experienced as a flow—giving the impression that time is real only in the eye of the beholder. For the French philosopher Henri Bergson, the character of temporal continuity of consciousness is constructed, not received. In "The Cinematic View of Becoming," the first chapter from his *Creative Evolution* (1911), Bergson rebukes Zeno's paradox: "every attempt to reconstitute change out of states implies the absurd proposition that movement is made out of immobilities."[3] Even so, film has retained this mark of Zeno. The film frame has become a received idea of what constitutes the basic unit of time.

With the invention of instantaneous photography, we uncovered a microcosm of time and the event. In "A Short History of Photography,"[4] Walter Benjamin describes how the photographic aura withered as the technical advances in photography allowed for shorter and shorter poses. As the photograph moved towards the instant, it was less able to capture the traces of duration that for Benjamin gave the photograph its charm and particular haunting quality. And as the image was drained of its aura, it took us into a world beyond our experience like the microscope drew us into a new unimagined world. As the microscope allowed us to understand and manipulate this minute world (such as fighting germs, etc.), so too the world of the instantaneous photograph led the way to the birth of cinema where it was discovered that combining discrete images in sequence could create the illusion of continuous motion. We had to kill duration to create the image of time.

When Eadweard Muybridge generated his first set of motion studies, he was met with disbelief that these flailing images of horses—each numbered in sequence—actually reflected discrete moments of a horse running. There was something unphotographic—or perhaps unauratic—about these images to the eye of the contemporary beholder who was used to long, torturous poses in front of the slow chemistry of the photographic plate. Muybridge had to animate the individual frames of his studies back into motion through a primitive device called the zoopraxiscope to convince the sceptics. The irony perhaps—that speaks more to the birth of animation than to live cinema—is the fact that Muybridge's zoopraxiscope images were not made from photographic images but of drawings made of each photographic image—a technique now known as rotoscoping.

The nineteenth century had seen a parade of animation technologies that lent themselves to our imagining of time as a succession of discrete moments. The zoetrope, praxiscope, kinetoscope, cinematograph, phenakistiscope, thaumatrope, choreutoscope, etc. all provided metaphors of discrete states for the intangibilities of passing time. With the development of movie cameras, animation became the poor cousin of cinema as the automated process of recording real-time events overtook the meticulous creation of an illusion of time created one frame at a time. As Lev Manovich describes it, "Twentieth century animation became a depository for nineteenth century moving-image techniques left behind by cinema."[5] However, in the digital age, animation has thrown off the shackle of laborious work and now the distinction is blurred. Manovich makes the point that "digital cinema is a particular case of animation that uses live-action footage as one of its many elements."[6]

The invention of the motion picture was another example of our giving over to the machine the authority of defining the real. Realism in painting had been radically displaced by the advent of the photograph in the same way that measurement displaced the human observation in the sciences. By the nineteenth century, science had been transformed by the use of scientific instruments, whereas art still relied on man as the measure of all things. Rodin's reaction to photography is typical. "It is the artist who tells the truth and photography that lies. For in reality, time does not stand still."[7] The fact that Muybridge's instantaneous photographs could make time stand still, and then turn around to create such a compelling realization of the movement of time, was an important contribution to the mechanization of the real. In cinema, that Jean-Luc Godard once defined as truth at twenty-four frames per second, Muybridge's truth has largely won over Rodin's.

Subatomic Cinema and Postcards from Godard

Godard had another analogy for cinema. He said "to make cinema or television, technically, is to send twenty-five postcards per second to millions of people."[8] The postcard, however, was an indiscrete construct. Postcards were introduced during the time of the Franco-Prussian War after the hostilities started to drag on and soldiers needed to have a system of communicating with loved ones that could be monitored by military censors. The marriage of text, address, and image in the postcard, as well as its military genealogy, may also serve as a powerful metaphor for digital cinema. New media is nothing if not indiscrete. Digital film has split the atom. The frame is no longer the basic unit of truth. A frame and a moment are no longer held together by the medium the way they were in film. They have been divided and reorganized. A frame of film is now a complex array of possible components each with a number of possible sources and controls. Truth is now a mixture of pixels and code—of images and communication systems. And the charm of the discrete units of digital cinema has the same intangibility of the charm of a subatomic particle.

And so the condition of animation these days is one of increasing abstractness as the image is removed from the hand of the animator and the index of time. The image in digital animation is derived not exclusively from optics but also from vectors and datastreams. A film is not a linear progression of frames along a timeline but the coordination of databanks, images, sounds, and code. And ultimately the basic unit of digital film is not the frame but the simplicity of binary machine code. In digital media, the progression of the image is not limited to the run/stop algorithm of the film projector but can now engage in the complex if/then logic of the computer code. With this code the physics of movement can be written and distributed separately from the image itself. The code can generate the image and the image can generate code. Just as live-action film can now be seen as a sub-set of animation, so too can animation be seen now as one particular simple example of this image/code hybrid. As Lev Manovich contends, new media is no longer an indexical medium.

The Hand of the Animator

The "hand of the animator" is a term used in the history of animation to denote the self-referential use of the animator's hand on the screen to interact with the drawn, animated figures in the frame. Its appearance in many early animations attests to how animators came to terms with the strangeness of this new medium. Through the hand of the animator, we are able to imagine our body inside the strange and foreign parallel world created by a new technology. It is part of the formal exploration of the medium that accompanies shifts in visual culture. With the loss of the indexical relationship to reality in digital cinema, a new ontology of the medium is emerging, and in contemporary new media art you can see this hand of the animator effect returning as artists once again explore the formal characteristics of the new medium. The "hand of the animator" effect now needs to expose us to the relation between the cinematic image and the code that controls it.

Joan Heemskerk and Dirk Paesmans are artists from Belgium and the Netherlands who work under the name of jodi.org. They are recognized as early innovators of net.art. Their work evolved from experiments with VJing to early hacking experiments with game code. *Untitled Game*, for instance, uses the game engine from popular commercial gaming software DOOM that they hacked, leaving the navigation system intact but the visuals reduced to a Mondrian-like abstract world. Jodi.org's websites exploit the way in which underlying HTML (hypertext markup language) and JavaScript code constructs a web page, and in particular the pop-up window, to create animated motion.[9] The experience of opening up the jodi.org site can make you feel like your computer has been possessed. Pop-up windows dash across the screen like frightened cockroaches. The web page is no longer the frame through which you look at the work. The frame is animated and, after you orient yourself to it, is the work itself. The normally quiet and obedient HTML has become an animator. The experience of their website draws your attention to the way the convention of the web page is an animated experience and evokes the uncanny feelings we ascribe to our computers as being controlled by viruses and spyware.

Jim Punk also exploits unconventional approaches to constructing web

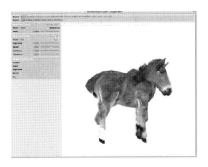 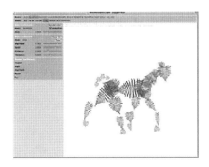

pages. For him, the web space is a place to explore the vocabulary of graffiti. His work owes a debt to the "tag" of the graffiti writer. Ironically HTML is also constructed with "tags" that separate the code from the content of the HTML. In Jim Punk's work, navigation functions are often disabled or confused, leaving the viewer to negotiate an unruly array of images and pop-up windows. This work disrupts the habits we have formed in navigating web pages and, like jodi.org's work, draws our attention to the animated experience of the web browser environment. The use of self-referential motifs like the qwerty keyboard or the animated window makes us consider these conventions in a different light. The titles of his works, *100.000.000.000.000—Headache & various musical temptations for International Computers *Error** and *paranoiacwww*, allude to the psychological dimension of web browsing.[10]

This work has its roots in the disruptive Modernist impulses of Dada and Absurdist theatre. Applied to the new conventions of the web-page, they contribute to a critical evaluation of the conventions being established on the internet. They also extend the tradition of the animated film beyond the frame of the internet. Under the banner "hacktivism," artists are discovering the potential of a wide range of new technologies and questioning their social use. For instance, jodi.org has used email spam as a system of distribution and the net.art collective 0100101110101101.org (with programmers "epidemic") released a virus called Biennale.py from the Slovenian Pavilion at the 49th Venice Biennale on June 6, 2001. Artists are realizing that almost everything is, or can be, animated in our new media landscape.

The Hand on the Ouija Board

The computer has incorporated the hand of the animator effect into the design of the machine itself. The computer mouse allows us to be the hand of the animator—to reach into and interact with this strange new world. The

still: LeCielEstBleu's *Puppet Tool* (2003)

GUI (graphic user interface) that paved the way for the popularization of computing is a continuation of that impulse of wanting our presence to be symbolized within the medium. Our way of negotiating the contours and parameters of the digital world is now offered to us through a proto-tactile experience termed "interactivity." The audiences of new media works now have a participatory role in the work that is somewhere between a user and a viewer, something the American media artist Bill Seaman has called the "vuser." Interactivity has created the possibility of a tug of war between you and the work and again opened up questions about what is alive and dead. The prototype of this experience is perhaps the Ouija board.

The new media artwork *Puppet Tool,* by the French collective LeCielEstBleu, allows the viewer to manipulate a bestiary of animals such as a horse, giraffe, or penguin, each created from photorealistic fragments.[11] These creatures are animated by a combination of the viewer's interaction and computer code that gives physicality and elasticity to the creature's movements. There is something akin to Muybridge's experiments in this work as it investigates the mystery of motion and how things work. But the image and the motion are not an index of reality as they are in Muybridge's sequences. The image is created through still photographic images, whereas the movement derives from how the code is able to move these fragments to simulate the weight and feel of a body in motion. It is through the viewer's interaction with this work that we understand the physicality of the world being described.

Another example of this puppet interface metaphor is the website *SodaPlay.*[12] This work allows the viewer to create wire-frame models in a virtual space by connecting dots together with lines. These simple constructions can then be subjected to the effects of gravity, tossed around by the user, or programmed to move by themselves. This piece also has an online communal toy box where constructions can be added to an archive or entered in races with other users. The simplicity of this tool underlines even more succinctly than *Puppet Tool* how new media work has broken apart the relationship between the image and movement. The viewer is brought into the animation process as the creator of the objects but it is the virtual world—the frame around the object—that animates them.

American net artist Erik Loyer combines traditional linear narrative with the responsive interface in his 2001 piece *Chroma.*[13] A voice-over guides us through a sci-fi scenario where characters discover and explore an abstract landscape—a "natural cyberspace"—through simple graphics and text. The mouse functions of point and click each control different aspects of the navigation. The click function moves the narrative ahead while the point function (moving the mouse around the screen) is attached to a code that controls how the graphic elements on the screen behave. An interesting push and pull happens with this piece. Although we are engaged in the progressive unfolding of a story, we also create some of the animation ourselves.

Andy Foulds has also explored the interactive possibilities of code-based animation combined with photographic images. A particularly poignant example of this technique is an animation called *Leader of the Free World?*, where an elastic image of George W. Bush can be led around the screen by his nose following a dollar sign cursor.[14] In another piece, Tony Blair obsessively follows an image of Bush. We only understand this work by participating in it, by using it. The animation is no longer an index of a determined motion but a record of our hand moving across the piece.

Hans Hoogerbrugge is a net.artist from the Netherlands who is known for his absurdist interactive animated figures.[15] Dressed in business attire, he appears as a recurring character in his work. He uses animation as a way to create a bizarre and surreal world where anything is possible. Through a click or a rollover or sometimes a keystroke, the viewer becomes the hand of the animator interacting with this world. His series Modern Living is an encyclopedia of small interactive visual gags; perhaps the figure's head explodes, or he suddenly plays air guitar, or rips off his face to release flies trapped in his head. The works *Flow* and *Spin* move forward through a progression of interconnected vignettes that inevitably loop back to the beginning again. The interaction is integrated with the progression of the music, making the work a semi-interactive rock video. In the work *Hotel*, Hoogerbrugge has added more complex gaming elements into his vocabulary of animation, allowing storylines and characters (albeit still quite absurd) to develop over a number of chapters and in a series of locations in his fictional hotel.

These works explore how the dynamics of interaction create meaning but they still fall in the tradition of character animation. The computer has allowed another branch of animation, abstract animation, to flourish as well.

Ghost in the Machine

Generative animation removes the hand of the animator even further. Also called software art or code art, generative animation creates images and motion through the use of computer algorithms. The computer's efficiency and speed at generating images has created new possibilities for abstraction in cinema. Programs can visualize the recursive mathematical functions used by programmers or reproduce mathematical descriptions of motion described by physics equations. But they are abstractions. Even the most obtuse films of Stan Brakhage are still an index of chemical and optical material processes. Computer-based artworks, where the images are generated by the underlying code, create a new level of remove from the material index of the work. As the image is constructed as it is being displayed, any distinction between animation and live action dissolves. It is work that exemplifies Bergson's idea of time as creative evolution and dissolves Zeno's paradox.

Generative art's genealogy includes John Cage's experiments with chance operations in composition, Duchamp's removal of the hand of the artist in his readymades, as well as the OULIPO movement in France, which sought to create a literature out of generative structures and constraints. Generative work also has an affinity with the rule-based work of Sol Lewitt and the geometric abstraction of Bridget Riley and the British school of op art and system art. This was work that prioritized the process of codifying and executing the artwork through mechanical and logical procedures. The ontology of cinema under these conditions is not one that is aligned with being—the pure presence of the indexical *this was* of live action film—but with that of becoming, the aesthetics of process and uncertainty.

The code of the early cinema could be seen as a crude mechanical system that simply replaced one complete image for another at a standard rate (eighteen or twenty-four frames per second), creating the remarkable illusion of a time image. The complexity of the parameters for the control of animation by computer code has now left the intuitive grasp of the viewer. New media work can now connect the process of generating the animation to any number of complex data sets or mathematical operations. There is a continuity of this work to the visual formalism and abstract language of painting and drawing over the last century, but there is also a new instability and unpredictability of the art object. Generative artwork dances on the grave of the death of the author and is perhaps the royal road to the unconscious of artificial intelligence.

The work of British net.artist Stanza continues this trajectory of system art and abstract painting from the 1960s. His works use the generative capabilities of the computer to create complex and ever-changing pieces. Works like *central city*, *amorphoscapes*, and *subvergence* create dynamic landscapes of text, image and sound.[16] Although the vocabulary of colour, shape, texture, and form have a lineage in Abstract Expressionist painting, the work also incorporates architectural, diagrammatic references, and artifacts from digital culture. The *ccityv* part of the *central city project*, for instance, uses video from webcams of cities as the source material for a series of distortions.

The field of generative art has flourished with the coming together of computer programming and animation. This world is populated by both artists who have taken up programming and designers and codeheads who aspire to work in the visual art world. Sites such as Praystation, Bodytag, Levitated.net, Incident.net, Liquid Journey, Bit.101, and uncontrol.com are all repositories of code-generated visual experiments and abstract animation that continue the tradition of experimental animation of Stan Brakhage and Norman McLaren. The exploration is often one that straddles or even transcends categories of art and programming just as the internet has blurred the line between professional and hobby practices. What is distinctly different, however, is how the sequential progression and temporal index of the creation and reception of this work has changed. Many of these works have no fixed temporal dimension. They simply run for however long they are left. And their creation is no longer inscribed in their form. They are generated in the instant the code is executed. They are, in essence, live animation.

A Year and a Day (Reprise)

John Cabral's web piece *Ground Zero* is an animation that works around the clock. It plays continuously over twenty-four hours and the narrative unfolds in correspondence to the time in the real world.[17] The cartoon characters in Cabral's world seem to live in real time and the banality of the everyday. This is somewhat uncanny given that we are used to the compressed and kinetic storylines of cartoon animations because of the labour intensive nature of animation production. But in Cabral's world—generated with video game character software—the time and duration of this medium has been extended. We have the impression that we are looking here at a webcam for cartoon characters. Cabral's piece reframes animation by playing with the scale of duration in a way that is similar to what Douglas Gordon did with *24 Hour Psycho*.

Of course, one of the important considerations for duration work on the internet is the fact that these works are not constrained by the reception of films in a theatre or the strict broadcast schedule of television. Film requires a considerable investment of time and the presence of the audience to attend the screening of a film. The internet is a domestic animal that extends the distracted viewing patterns of the television audience but with random access to the content. Web work and video games are more like a novel that you pick up and put down as it fits in with your schedule.

This idea of duration and time is the subject of a work by MTAA (M. River & T. Whid Art Associates) called *1 year performance video (aka samHsieh-Update)*.[18] They have been updating classic conceptual art for the internet in a series that includes remakes of On Kawara and Vito Acconci works. This work is a pastiche of Sam Hsieh's 1978 performance where he locked himself inside a small room for a year. For the web piece, the two artists appear in what seems to be a live streaming video of two identical ten-foot by ten-foot by ten-foot rooms. The viewer is asked to log in and observe the performance in progress as they go about a mundane series of actions of sleeping, reading, and working on a computer in their self-imposed confinement. The duration of the piece indicated in the title is not actually the length of the performance event: The live video has been stitched together from video fragments that seamlessly create the illusion of real time, similar to the technique used to create the Subservient Chicken video sponsored by Burger King, where a video of a man in a chicken suit in an apartment would seemingly respond to instructions typed into the site.[19] The real duration of the piece depends on how long the viewer watches. The piece will be over when someone has logged on and watched the piece for a year. The piece presents an illusion of real time "live" video using the constructed techniques of animation. It also highlights the fact that new media work is often more about the index of the viewers' experience than an index of the event of the object.

Animation's trajectory into new media has radically altered the techniques of the medium, but perhaps more importantly it has fundamentally altered the metaphors by which we imagine time and change. Time is that most intangible of concepts and artists continue to frame questions about time from within digital culture. How we understand duration and represent time through an indexical process has changed in a way that is analogous to how physics' understanding of matter shifted from the nineteenth-century intuitive conceptions of atomism, which proposed that matter was like our reality, only smaller, to the surreal twentieth-century world of quarks, charm, spin, uncertainty, incompleteness, and chaos. And so the experiments with time and duration that constituted the formal phase of examining the media arts have been updated. Hsieh's year and Gordon's day are different things on the internet.

Endnotes

1. Peter Osborne, 'Distracted Reception: Time, Art and Technology' in *Time Zones, Recent Film and Video*, (Tate Publishing, 2004), 70.
2. Lev Manovich, *The Language of New Media*, (Massachusetts Institute of Technology, 2001), 294
3. Henri Bergson, *Creative Evolution*, trans. Arthur Mitchell, (University Presses of America, 1983).
4. Walter Benjamin, "A Short History of Photography," trans. P. Paton. *Classic Essays on Photography* ed. Alan Trachtenberg. (New Haven: Leete's Island Books, 1980).
5. Manovich, 298.
6. Manovich, 302
7. Marc Gotieb, *The Plight of Emulation: Ernest Meissonier and French Salon Painting*, (Princeton University Press, 1996), 181.
8. Quoted in Richard Dienst's *Still Life in Real Time* (Durham: Duke UP, 1994).
9. www.jodi.org
10. www.jimpunk.com
11. www.lecielestbleu.com/html/puppettool.htm
12. www.sodaplay.com/
13. www.marrowmonkey.com/menu.html
14. www.andyfoulds.co.uk/flash_design.html
15. www.hoogerbrugge.com/
16. www.stanza.co.uk/
17. www.turbulence.org/Works/groundzero/
18. www.turbulence.org/Works/1year/index.php & www.mteww.com/
19. www.subservientchicken.com/

Jeremy Blake: "I blacked out and had some very vivid dreams..."[1]

Lia Gangiatano

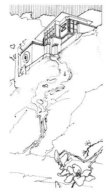

I've always thought of animation as the closest thing to a recorder of the free associations of dreams. Its prolific digital status, although dematerializing the animated image, has also blurred itself into everyday waking life (on cellphones, taxicabs, etc.). If everything's becoming like a wayward animation, then two quiescent, imagined stills frame my understanding of the work of Jeremy Blake, both geographically and temporally relating to the context of our acquaintance in New York around 1997: a glass structure by Dan Graham sits upon the roof of DIA; and on the east side where we used to live, the last Marlboro man presides on a lone billboard high above Delancey Street, as if he's paused on a drive-in movie screen. These things are both gone now, ostensibly, but it seems to me that Blake's manifold, unfolding interests in flawed utopic architectures and absent yet larger-than-life characters are somehow connected to these once real, now ephemeral, images. Aided, in part, by animation, they branch, in Blake's work, into historical, cultural, and personal references ranging from Philip Johnson's glass houses to Richard Prince's cowboys; from *Get Smart* to *Junior Bonner*; from Ossie Clark to his dad; and so on. The dates might not synch up, but when Blake left New York, the billboard was gone, too. Blake has said of the Sunset Strip's last Marlboro man: "He was like a land-based astronaut, which, in my opinion, can also be one definition of a successful artist."[2]

Perhaps it was a job-turned-collaboration, working on drawings for an animated short film by Theresa Duncan, *The History of Glamour* (1999), that ushered Blake's practice, formerly rooted in painting and drawing, into the unique application of computer animation that, around 2000, placed him at the forefront of new media art. Like Duncan's protagonist, an aspiring rock star named Charles Valentine, who, after numerous episodes of getting drunk on Chanel No. 5 and unleashing friendly critiques on the worlds of art, fashion, and music that spawned her fame, Blake also unwittingly rose to the top by using all the right tools, only to return to his roots to seek happiness. In both Valentine and Blake's cases, however, the typewriter and the paintbrush were always there—inextricably linked to the preferred, popular formats of the day, and, in fact, consistently informing their particular usage of them.

Perhaps Blake saw this coming? His *One Hit Wonder* (1999), a screenplay

drawing by Jeremy Blake, courtesy of Feigen Contemporary

consisting of ink drawings, hand- and typewritten fragments of narrative, and an apparent cast of losers—although loosely based on the spooky yet uplifting *Wizard of Oz*—is a story of mishaps, missed opportunities, and descent into LA-style misguidedness. The A-frame house of his protagonist's guru, when stripped of its drug-induced sparkle, looks more like the top gangster's stronghold in *The Killing of a Chinese Bookie* than Emerald City.[3] Like the glimmering cocaine dust that populated the shag rugs of his earliest computer-generated set designs for non-existent films—the dust, or aura, of Blake's later paintings insinuates equal distrust in the ability of any of his chosen mediums, taken separately, to adequately represent his dreams.

> Walter Benjamin employs the metaphor of dust to describe the rundown state of dreams in modernity. Attuned to the fate of the aura, he says, dreams are no longer removed from concrete experience, but tangible and near. They have lost their romantic dimension, their "blue distance," fading into a sad grayness that figuratively represents the disintegration that befalls dreams when they cease being imaginary and enter the polluted atmosphere of everyday life.... And, as is always the case with the aura, the loss of distance is occasioned by technology....[4]

Blake's connection to the presumably sunnier West Coast—where the blue distance of dreams is preserved, bought, and sold every day—was always there, too. Having attended graduate school in the desert outside Los Angeles, Blake's cinematic style, lifestyle, and aesthetic never completely succumbed to New York's down-and-out urban darkness. His work at the time of our 1998 collaboration (on the exhibition Spectacular Optical at the late Thread Waxing Space) consisted of scripted drawings (or scripts), light box movie posters, and digitally rendered set designs. His artist's statement back then read:

> The sensibilities and techniques of Hollywood cinematographers, set-builders, make-up artists, etc., have lately been widely borrowed by artists and employed to produce much of contemporary sculpture, photography, and video art. In some cases, this borrowing may be an effort to promote the trusses and supports for thespian delusion as the only realizable utopic architecture. In other cases, it is a seemingly cold-hearted, but ultimately philanthropic effort to point out that the world is full of half-assed actors, badly scripted dialogue, and almost too dazzling special effects. Other work is designed to demonstrate the delirious potency of the artist's imagination by offering fragments that may be pieced together to form ridiculous dream sequences, and then broken down and sold separately.[5]

still: Jeremy Blake's *Reading Ossie Clark* (2003). Sequence from DVD with sound for plasma or projection. 9-minute continuous loop. Courtesy of Feigen Contemporary

These ideas seemed to aptly describe the cultural moment and the tendency in artistic practices of the late nineties to aspire to other media and modes of production, in particular, cinematic sources and their byproducts —ideas that instigated *Spectacular Optical*, an exhibition that aligned the work of contemporary artists with the early experimental films of David Cronenberg. As well as featuring Blake's work, this exhibition drew upon a well-worn book loaned to me from Blake's library, *Dan Graham's Kammerspiel* by Jeff Wall—a book that had been passed on to him by his teacher, David Reed. The author describes the nature of his book as follows:

> Dan Graham's unrealized (and possibly unrealizable) project *Alteration to a Suburban House* (1978), generates a hallucinatory, almost Expressionist, image by means of a historical critique of conceptual art. In this work, conceptualism is the discourse that fuses together three of the most resonant architectural tropes of this century (the glass skyscraper, the glass house, and the suburban tract house) into a monumental expression of apocalypse and historical tragedy.[6]

For Cronenberg, as well, the inevitable sprawl of institutional bleakness served as much as a main character as the numerous overly-creative (mad) scientists who sought to conquer rationality with their experiments in exploded repression. The projects pursued by his "heroes" were generally driven by misguided utopian goals and involved various drug-filled communes poised against menacing corporate entities. Because of the relentless austerity of Cronenberg's early films, tracing his development in terms of the artistic precedents that coincided with their production, namely, minimalism and conceptual art, provided a link to Wall's observation that

> reductivist tendencies formed a primary fascination in the sixties because they resulted in the production of austere and mechanistic objects whose aggressive passivity and stylish indifference toward the spectator evoked feelings of alienation and dehumanization reminiscent of those experienced in everyday life.[7]

This historical lineage and its fallout seemed particularly relevant to Blake, and to numerous practitioners of contemporary art toward the end of the century. Wall's meditation on "profound estrangement," and the disturbing qualities embodied in the "disorienting, mirroric invisibility" of presumably rational architectural forms served to outline the haunted, vampiric state of things that, although momentarily trivialized by millennial hype, has remained an increasing preoccupation in Blake's work.

> The vampire is neither alive nor dead, but exists in an accursed state of irre-

mediable tension and anxiety. Although his symbolic identity is complex and goes beyond its function in this analysis, he embodies a certain sense of cosmic grief, which is a diffracted image of a concrete historical uneasiness.... [T]he vampire signifies not simply the unwillingness of the old regime to die, but the fear that the new order has unwittingly inherited something corrupted and evil from the old, and is in the process of unconsciously engineering itself around an evil centre.[8]

Blake's literal invocation of the vampire, or, more accurately, a residence devoted to "itinerant vampires," in *Berkshire Fangs* (2001), seamlessly incorporates architectural as well as art historical monoliths from the previous century—mixing his homage/critique of modern masters with references to some of his favorite, real and imagined, iconoclasts. He has noted of the larger work, *Mod Lang* (2001): "There are plenty of inspirations for the work: Morris Louis, Rothko, Archigram, Ruscha, Keith Moon's various nouveau riche residences. But I lifted the title from a song by Big Star."[9] Regarding his generous quotation of modernist painters, he continues:

> I use that kind of abstraction to haunt representational space. Mixing architectural and abstract imagery into a kind of time-based, painterly hallucination is the most satisfying way I've found to represent the uncanny. I got a push in this direction from the writings of Anthony Vidler, and Jeff Wall's take on Philip Johnson's houses, and also from reading Walter Benjamin, who said that modern painting should take note of the innovations of architecture and film. I was foolhardy enough to actually try it.[10]

Against the repressive forces concretized in institutional architecture, for example, the wild futurisms of the past and the visionary authors who imagined them have always existed—with or without the actual technological means to realize their dreams. The current availability of tools that enable the rendering of widespread hallucinatory spectacle, global communications, etc., across real space and time doesn't necessarily make them better, or more real, than the speculative projects of the sixties by Archigram, Utopie Group, or Buckminster Fuller, to whom Blake refers in his work. These artists and groups integrated themes from popular culture and politics within radical intellectual frameworks to expand the fields of art and architecture—mainly through works made of paper, cardboard, toothpicks—and unaided by computers. Blake's engagement with the imaginations of the past at a moment when technological advances have made increasingly tangible the theoretical experiments of prior generations is deliberately hesitant. His grafting of traditional drawing and painting techniques with, by today's standards, already obsolescent, old-fashioned computer programs such as PhotoShop and After Effects, does not wholeheartedly embrace new technology—it just ups the ante a little bit, as if to call each of his practices (in his painting studio or in front of a computer) into question. This desire to integrate, and thereby obliterate, easy understandings of existing formats, genres, and mediums is perhaps the domain of every generation's artistic mavericks. And by referencing his favourite rogues and badasses across disciplines—Archigram, Robert Evans, Keith Moon, Ossie Clark, Sarah Winchester, and David Berman (a poet/musician with whom Blake is currently collaborating)—Blake acknowledges their stylish contributions to progress.

In reference to the "intersection of cosmopolitan and utopian fantasy" insinuated by works such as *Reading Ossie Clark* and *Autumn Almanac* (2003), Blake has noted, "There was a belief that good design or good drugs or good clothes would actually lead to a better world, and there was an optimism in that."[11] The predominantly ephemeral histories of utopian art and architecture collectives of the sixties, for example, run parallel to the still-persistent inheritance of modern rationalist methodologies—outlining that there were other, less tangible, societal dreams at play. Not always explicitly oppositional (although hostage-taking did occur at conferences involving Utopie, Archigram, Superstudio, and Archizoom), these projects were oriented toward a different future than the one we typically experience today, and they achieved this alien status by challenging the accepted links between artistic forms and representation—seeking, instead, to demystify the objects of art and architecture.

> Basically they [Utopie] attempted to transcend architecture itself, as they transcended urban planning itself, like the Situationists could scrap the university milieu itself.... Everyone found himself at ground zero of the destruction of his own discipline. There was a kind of dissolution by excess on which everyone could agree.... Within the framework of *Utopie*—and that's what Utopie was, too—we were searching for an intellectual center of gravity from where we could branch out to all the other disciplines.[12]

I would venture that Blake's ambivalence toward the label of new media artist has something to do with the "evil centre" to which Jeff Wall referred (and against which freethinkers of prior generations rebelled) in that hierarchies of medium propped up by institutions of power (such as those that place technological prowess as a pinnacle of art) necessarily drain the dreams of artists of their revolutionary potential. The fact that digital animation has given Blake's "paintings" a "jolt of life,"[13] is predicated on his particular mixing of new media with more traditional, static forms (architecture and painting) to advance these forms towards a more eloquent articulation of generational, societal, and cultural concerns. Often, when formal conventions are seamlessly broken and the status of the image is not easily extrapolated, a disarming of intellectual structures gives rise to the forwarding of deeper, more complex inward turns, as has often been the case in tracing more meaningful trajectories, for example, in cinema.

> What Lev Manovich wrote in relation to the history of cinema can be applied to Blake's expanded computer-generated images: "We no longer think of the history of cinema as linear march toward only one possible language, or as a progression towards more and more accurate verisimilitude. Rather, we have come to see its history as a succession of distinct and equally expressive languages, each with its own aesthetic variables, each new language closing off some of the possibilities of the previous one."[14]

Roman Polanski, a cinematic innovator, who, prior to the unquestionable end of the optimistic cultural imagination of the sixties (as signaled by, among other things, the Manson murders) foreshadowed its demise by fashioning a distinctive interior dread—from which there was necessarily no return—entirely through hand-built sets and camera lens effects in his 1965 film, *Repulsion*. The rooms of the apartment of Carol Ledoux (Catherine Deneuve) become the site of Carol's increasingly hallucinatory vision and form a key expression of neurosis in his work—the Ledoux sisters' top-floor flat near Earls Court Station in London is closely scrutinized. Polanski has noted of this choice of location: "... I wanted to show precisely a kind of disorder and not another. Therefore I had to do so where that disorder exists."[15] While riffing on important Gothic tropes, Polanski significantly conflates architecture and event so that there is no exteriority toward which his characters can flee. His now iconic elongating corridors, attenuated shadows, and soft, groping walls resonate Carol's inner turmoil. The spatial distortions deployed by Polanski are perhaps the most formally compelling aspect of the film and contribute to the lack of cinematic distinction between the real and the hallucinatory—aptly describing the characteristics of Carol's distress.

> Towards the end of the film the sitting room and bathroom become, in Carol's eyes, enormous, menacing caverns. Polanski obtained these extraordinarily terrifying effects by a combination of wide-angle lens and duplicate sets built not only on a much increased scale but with grossly distorted angles and curves."[16]

Initially, Blake's spatial distortions, generated by computer graphics software, took the form of endlessly sliding glass doors, morphing après-ski fireside lounges, and R2D2-style blinking light banks to insinuate the lavish alienation of excess comfort—a new kind of architectural menace. In his *Black Swan* (one of a series of three digital projections that comprise *Bungalow 8*, 2000),

> The lights of the city then dissolve into a figure-eight hot tub, eponymous of the bungalow itself and of Hollywood decadence more generally. As the lit steam from the hot tub rises, it is suddenly transformed into search lights to the accompanying roar of a helicopter, the paranoid double that hovers above and helps maintain the land of dreams.[17]

In Blake's work, however, the characters themselves are conspicuously absent—they are the fictitious authors, unseen architects, or in the case of the *Winchester Trilogy* (2004), the historical eccentric whose constructed environment serves to mirror the inner workings of her distressed mind. Blake's luxurious depictions of cumulative cultural malaise, as well, tend not to derive from actual, real, or built spaces (except in the case, again, of the *Winchester Trilogy*, which incorporates actual footage from Sarah Winchester's house). His works instead emerge from hand-drawn, computer-animated images woven into looping DVD projections. "Blake calls the DVD loops 'time-based paintings,' since, as he likes to point out, they are built up with layers of translucent color."[18] Prior to his actual return to painting as such, Blake's *Mod Lang* explored the potential disappearance of painting in a DVD whose morphing abstractions derive from a made-up story articulated in a series of drawings. Placing a roguish fiction as the basis of destabilized painterly concepts further emphasizes his idiosyncratic approach to this presumably autonomous medium.

> But despite Blake's painterly approach to digital animation and his interest in high Modernist formal conventions, there is still no painting here. At least no Modernist painting, which depended upon the belief in being able to isolate and render semi-autonomous painting as a practical discipline. In extending the history of that practice, its long tradition of achievements, by revolutionizing such isolatable material and ontological parameters... Blake only simulates the effects of painting; otherwise he participates in the dissolution of its material identity, and so its chances to advance a history of its own. That history is shown stalled in the past, caught in the purgatory of an endless playback loop.[19]

In tandem with his rigorous engagement with the dissolving of forms (ani-

mation as painting, painting as animation), Blake's project maximizes the potential of the moving image—its ability to encompass a complete world-view—by fracturing its parts. Incomplete scripts, fragmented narratives, disparate set designs exist, but they are kept separate, resisting the cumulative goal of making a picture in the traditional sense. While his drawings

still: Jeremy Blake's *Winchester* (2002). Sequence from DVD with sound for plasma or projection, 18-minute continuous loop. Courtesy of Feigen Contemporary

may provide "a skeletal back story," perhaps insinuating some kind of beginning and end, his DVDs perpetually loop, allowing evolvement and dis-solution to coexist in narcotic waves. Blake has noted: "A scene in *Berkshire Fangs* shows what appears to be a pristine Ellsworth Kelly composition that slowly changes tone and goes out of focus until it becomes unbearably infernal. It's important to me that the threat of narrative intrusion trans-forms the work."[20]

Blake's *Winchester Trilogy* flirts with the notion of telling a story, as well, but focuses instead on the ambience authored by Sarah Winchester, heir to the Winchester firearms fortune, through her life's project—building hun-dreds of rooms to house the ghosts that haunted her. Tracing a particular form of West Coast popular mythology—spirituality and its related cults—back to its early roots, Blake's interest in the Winchester Mystery House stemmed from its formal as well as psychological resonances. As Steve McQueen would be warned decades later (that, following his fortunate detour on the way to Sharon Tate's for dinner, a coven of witches was wish-ing him dead), Sarah Winchester was told by a spiritualist that she was the object of haunting by the spirits of the victims of her family's invention. While specific reference is made to violence through logo-like images of cowboys with guns, the locus of internal fear, in classic gothic form, is expressed through the haunted house.

And while discussions of colour in Blake's work have centered around the colour field painters whom he directly quotes in his works, it is tempting to

still: Jeremy Blake's *Reading Ossie Clark* (2003). Sequence from DVD with sound for plasma or projection. 9-minute continuous loop. Courtesy of Feigen Contemporary compare, in terms of structure and themes, as well, Blake's *Winchester* project to the films of master colourist Dario Argento. A character in Argento's *Inferno* says, "the only true mystery is that our very lives are governed by dead people." His unfinished *Three Mothers* trilogy (including *Suspiria*, 1977, and *Inferno*, 1980) involves houses populated by powerful covens of witches. Their stories are left mainly unexplained in Argento's films; their dominant presence, instead, is expressed through architecture, colour, and soundtrack. *Inferno*'s famous (and technically demanding) underwater parlour scene underlines the dreamlike vision Argento strove to achieve in his films, but, strangely, he accomplished equally fantastical effects by using coloured gels, and in the case of *Suspiria*, a soundtrack by Goblin. Unlike the extreme "mood control" exacted by Argento's deployment of Goblin's distinctively scary music, Blake offers ambient sound in the form of DVD soundtracks as well as CD accompaniments to his exhibitions (such as his collaborative soundtrack for *The Forty Million Dollar Beatnik*, 2000, with Neil Landstrumm and Mike Fellows, that includes generous samples from Bob Evans's book on tape, *The Kid Stays in the Picture*). As another form of repressed narrative, the sound of a film travelling through a small gauge projector opens *Winchester*, further mingling understood formats.

While Polanski built duplicate, exaggerated sets, and Argento augmented already imposing architectural spaces through eccentric, theatrical lighting effects to express internal fears, their innovative artistic methods reflected a stretching of available means relative to their times. However, discourses of technology did not necessarily dominate the reception of their otherwise groundbreaking films. Today, as technology's advance is ubiquitous and accelerated, its effects cannot be disentangled from current understandings of art and its relationships to popular culture, media, entertainment—and the historical predecessors who seemed to pre-imagine this hybrid state, as well, have become a preoccupation for new generations of artists. Blake has noted of his collaborations outside the "art world," such as his animated passages for P.T. Anderson's *Punch-Drunk Love* and album cover art for Beck's *Sea Change*,

> All three of us have something in common, which is that as artists we're all looking at previous generations as kind of rifling through the files of history, trying to find something that matches how we feel.... But at the same time as we're inspired by our sources, we're still trying to do something totally new.[21]

Tracing the architectural activities of Sarah Winchester in the first two parts of his trilogy, Blake continues through *Century* to the commercial cinemas built around the house: "These buildings are space-age domes, but to my mind just as 'haunted' by specters of the American West as the mansion. In other words, I am tracing the mythology of the gunfighter away from the house, and dealing with the Hollywood Western."[22] Blake's choice of digital animation, an available method that formally matches the temperament of his actual and imagined inheritance of dream/nightmare scenarios—and one that can accommodate the spontaneous flow of (past, present, future) images[23]— is consistently countered by his placement of paintings, shadowy mirror fragments of methodologies of the past, to ground his DVD projections in the however tainted present.

> These paintings predicated on the miscegenation of media stand in direct opposition to the modernist mantra of medium specificity. Purposefully unfinished, Blake's paintings point out how painting alone cannot achieve a critical function—painting is now a mere ghost of what it once was. At the same time, the paintings' delicate layering and caustic colour combinations proclaim their status as objects in a way that the projection's spectral play of light can never achieve.... As both painting and projection, as new combinatory art form, Blake's work has the revolutionary potential to change the way the object of art is defined today. In this way his art is what Gilles Deleuze defined as the objectile. Objectile is the term for a new type of object that intrinsically expresses the variability and multiplicity endemic to the computer age.[24]

Even so, works such as Blake's *Autumn Almanac* (2003), a series of fifty-two paintings installed "to echo the even, grid-like display of the scene lengths on an Avid editing program,"[25] live together with DVD animations (in this case, integrally linked with *Reading Ossie Clark*) to provide a structural key just verging on narrative, resonating the form of his DVDs. His *Almanac* includes paintings of patterned fabrics photographed at a thrift store in Topanga Canyon; inscriptions from Ossie Clark's day planner; images of Twiggy, Viva, Michel Auder, and Barnett Newman, for example— both strangers and friends. With *Almanac*, Blake expands the loose storytelling of his drawings, borrowing the title of The Kinks song in which Ray Davies "finds poetry in the everyday stuff he sees strolling through a somewhat drab post-war London district."[26] Titled as a deliberate "class distinction" from Gerhard Richter's *Atlas*, Blake has noted,

> An atlas is the guidebook for a traveler, and calls to mind images of well-funded expeditions; whereas the almanac is the guide for the humble farmer and working men and women in rural cottage industries. Weather patterns, folk wisdom, bawdy jokes, etc., all get an airing in *Almanac*.[27]

Some people think it was the bubbles in Coca-Cola, "the beverage choice of a generation," that inspired change in the sixties, too.

Endnotes

1. LAPD Police Detective Spike Punch in Jeremy Blake, *One Hit Wonder* (Los Angeles: works on paper, inc., 1999): unpaginated.

2. Martha Schwendener, "Technical Knockout," *Time Out New York*, (December 11-18, 2003), 20-21.

3. For John Cassavetes' surrogate artist, Cosmo Vitelli (played by Ben Gazzara in *The Killing of a Chinese Bookie*), who traverses Los Angeles to exact the hit on the Chinese bookie, "His club was his life, and the gangsters were the nuisances—the anti-art, the people who come into your life and impede your soul, your dream." Ben Gazzara quoted in *Cassavetes on Cassavetes*, Boston University, unpublished manuscript, this selection and arrangement 1989: 115.

4. Celeste Olalquiega, "Dust," *The Artificial Kingdom: A Treasury of the Kitsch Experience* (New York: Pantheon Books, 1998), 87-88.

5. Jeremy Blake, artist's statement, 1998.

6. Jeff Wall, *Dan Graham's Kammerspiel*, (Toronto: Art Metropole, 1991), dustjacket.

7. Ibid., 16-17.

8. Ibid., 61.

9. Tim Griffin, "H-h-h-his generation," interview with Jeremy Blake, *Time Out New York*, (October 18-25, 2001), 75.

10. Ibid., 76.

11. Eve MacSweeney, "Strange Days," *Vogue*, (October 2003), 284.

12. Jean-Louis Violeau quoting Jean Baudrillard in "Utopie: In Acts," *The Inflatable Moment: Pneumatics and Protest in '68* (Princeton Architectural Press and the Architectural League of New York, 1999), 53.

13. "When I started making the DVDs I'm best known for, I wanted an artwork that would be equal parts painting and time-based. To give my painting a jolt of life—even if it risked creating a Frankenstein. Richard Prince once said that Frankenstein was a handsome guy. I think so too." Boris Moshkovitz, "Changing Gears," *Berliner*, (October 2002), 72.

14. Berta Sichel, quoting Thomas B. Kuhn, *The Structure of Scientific Revolutions* (2nd ed. Chicago: University of Chicago Press, 1970) in *Jeremy Blake: Winchester*, exhibition catalogue, (Madrid, Spain: Museo Nacional Centro de Arte Reina Sofia, 2003), 45.

15. "Landscape of a Mind," from an interview with Roman Polanski by Michel Delahaye and Jean-André Fieschi, in *Cahiers du Cinema*, February 1966, No. 3; reprinted in *Polanski: Three Film Scripts* (London: Lorimer Publishing Limited, 1975), 207.

16. Ivan Butler, "*Repulsion*," in *The Cinema of Roman Polanski* (New York and London: A.S. Barnes & Co. and A. Zwemmer Limited, 1970), 76.

17. Andrew Perchuk, "Jeremy Blake: Bungalow 8," *Artforum*, (Summer 1999), 157.

18. Lane Relyea, "Jeremy Blake Now Playing," in Lane Relyea and Terry Sultan, *Jeremy Blake: All Mod Cons*, exhibition catalogue, Blaffer Gallery, (Houston, Texas: The Museum of The University of Houston, 2002), 4.

19. Ibid., 4.

20. Griffin: 76.

21. Jessica Hundley, "A Mix Master," *LA Times*, (November 14, 2002), E14.

22. Manuela Villa, "Pixeles y Rifeles de Repeticion," *El País de las Tentaciones*, (July 23, 2004), 8.

23. "The fluidity of information rushing from every direction, and the way we process it, define our culture now. And Sarah Winchester interested me because the jumbled free flow of the house she built seemed like an architectural metaphor, a 3-D symbol for that fluidity. Then there's the psychological aspect of the place... the neurosis and mad logic and creativity all flowing together in this crazy quilt of rooms." Steven Henry Madoff, "Guns and Ghosts: The Winchester Witch Project," *The New York Times*, (February 27, 2005), 38.

24. Rachel Teagle, "*Cerca Series*: Jeremy Blake," Museum of Contemporary Art San Diego, (October 3 to November 24, 2002).

25. Jeremy Blake, email correspondence, April 2005.

26. Blake.

27. Blake.

Meticulously, Recklessly Worked Upon:
Direct Animation, the Auratic and the Index
Tess Takahashi

In the last decade, direct animation, along with other practices that emphasize the physical presence of the artist, has emerged as one response to the ubiquity of easily produced digital effects. Since the early 1990s, an increasing number of contemporary filmmakers have produced films without cameras. They work directly on the body of the celluloid, using drawing, painting, scratching, contact printing, and the application of materials, in what often is called "direct" animation. The films considered here are not all animations in the narrow sense that they produce the illusion of coherent movement (or gradual change within a stable pictorial field, as in Norman McLaren's *La Poulette Grise* (1947) or the contemporary animations of William Kentridge). For the most part, there are no running animals or human figures; most of these films present moving abstract shapes and colours in sometimes unpredictable sequence. Likeness is unimportant. Rather, as an artisanal approach taken up by filmmakers who associate themselves with the tradition of avant-garde production, direct animation emphasizes the contact between the artist's hand and the film's surface. In a move that harkens back to the materialist investigations of the so-called "structural" films of the 1960s and 1970s, these films investigate film's celluloid base: not just its emulsion, but its capacity to take colour, to be glued, cut, scraped, xeroxed. At first glance, direct animation processes seem to promise a closer relationship to the image's origin and a guarantee of artistic value.

still: David Gatten's *Fragrant Portals, Bright Particulars and the Edge of Space* (2003)

Within discussions of avant-garde film, the digital has been articulated as a threat not only to the medium of film, but to the filmic "avant-garde." For example, in a recent *October* round table, film was said to be threatened with obsolescence, even "death," by the proliferation of the digital.[1] In this round table, the digital was seen as a potential hazard to artistic innovation, the tradition of American avant-garde film, and to avant-garde community. In more practical terms, the ubiquity of digital consumer goods has coincided with the rising cost and outright discontinuation of a variety of film stocks, chemical developing agents, cameras, screening equipment, and related services such as professional film processing. The ongoing disintegration of older films and the loss of 16mm classroom rentals to the newer (and ironically less stable) media formats of VHS and DVD has also been cause for concern. At the same time, as noted by the *October* round table participants, the filmic avant-garde seems to be undergoing a revival; it has not been this vital since the 1960s and 1970s. Over the past ten years, there has been an explosion of avant-garde film and media exhibition, increased scholarly work, and the revitalization of long-abandoned avant-garde filmmaking practices.[2] Avant-garde filmmaking seems to have enjoyed a resurgence of activity and popularity just at the point at which the medium of film seems most threatened with obsolescence, both figuratively and literally.

While contemporary avant-garde "film" is now regularly produced and screened in a variety of combinations of media, including digital, video, slides, and various film stocks and gauges (such as 8mm, super 8mm, 16mm, 35mm, and 70mm), a significant portion of this work can be described as devoted to the medium of film in its specificity.[3] Generally speaking, the most prominent characteristic of avant-garde work produced on film in the last decade is its attention to the specificity of the filmic medium, its processes of production, and film's indexical status. Current discourse on medium-specificity within the contemporary filmic avant-garde re-opens questions about the status of authorship, of film as a "work of art," and of the very possibility of a filmic avant-garde capable of influence within both the art world and the larger culture.

On one level, contemporary avant-garde film seems to respond to the encroachment of the digital through a reclaiming of the auratic qualities of the work of art for film and a re-establishing of the centrality of the filmmaker as artist. This movement appears to reclaim aura through a construction of film's specificity as singular, old-fashioned, and one-of-a-kind in its attention to the "craft" of filmmaking. However, this trend does not simply point to a longing for a set of historical conditions set in the past (pre-1960s), when the status of artist and work of art were ostensibly unproblematic. Rather, appeals to film's aura can be read as symptomatic of the ways in which the proliferation of the digital image is forcing artists and laymen alike to renegotiate the status of all images.

At stake are questions of what constitutes the ground or guarantee of artistic value when the author has long been dead, the work of art has lost its aura, the filmic medium has lost its specificity, and the individual "work of art" has extended into a textual system in which personal vision is put to the side. However, the emphasis currently placed on the presence of the artist's hand in discourse surrounding contemporary avant-garde film (in program notes, artist's descriptions, and film reviews) obscures other issues that have been crucial to the rise of films concerned with various aspects of film's medium specificity. More than recentring the author and reclaiming the nostalgic work of art, contemporary avant-garde film made on the medium of film can be read as a product of the current crisis of the image. As W.J.T. Mitchell and others have noted, such crises occur at historical points in which an "old" medium is being encroached upon by a "new" representational technology.[4] The implication of the filmmaker's bodily contact with the image thus emerges as the most important point of reference in its guarantee of authenticity and claims for auratic presence in contemporary avant-garde filmmaking.

Within discourse on avant-garde film, the capacity of digital media to edit within the frame (as opposed to between frames), along with its capacity to alter an image seamlessly, seems most threatening to artistic intention. The work produced by the digital apparatus is considered too "automatic," the options it provides too "cookie-cutter."[5] As Lev Manovich observes in *The Language of New Media*, the computer's capacity for "automaticity," its ability to perform previously time-consuming operations such as collaging, animation, and the repeating or looping of images at the click of a button, seems to remove human intentionality from the creative process.[6] Such so-called "avant-garde strategies," Manovich continues, now "have become the normal, intended techniques of digital filmmaking, embedded in technology design itself."[7] While Manovich sees these innovations as cause for celebration, for the contemporary avant-garde filmmaker they constitute an implicit threat both to his or her place as artist and to the definition of what constitutes a so-called avant-garde film.[8] Little wonder that a recently reclaimed and increasingly preferred term, "artists' film," has achieved currency in avant-garde film discourse.

Within the traditional fine arts at both the turn of the last century and the turn of this one, the uniqueness and contingencies involved in human production have been opposed to, and valued over, what is produced by the machine.[9] Many programmers' and filmmakers' protests against work that utilizes the computer's automatic functions reveal a continuing anxiety about the relationship between human being and machine. It is in this context that the digital is figured discursively as unavailable to physical manipulation. One cannot go into the machine and rearrange pixels by picking them up with one's fingers. By contrast, film, figured as a material medium, is constructed as having the capacity to "index" artistic intervention through its celluloid, its chemistry, its ability to be cut physically, and even in its mechanical projection. The physical variability and irregularity of film have become newly important aspects of its ontology. Thus, the medium of film has been reconceived in recent years according to its ability to bear the artist's physical intervention, as well as the indexical touch of light. Direct animation's emphasis on artisanal processes and homemade qualities is reinforced by textual support that exploits the artist's retreat from not only digital techniques but the traditional mechanical technologies of filmmaking, such as professional chemical processing labs, lenses, and even the camera. In turn, much of this writing celebrates the turn toward film as handmade object. For example, filmmaker Sandra Gibson's process is described in terms of its intricacy and craft. As one programmer writes, Gibson's films are comprised of "painted, scratched upon and braided strips of film-surfaces meticulously and recklessly worked upon, until blistering and flowering with the maker's material mark, [they are] further reworked and rephotographed through optical-printing."[10] In this description of Gibson's work, her use of an optical printer is carefully downgraded in its importance to the film's production. "Setting aside the stop-action-of-frames characteristic of the optical printer," the note continues, Gibson's *Tablecloth* (US, 2002) and *Precarious Path* (US, 2003) "were made without the optical aids of camera, projector, and sometimes even circumventing a trip to the lab." Such descriptions produce the impression of a complicated, but highly personal, artisanal process that takes place in a space set apart from the industrial world of the "camera," "projector," and "lab."

Many films that use direct animation techniques suggest a desire for the pure communication of an image through techniques based on the impression of an implement held in the filmmaker's hand. This can be seen in films in which the filmmaker draws on the surface of the celluloid by hand: for example, the films of Goh Harada, Nina Paley, Richard Reeves, and Carol

Beecher.[11] Much of this work is highly abstract, presents simple geometric or organic shapes, and recalls animations from the early twentieth century, like those of Walter Ruttmann, Hans Richter, Viking Eggeling, and Oskar Fischinger.[12] The framing of these contemporary animations suggests that they do not want to be an illustration of music but rather seek to be a presentation of processes. Reeves's *1:1*, which was drawn and painted directly on the surface of the celluloid, proudly announces that its colourful, geometrically expanding animations were hand-drawn on the film stock itself. Not only were no computers used, but the film's caption claims that no cameras were employed in the film's creation. There is, the film announces, a literal "one to one" correspondence between the mark of the implement and the image produced. Here, Reeves claims a direct, existential link between artist's pen and the strip of celluloid, a link that seemingly avoids the machine altogether, despite the fact that what is screened is surely a print.[13]

Likewise, hand-painted films such as those by Robert Ascher (*Cycle*, us, 1986), Jeremy Coleman (*I, Zupt 49*, us, 1994; *Ecclesiastic Vibrance*, us, 1995-6), Bärbel Neubauer (*Passage*, Germany, 2002), Zoran Dragelj (*Simulacra*, Canada, 2000), Rena Del Pieve Gobbi (*Insurrection*, Canada, 2000), Courtney Hoskins (*Munkphilm*, us, 2001), and Stan Brakhage emphasize the presence of the artist's body in the production of its image through allusions to the tradition of Abstract Expressionism.[14] The work of Stan Brakhage, who produced hand-painted and scratched film for three decades before his death in 2003, has been aligned with the Abstract Expressionist tradition, and his written descriptions of this work would seem to confirm that observation.[15]

Descriptions of these pure colour abstractions tend to suggest that they function as direct presentations of the experience of human emotion or of physical encounter with the natural world. They imply a desire for a pre-linguistic, primal form of communication based on texture, colour, form, and rhythm. Program notes and artists' statements draw connections between the colours presented and the embodied experience of the movement and hues of nature such as vegetable and animal life, rocks, lava flows, the ocean, stars, and branching of roots. There is also the implication that the films communicate human emotion in a visceral, unmediated way. For example, *Numerical Engagements* (us, 2004), by Chelsea Walton, is described as a "lush... love poem" in which colour, through "the film's rhythm of editing is like a heartbeat." Similarly, Brakhage's *Sexual Saga* (us, 1996) is a hand-painted, step-printed film in which the form is intended to express the movement of sexual arousal, beginning with "'explosions' of white, yellow, orange (deepening into reds), vermillion, and darker red flame shapes."[16] Communicating a very different mood, Brakhage's *Self Song/Death Song* (US, 1997) produces the struggles between "glowing ambers" and blacks that threaten to take over the image in order to "document a body besieged by cancer."[17] Films such as these imply a desire for unmediated communication and a distrust of both the indexical image and the written sign's capacity to translate adequately the natural world, human emotion, or individual experience.

These abstract animated films produce their "guarantee" through a building of extra-textual evidence that draws on the idea of the pure presentation of colour (as opposed to the presentation of the inadequate sign), the visible material properties of paint, the implied physical presence of the painter/filmmaker, and the communication of an experience. Their presence and veracity are figured as abstract and therefore potentially more immediate for a potential spectator. Many films produced in this mode are described in ways that exhibit a desire to achieve a basic, universal communication attainable through the medium of film that depends on its figuration as *material* and *present*, unlike the digital image, which is figured as ephemeral and always somehow mediated. In some ways, the process of painting on film seems to promise a pre-linguistic fullness, in the sense that it is figured as able to communicate on the level of the emotional, the universal, and the natural.[18]

Some contemporary avant-garde filmmakers reference the tradition of direct animation in the work of Len Lye and Norman McLaren, who began working in the 1920s and 1930s, and the mid-century "early abstractions" of Harry Smith.[19] However, many contemporary filmmakers' interpretations of the relationship between film and image have shifted from Lye's suggestion that direct animation is a way for the artist to imbue the film with the imprint of the filmmaker's essential self, and suggest that it is human physical contact with the materials of filmmaking that emerges as most important today. As Arthur Cantrill writes, Lye asserted that "his 'absolute truth' was in 'the gene-pattern which contains the one and only natural truth of our being.'"[20] When film art draws on this information through direct contact with the artist, Cantrill continues, paraphrasing Lye, "it resonates with our sense of essential selfness, and we experience the aesthetic value as happiness. For Lye, this 'selfness' was anchored to the body and to bodily weight and motion."[21] The filmmaker's essential self, represented for Lye by the then-new discovery of DNA, was transmitted in the process of direct animation.

Stephanie Maxwell, one of a number of young filmmakers inspired by Len Lye, adjusts his theories to suggest that all that is transferred in the process of filmmaking is evidence of physical contact—though that contact is crucial to the individual work of art. Maxwell describes direct animation as a "process which reproduces very exactly the individual physical impulses of the artist: the artisanal images reflect the vibration of the fingers, the variations of pressure, the internal rates/rhythms externalized."[22] There is no claim for the transfer of "essential selfness" through direct animation. Rather, Maxwell and others point to the importance of the physical proximity of the artist's body to the film. This contact is between the physical human body and the material embodiment of the image on celluloid, not a transmission of the "self." However, still present is the idea that working on film "directly" produces the artist as a guarantee of meaning. More often, direct animators claim the capacity for direct, primal communication via the filmstrip, the communication of bodily "rates" and "rhythms externalized" as opposed to the communication of emotion, vision, or artistic genius.

While all direct animation film produces a gap between the image projected and the image on the celluloid, these abstractions eliminate the problem of the gap between indexical representation on film and material referent. Hand-drawn and painted films such as those described above index the process of their production. Films that use the techniques of the photogram, layering objects onto the celluloid, or using bodily fluids to produce an image, introduce the problem of indexical *representation*. They point to the direct, unmediated experience of an object (often taken from the natural world) and to the necessary gaps between the image's point of capture, its index on celluloid, and screened projection.[23] However, the desire for the immediacy of presentation rather than the gap in time and space associated with representation can be observed in the discourse surrounding contemporary photogram films such as Izabella Pruska-Oldenhof's *Light Magic* (Canada, 2001) and Jeanne Liotta's *Loretta* (US, 2003). This suggests a desire to align film with nature rather than with the world of machines and computers. In reference to *Light Magic*, Pruska-Oldenhof writes that "images created through this technique are traces of light that passes through each object leaving its mark on the film surface." She continues, "Photograms bring both the maker and the viewer closer to the object, thus revealing the *essence*, that neither the naked eye could see, nor the camera lens could capture" (my emphasis).[24]

Something similar occurs with films that not only eliminate cameras but incorporate actual objects and transparent materials into the celluloid itself. For example, Jon Behrens's *Anomalies of the Unconscious* (US, 2003) uses bleaching, baking, painting, inking, and chemical hand processing in conjunction with the inclusion of leaves, flowers, hair and insects. San Francisco collective silt's *Ouroboros* (US, 2000) incorporates cast-off snake-skin, and Rena Del Pieve Gobbi's *Interception* (Canada, 2003) uses dried fruit as negative. Johanna Dery's *The Natural History of Harris Ave, Olneyville (RI)* (US, 2002) utilizes actual plant life found during her walks along this avenue and attaches it to the celluloid in a way reminiscent of Brakhage's *Mothlight* (US, 1963) and *Garden of Earthly Delights* (US, 1981). In ironic contrast to the natural objects incorporated into most films in this genre, Rock Ross's *Baglight* (US, 1998) was made by ironing plastic bags onto film stock. Here, it is the filmmaker's engagement in the process of selection and application of materials that is narrativized. Films in this mode rely on the assertion that artist, worldly referent, and medium were present together at the site of the film's production for their claims to immediacy, presence, and singularity. Although the spectator cannot touch the film, the material body and testimony of the filmmaker can serve as a guarantee of authenticity. "I saw" is supplemented by "I found," "I touched," "I made," and "I bring to you."

Like films that incorporate material objects, films that incorporate the artist's own body seem to want to present those bodies as physically present in the film, rather than represented. Filmmaker Thorsten Fleisch's films are striking in that they present the filmmaker's bodily fluids and oils directly on the celluloid and on the audio track. *Blutrausch* (Germany, 1999), translated as "bloodlust," was made through the application of the filmmaker's own blood to both the optical audio track and the picture area in order to produce a "dizzying variety of splotches, drips, and cracks in dried blood which fleetingly resemble butterfly wings and stained glass windows."[25] Fleisch's *Hautnah* (Germany, 2002) begins with sounds "produced by running a finger on a phono cartridge" and images produced by the filmmaker's fingerprints where they made contact "directly" with the celluloid.[26] In a film that points to its status as a direct index of the filmmaker's body, Emma Hart's *Skin Film* (UK, 2004) uses cellophane tape to produce a map of the artist's body from head to toe as the tape picks up pieces of her hair, body oils, and skin.[27] This film fluctuates between presenting bits of hair and skin as objects for the eye and producing a readable map of a woman's body that must be mentally reassembled. In their use of materials from the filmmaker's own body, films like this literalize the filmmaker's physical role in their production. However, their implicit reference to the traditions of conceptual, performance and body art draws attention to the gap between image and the presence (or absence) of the filmmaker's body in the exhibition space. Despite the desire for presence implied, such films inevitably draw attention to the spectatorial experience as an act of reading rather than of immediacy.

Many contemporary hand-scratched films, in which filmmakers scratch directly into black leader, tie the specificity of celluloid and its emulsion to the idea of an originary language, making reference to ancient, hieroglyphic, cuneiform, and non-Western alphabets. However, they also invoke problems of translation, between written language, image, and worldly referent. Donna Cameron's *World Trade Alphabet* (US, 2001) utilizes oil, charcoal, and ink on paper emulsion to combine drawing and scratching in the production of cuneiform symbols.[28] Bärbel Neubauer's *Passage* (Germany, 2002) and *Moonlight* (Germany, 1997) utilize basic, geometric shapes meditating on the evolution of the alphabet. Brakhage's *Chinese Series* (Canada, 2003), made while bed-ridden in the last months of his life, was produced by "scratching on spit-softened emulsion with bare fingernails."[29] It is the last of a series of major works based on ancient languages undertaken by Brakhage in the last two decades of his life. Such practices, and their framing discourse, suggest a desire to get back to an original, primal language of film, made through direct contact with the most basic of materials—fingernails, spit, wood (celluloid). In the *Chinese Series*, there is no tool mediating between the filmmaker's hand and the film in the creation of such an image. Scratched films suggest that the filmmaker's body is essential to the representation of the basic forms they image, and yet they point to the problems and gaps inherent in the process of translation and the need for the caption in order to be understood.

Likewise, David Gatten's *Fragrant Portals, Bright Particulars and the Edge of Space* (US, 2003) presents stick-like forms, scratched individually into the emulsion, based on the Ogham alphabet. Most spectators would not guess that these are the letters of an ancient writing system until reading the program note, in which Gatten describes the film as spelling out one "early" and one "late" Wallace Stevens poem, "both about making sense/language from the natural world—the palm tree and the ocean." These were then "translated into Ogham, the 5th century 'tree alphabet' derived from a notational system used by shepherds to record notes on their wooden staffs," Gatten's note continues, "and carved a letter at a time into a piece of semi-transparent flexible wood (black leader)."[30] As such, *Fragrant Portals*, like much of Gatten's work on film, invokes the relationship between written text, image and material world through the use of an early alphabet, whose letters bear a striking, if abstract, relationship to the trees on which their form is based.

The problem of translation between spoken text and image can be seen in Québecois avant-garde animator Pierre Hébert's live enactment of the process of hand-scratched animation. Sitting at a light table in front of an audience, Hébert progressively adds scratches and shapes to a loop of black leader as it repeats its lengthened path around the room and back through the projector.[31] In one Montréal performance, for example, Hébert collaborated with his partner by animating a poem she wrote about a homeless woman falling on the street. Hébert animated the poem using simple, gestural figures as it was read aloud, a few lines at a time, in French by his partner. Both markings and language gradually accumulated over the period of time in which the poem was read and the marks were scratched. As the performance progressed, the image was transformed from a series of unreadable marks to a legible animation of a stick-figure woman falling on the sidewalk. In such performances, the filmmaker's presence before the audience anchors the image to his readily observable handiwork, while the poem/narration directs the reading of the images. However, the gaps between written language and spoken language, French and English, still images and moving images, dark and light, one person and another (whether an intimate like his partner, or a stranger like the homeless woman) resonate with one another in their various translated versions.

While most of the filmmakers discussed do not incorporate photographic film images within their texts, quite a few do, including Naomi Uman (*Removed*, Mexico/US, 1999), Lawrence Brose (*De Profundis*, US, 1997), Christophe Janetzko (*Axe*, Germany, 2004), and Steven Woloshen (*The Babble on Palms*, Canada, 2001 and *Two Eastern Hairlines*, Canada, 2004). Hébert himself has produced a large body of work over the course of his career that deals with the relationship between image and text, world and representation, and the aesthetic in relation to the political. Steven Woloshen has produced films that combine filmed images with scratched and painted animations. In *The Babble on Palms*, Woloshen paints over a filmed 35mm colour image of a hand and forearm blocking the camera's view of a sequence of seemingly unrelated scenes. The painted hand pulsates and transforms itself in bluish purples, drawing attention to its status as an intruder within the frame of the camera's indexical view. However, the painted hand transforms quickly into the film's point of interest, contrasting with the film camera's stasis. The paint, messy and throbbing, draws attention to its own "life," to the celluloid as a surface, and to the indexical scenes' illusory impression of depth.

It produces the celluloid as a material, embodied medium, rather than a window onto the world. *The Babble on Palms* thus thematizes the role of the filmmaker/animator as having a direct "hand" in the production of the image in an explicit way that emphasizes the physicality of the animation process.

The body of films discussed here, in their attention to the material aspects of film, can be read as commenting on the problems of representation, translation, and experience in the age of the digital. Unfortunately, many contemporary avant-garde animations have been categorized as purely formal, decorative, or conservative in their preference for film over the digital. As such, some see these films as hermetic and inward-looking, a charge leveled at many of the medium-specific investigations of so-called structural films of the 1960s and 1970s, a period also marked by the introduction and convergence of new and old media forms. However, there is a complicated politics at work in the aesthetic choices made in these films that evokes contemporary problems of relationship and communication over both distance and difference.

still: Steven Woloshen's *The Babble on Palms* (2001), courtesy of Canadian Filmmakers Distribution Centre

Endnotes

1. "The Obsolescence of the Avant-Garde," *October, 100* (Spring, 2001).

2. There has also been a remarkable development of individually or collectively-run microcinemas devoted to the avant-garde, such as The Robert Beck Memorial Cinema (NYC), Movies With Live Soundtrax (Providence), and Pleasure Dome (Toronto). There has also been increased activity among avant-garde film festivals and organizations such as Black Maria (Jersey City), Ann Arbor (Ann Arbor), Images (Toronto), Views from the Avant-Garde (New York), Wavelengths (Toronto), Anthology Film Archives (New York), Northwest Film Forum (Seattle), Pacific Film Archive (Berkeley), the iotaCenter (Los Angeles) through its touring programs, Cinematheque Ontario (Toronto), Harvard Film Archive (Cambridge, MA), Bangkok Experimental Film Festival (Thailand), Seoul Experimental Film Festival (Korea), Image Forum Festival (Tokyo), Oberhausen Film Festival (Germany), London International Film Festival (UK), Rotterdam International Film Festival (Netherlands) and the Videoex Festival (Switzerland).

3. Some of the most prestigious festivals, like the now 8-year-old Views from the Avant-Garde (a part of the New York Film Festival) privilege work made almost exclusively on film, although this is a practice that has been criticized by some (e.g. Ed Halter in *The Village Voice*).

4. WJT Mitchell. "Cloning Terror: The War of Images, 2001-present." Lecture at "Urban Interventions: A Symposium on Art and the City," (9 April, 2005, Toronto). See also Raymond Williams, "Base and Superstructure in Marxist Cultural Theory," in *Problems of Materialism and Culture* (London: Verso, 1980).

5. In terms of its threat to artistry and singularity, the threat of digital technology to analog media closely resembles nineteenth-century disputes about the artistic value of photography in relation to painting. According to popular nineteenth-century claims, photography was not an "art" due to its mechanical nature. Now, film and photography have taken on the status of "art" and it is the digital that is too automatic.

6. Lev Manovich, *The Language of the New Media* (Cambridge: MIT Press, 2001), 32.

7. Ibid., 307.

8. Ibid., 32. This is despite the claims of Manovich and others who see the artist's ability to manipulate pixels as more akin to painting (and thus more easily under the control of the artist). Paul Arthur also found this formulation troubling in his review of Manovich's book, "What Makes the Digital Tick?" in *Film Comment* (November/December, 2001), 35.

9. As has been discussed by theorists from Walter Benjamin to Peter Bürger, the historical avant-gardes in the form of Dada and Surrealism embraced mechanical reproduction, looking to the machine (and to film) as a way to escape the hold of the bourgeois museum and the traditional fine arts.

10. 21st Annual Olympia Film Festival program, <olympiafilmfestival.org/movieDetail.asp?id=55>

11. Goh Harada's *Lampenschwartz* (Japan/Germany, 2001); Nina Paley's *Pandorama* (US, 2000); Richard Reeves's *Linear Dreams* (Canada, 1997) and *1:1* (Canada, 2001); Carol Beecher's *Ask Me* (Canada, 1994); and Sandra Gibson's *Edgeways* (US, 1999), *Soundings* (US, 2001), and *Outline* (US, 2003).

12. Walter Ruttmann (*Lichtspiel Opus I*, Germany, 1921), Hans Richter (*Rhythmus 21*, Germany, 1921); Viking Eggeling (*Diagonal Symphony*, Germany, 1925); Oskar Fishinger (*Study No. 7*, Germany, 1930-31); and others. Such techniques can also be seen in avant-garde films from the 1960s and 1970s, such as Michael Mideke's *Twig* (US, 1967), Storm De Hirsch's *Peyote Queen* (US, 1965), and Margaret Tait's *Colour Poems* (UK, 1974).

13. Reeves is a founding member of the Calgary-based Quickdraw Animation Society, founded 1989, which works to support artists engaging in direct animation and to spread the practice.

14. For example, "Damonte's films are motion graphics made up of abstract imagery edited in streams of color, pattern and rhythm—much like a moving painting"
<www.coolidge.org/balagan/animation_spring2001.html>

15. Brakhage explains he was "strongly drawn to the Abstract Expressionists—Pollock, Rothko, Kline—because of their interior vision... To me, they were all engaged in making icons of inner picturisation, literally mapping modes of non-verbal, non-symbolic, non-numerical thought. So I got interested in consciously and unconsciously attempting to represent this" (Stan Brakhage quoted in Suranjan Ganguly, "All that is Light: Brakhage at 60," *Sight and Sound*, v. 3, no. 10 (1993), 21). Sam Bush, Courtney

Hoskins and Phil Solomon, among others, have optically printed Stan Brakhage's hand-painted films, which he produced steadily from the mid-1980s on. Brakhage describes these films as collaborations with the printer. Among the most recent of these are the hand-painted, step-printed shorts *Autumnal* (US, 1993), *First Hymn to the Night—Novalis* (US, 1994), *The Preludes 1-24* (US, 1996), *Shockingly Hot* (US, 1996, made with his young sons), *The Birds of Paradise*, (US, 1999), and *Lovesong*, (US, 2001).

16. *Canyon Cinema Catalogue*, <canyoncinema.com/B/Brakhage_1990-1999.html>

17. Ibid.

18. In this way, contemporary avant-garde filmmaking practice recalls one of the fundamental questions of film theory—the tension between film's status as language (Eisenstein) and its capacity to represent the world (Bazin).

19. For example, Len Lye's hand-painted and scratched *A Colour Box* (UK, 1935), *Free Radicals* (UK, 1948) and *Color Cry* (US, 1952); Norman McLaren's *Hen Hop* (Canada, 1942) and *Begone Dull Care* (Canada, 1949); and Harry Smith's *Early Abstractions #1-5, 7*, and *10* (US, 1950s).

20. Cantrill, Arthur, "The Absolute Truth of the Happiness Acid," *Senses of Cinema* (2002), <sensesofcinema.com/contents/01/19/lye.html>

21. Ibid.

22. http://gsd.ime.usp.br/sbcm/1998/papers/cSchindler.html

23. If early uses of photogram techniques, such as those of Man Ray, imaged man-made objects (like nails), today the objects imaged are overwhelmingly taken from the natural world.

24. *LIFT Newsletter* (March/April, 2001).

25. *Blutrausch*, note by David Finkelstein, <hi-beam.net/hi-beam/finkelstein.html>

26. *Hautnah*, note by David Finkelstein, <hi-beam.net/hi-beam/finkelstein.html>

27. A.L. Rees, personal communication, September, 2004.

28. "Film begins with primitive carving into handmade paper emulsion of ancient cuneiform glyphs, evolves into painting and drawing of glyphs, then floating type, using digital print-outs of helvetica type, and concludes with multi-material words: World Trade Alphabet. A Visual Meditation on the evolution of the alphabet which we use, its origins in ancient Phoenicia, and the fact that it was invented as a shorthand from 360+ character cuneiform to better the efficiency of communication in ancient international world trade. Made at the MacDowell Colony." *Canyon Cinema Catalogue*, <canyoncinema.com/C/Cameron.html>

29. New York Film Festival's Views from the Avant Garde 2003 program note.

30. David Gatten, program note, 2004 Onion City Festival, <chicagofilmmakers.org/onion_fest/onion2004.htm>

31. Related by Toronto International Film Festival curator Elizabeth Czach and avant-garde film and video curator Chris Gehman.

Cinema, Animation and the Other Arts:
An Unanswered Question

Pierre Hébert

This essay is a revised version of a lecture presented on November 23, 2001 at the Symposium on Art and Animation (Porto, Portugal, November 22-25, 2001). The symposium was organized by the Casa da Animaçao and curated by Jayne Pilling. The text is reprinted by permission of the author.

Since we are here to discuss the relationship between the arts, I thought I would use a musical quotation as the title of my presentation. (Music plays for ninety seconds, fades out.) That was the beginning of *The Unanswered Question*, by American composer Charles Ives. As in the Ives, questions are going to be asked and remain unanswered. I am sorry that I am going to be reading this paper. I always think it is a bit dull to hear people reading. But in the process of preparing this, it became obvious that it had to be written. Maybe because English is not my first tongue, maybe because the ideas are intricate. Rereading it, I found it too authoritative and too theoretical. So I would like to warn you to not be too impressed. This talk didn't come out of any pre-existing, well-thought out theory, but emerged out of the activity of writing itself and my primary need to accompany everything I do with a parallel flow of writing. Writing is my first, most intimate, way of putting animation in relation to other arts. I always write. All the better if it also has some theoretical significance.

still: Pierre Hébert's *Entre chiens et loup* (1978), courtesy of the National Film Board of Canada

In order to discuss the relationship between animation and other arts, we should first question the ground on which it is raised. What is the basis by which different arts become separate and distinct disciplines? It has to do with what is sometimes called the system of the Fine Arts (*le système des Beaux-Arts*). It is not a new problem. Every epoch, every civilization, has developed its own approach to deciding what "art" is and how "art" can be divided into different disciplines. The division of "art" into different arts is an ever-changing thing. In order to establish disciplines, objective ground has to be cleared in the form of transcendent, universal categories. I'll give you three. First, the very matter which is given form (sound, voice, colours, the human body, etc.). Second, a specific body of technical skill and knowledge. Third, the way art fulfills certain functions in the social system (religion having been the main way this condition was implemented for much of the time).

I will not try to go through a whole history of this problematic—I am not an art historian—but I will try to keep this outlook in mind while discussing the specific problems regarding the relationship of animation to other arts. I should say that in my own practice of relating to other arts (it would be more precise to say "relating to artists of other disciplines"), this historical outlook has always been a conscious background concern. Two remarks of historical significance should first be made.

First, there are two different—almost opposite—perspectives to this question. Internally, animation is a combination of different arts (graphic art, photography, music etc.). This is also true of cinema. The combinatory nature of certain disciplines is nothing new. For instance, it is often said of both opera and cinema that they are an ultimate point in the fusion of the different arts. This was Wagner's position concerning opera, which he saw as the global art. Even though this question runs back almost to the origin of theatre, it has acquired a new significance in the technological era.

It seems that the emergence of technology (cinema, video, digital technology) has greatly enhanced the possibilities of mixing the different arts. We can discuss the relationship between animation and the other arts from

stills: Pierre Hébert's *Souvenirs de guerre* (1982), courtesy of the National Film Board of Canada two points of view: external and internal. From an internal perspective, if I collaborate with a musician, the result is a piece of film music. From an external point of view, the result would be a multidisciplinary piece.

Conceptually, this might not be so simple. I see artists as having autonomy determined by their disciplines. One is categorized as a filmmaker, say, or a musician. This is why I tend to see multidisciplinary works as being first and foremost characterized by the relation between the artists rather than any formal relation between the arts. But it raises a difficult question. When a filmmaker is having a multidisciplinary relationship with a composer, and each of them is a total master in his/her own field, how can it be said that music is an integral part of cinema? Does this situation change the very definition of cinema?

For example, when I worked with the trio of musicians Jean Dérome, Robert Marcel Lepage, and René Lussier in what I was calling cinema/music performances, we were equally responsible for our respective fields. Consequently, my field of cinema was stripped of sound, which normally I would consider an essential component. Being left only with the visual aspect of cinema, could I still be called a filmmaker? This leads us to question the significance of the distinction between internal and external relationships which, in turn, results in weakening the ground which all those new arts, starting with photography, claimed for themselves: to be autonomous.

This also leads to a second remark concerning the claim of photography, cinema, video, computer art, multimedia to be separate and autonomous disciplines. It is understandable that this claim was made because these new technology-based arts, especially photography and cinema, were facing a tightly locked nineteenth-century definition of art. But the claim tended to be made by the very standards and criteria of the nineteenth-century definition of art. For instance, photography in the pictorialist period imitated painting in an attempt to be granted the status of fine art. Likewise, cinema was said to be "the seventh art." In the light of further developments, it is now possible to see that none of this is relevant. Not that there is no art in cinema, photography, video, digital art, etc., but that the whole model in which they all fit has changed radically with the intrusion of technology. Some of the arts made with traditional means may still have a claim to the kind of autonomous definition of specific arts that was traditionally dominant. But technology, especially digital technology, has created a field where different artistic practices relate between themselves in a totally different way. Traditional distinctions between the arts no longer apply, at least not in the same way.

So, in my opinion, the claim of cinema to be an art of its own needs to be seriously questioned. Then what about animation? Here again if we examine things critically, we find a very uncertain situation. It is common sense to consider animation as part of cinema from the fact, I suppose, that it shares a common technical ground and a common interface with audiences. But the use made by animation of this common technical ground is enormously different from what we observe in live action cinema and, due mainly to its totally different relationship to the claim to "realism" associated to the photographic nature of live action cinema, its significance, its way of making sense, is very different. Because of this, but also as a corporatist reaction to the dominant and imperialist forms of cinema, the animation community has tended to act as if animation was an art of its own. For example, the expression "the art of animation" is quite commonly used.

To my knowledge, this autonomist view of animation is usually not developed theoretically into a formal position, but the ambiguity that stems from it can be seen everywhere. I must admit that I personally have an ongoing struggle with this question. On the one hand, I never accepted what I see as a corporatist syndrome which tends to isolate animation from cinema, raising the "frame by frame" criterion to a fundamental definition, the dividing line between animation and everything else. This widely accepted definition of animation implicitly puts the trade of animation at its center. This is why I call it "corporatism." It is a definition more for animators than for directors and I think it is responsible for the general weakness of aesthetics in the field of animation.

On the other hand, scratching animation directly on film led me somehow to acknowledge some kind of specificity to the act of animating. Most of my questioning about my own work boils down to one question: What do I really do when I animate? I have the objective of attributing some kind of philosophical weight to the activity, and refuse to see it simply as creating the illusion of motion frame by frame.

Animation is embedded in the invention of cinema, and it draws all its value, weight and significance out of this precise anchoring in history. I must admit this is not a very common idea, though I've carried it in my mind for some years. It's an idea I like. I like to imagine that every time I was animating, I was reviving the invention of cinema, that I was setting the stage for a renewal or a remembrance of the invention of cinema, short-circuiting historical time. In a way, it was just a phantasm, a story I was telling to myself in order to make myself happy. I did not attach any deep meaning to it until I saw this same view expressed in a more developed and formal manner by

Hervé Joubert-Laurençin in his book *La lettre volante*. This actually is the only other explicit occurrence of this view I know of. Giving it further attention, it appeared to me as quite a powerful thought that could help to reset the whole question of the definition of animation, its relationship to cinema, and how it relates to other arts.

The invention of cinema is at the meeting point of two different vectors of technical development: photography and the pre-cinema motion games popular during the nineteenth century. It resulted in this principle of capturing and reproducing motion through a series of discrete images driven by a mechanical device. For live action cinema, once this mechanical image processor was invented, it readily became a black box that was taken for granted, unquestioned, a totally neutral ground beneath the level where artistic decision-making was taking place. On the contrary, animation is constantly reopening the technical black box. Some of its key elements, such as the very idea of reconstructing motion frame by frame, are contained in that black box. So every time an animator animates, he is potentially reactivating this memory of the moment in which the elements of cinema got together to form the tightly-knotted entity that is live action cinema. Animation is thus based on a dissociative, disjunctive action inflicted upon the very structure of cinema. Animation sends cinema back to the moment just prior to cinema's very existence.

From this perspective, it is impossible to simply see animation as a branch of cinema (fiction/documentary/animation). Nor can it be seen as an almost distinct art that just happens to share with live action cinema the same technical substrate. The relationship between the two is much more intricate. It has historical significance. Both share a common origin, which makes them dissociable, but their respective connections to this common origin are highly specific. The live-action cinema developed by concealing the technical apparatus it was based on. It also maintained its claim to realism by asserting a direct connection between its moving photographic images and the real world. The claim to realism necessitates that the cinematic apparatus be hidden.

Animation was in a radically different situation, as it made no claim to

stills: Pierre Hébert's *La plante humaine* (1996), courtesy of the National Film Board of Canada

literal realism. Nevertheless animation, except for marginal examples of an experimental nature, did not seem to take advantage of the strengths related to its unique and peculiar position. On the contrary, for the most part animation has been mimicking live action cinema. Where live action has based itself on the idea of realism, animation has based itself on fantasy. Live action cinema has not benefited to any great extent from the light animation could have shed on its profound origin and possibilities; nor has animation benefited from its crucial and critical position in relation to cinema. Instead, it has used all its energy trying to establish itself as an autonomous art.

I find it puzzling that this perspective, which could have given animation such historical depth and leverage, has not attracted much interest amongst animators. This may be because it is an awkward idea, merely an insignificant theoretical phantasm that appeared in a few overheated brains, like mine. Soon to be forgotten. It may also be that this idea, which points toward the origin of cinema and thus questions its very essence, could only appear in the period where cinema in its canonical form seems to be disappearing at an increasingly fast rate. Because all of this is changing quickly, especially since the appearance of digital technology, which blurs what may have seemed to be clear distinctions between different audiovisual disciplines.

With the fast development of very convincing digital photographic manipulations, live action cinema is quickly losing its pretence of realism. Animation, in the form of extended and very diversified possibilities of image manipulation (again thanks to digital technologies) has been contaminating almost all areas of the moving image so that it becomes very difficult to define its limits. In particular, the reference to the frame by frame process as a fundamental criterion is increasingly irrelevant. Not that the ability to do frame by frame work threatens to disappear—on the contrary, its field of application is widening. But it is becoming more and more one image manipulation possibility (versus the

still: frame enlargements from 16mm loop performance by Pierre Hébert image capture possibilities) amongst many others and that can be associated with other ways which are not based on the frame by frame process.

Now how does all of this relate to our central question: animation and other arts? For me it all has to do with how tight or how loose the integrative strength of cinema turns out to be in its ability to swallow just about any other discipline. In order to have relations with other arts in which those "others" retain their autonomy, a loosening of the structure of cinema is necessary. As I have said earlier this integrative strength is organized either around the claim to realism, or the access to fantasy. And maybe those are just two different types of fantasy anyway. My own approach to cinema (or animation) has always been dissociative and disruptive, critical of any tendency toward realism or fantasy.

This is probably why I like to anchor the essence of animation to the precise moment when the pre-cinematic coalesces into the cinematic. Why, in my performance work, I like to tinker up shaky montages that display a disintegrated image of cinema as if on the verge of appearance or disappearance. Why I consider that my free interrelations with other arts are just another aspect of my questioning the fixed borders between cinema, animation, video, and all the other technological arts. Why in particular I don't think it was a good thing for the "art of animation" to try to set itself up as a more or less distinct entity. I think we should admit that the rise of technology has established an era in which the distinctions between specific arts has become volatile and unstable, with a chaotic alternation between effects of absolute coalescence (the dream of virtual reality being an extreme case of this tendency) or of sudden disruption. I believe that the pole of coalescence (by "pole" I mean not just a geographical point or an axis but something that has to do with an electromagnetic field) is always a pole of darkening of the real challenges of technology, a pole of mythologizing the common experience of technology, the infernal core of modern life. I believe disruption is more enlightening.

Should I continue with the use of the word "animation"? I think animation had meaning only as long as cinema remained the major discipline of the moving image. This is no longer the case. For me, the power that remains in the word "animation" resides solely in the fact that it still is—and will continue to be forever—an arrow pointed toward the magic moment when cinema was invented, a moment that will remain forever a major breaking point in the history of art. The message associated with this pointed arrow is that the technological black box could remain transparent, could be open at all times. This is an important message now that cinema (in its restricted historical form) is being totally overtaken by constant waves of technical novelties.

What to do with what is left of cinema, the heritage of cinema, the body of works and the body of aesthetic thinking it includes? How can it be disrupted in a way which becomes useful in this period of exploding technology in which things are happening too fast to leave much time for thinking and remembering, where the priority always seems to be learning the new update of the software or waiting for the new upgrade to finally decide to really learn the software? How can the interaction of different arts within the complex of cinema, through critical analysis, be useful to the current interweaving of arts and media? I propose this as a very personal problem. I am totally submerged in this world of exploding technology, surrounded by very dynamic and very excited artists and computer addicts of another generation. The cinema/animation couple is the absolute formative structure of my creative mind. How can this fit? How can I fit at fifty-seven not making believe I am twenty-seven?

The conceptual triad of speech, body, and technology is the matrix of any practice of art today (or, at the very least, it is for me). Technology is, of course, an issue, but in the context of technology, the fate of the human body is also an issue. I suppose my position about the importance of technology and the crucial importance of relating to it in a thoughtful and conscious manner is now understood. Technology is an issue for art because it is an issue for just about everybody. It has changed the way the arts relate between themselves. It has changed the time structure into which all of this is happening. It has also changed the way the human body relates to the process of art. And, through the generalization of mechanical and digital reproduction, it may have changed the nature of the work of art itself. As I said earlier, it matters whether technological art tightens itself around a self-contained idea of realism or fantasy or loosens its components and makes its technological nature transparent. The second case goes with a potential of free and problematic relationships between different arts and above all makes the human body visible at the center of the artistic activity even if it is of a technological nature. In the first case the human body tends to be obscured and the interrelations between disciplines aim at being fusional. Then the whole thing works like magic.

I guess this is why multidisciplinary practices tend to evade the reproductive circle and set themselves in real-time theatrical presentations where they can be fully transparent, fully free, and fully problematic both in term of technical and human presence. Not to say that only live presentations can

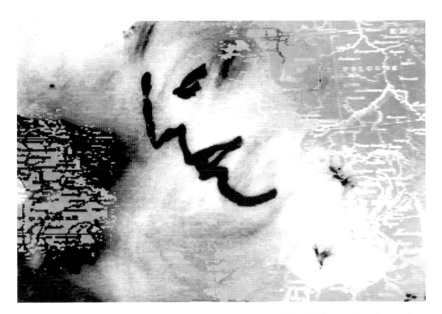

be transparent and critical of the mythologies of the high-tech culture, but for me this is where the centre of gravity lies and where the lesson can be learned more thoroughly and explicitly. That the interrelations are problematic is of primary importance, because questions must be raised concerning the possible relation between people and machines. Real encounters with people and with machines are always problematic, unlike the simulated universes displayed by the technological arts when they set themselves as a tightly closed circle and invite the viewer to just accept being submerged in them. Interactivity is a way to be even more deeply submerged.

The expression "relationship between different arts or disciplines" doesn't really fit what I'm interested in. Formal relationships between arts are a speculative varnish that cover what is really important: relationships between artists, that is relationships between people, which are always problematic. Contra Wagner, I don't believe in the fusion of the arts. I'm interested in the problematic relations between the arts. For the last fifteen years, live performances of the disjointed elements of cinema, in which the human body (my body) is central, have been, not only a theatrical presentation, but a workshop in which films (or any other type of finished, reproducible, and autonomous objects) could emerge. It was my hope that these objects would keep, within their closed constructions, some of the openness and some of the critical problematics that derive more easily from a live performance. This is still my hope today.

still: Pierre Hébert and Bob Ostertag's *Between Science and Garbage* (2001)

A last remark. It could be that recent events may force some disruptive changes in the way technology is discussed. Until recently, we could say, for example, that the discussion about technology centred on things like "how to build an airplane" or "how to build a skyscraper." Now we have new, unexpected questions for which there is no answer, like "what happens when a plane hits a skyscraper?" Questions about falling bodies, questions that are hard to explain to children and hard to explain to adults. Catastrophe has suddenly migrated from the domain of simulation to real life. The perverse pleasure mankind was getting out of being a virtual witness to its own destruction has blown out like a balloon. This may have some effects on the way we now let ourselves be submerged in the magic of technology. It may also have some effects on deciding what kind of art is needed to counterbalance mankind's new fear of its own creations and how those arts can connect together.

I will now show you the last fourteen minutes of the video capture of a live animation performance called *Between Science and Garbage*, which I currently perform with the American musician and composer Bob Ostertag. It reflects all the thoughts I have been trying to convey to you in this talk. It is a mixed-media animation (oil pastel on paper, paint on glass, chalk on blackboard, paper cutouts, and objects) done live and captured in a computer to be digitally processed as it goes, accompanied by improvised sampler music. It focuses on the association between live human actions done on stage and digital processing. Visually, it combines, first, the view of live manipulation of drawings and objects which may resemble puppetry; second, animation in the usual meaning of the term; and, third, live video processing of a continuous flow of images. Quite importantly, the frame by frame criterion is totally exploded: there is frame by frame work, but its flow is measured in thousands of a second (here, 1/24th has no special significance) and is conceptually distinct from the frame rate of the video projection.

We had decided to relate the performance to current events in the news, a very garbage intensive area of human activity. When we performed it in Minneapolis, in the USA, on the nineteenth of September, 2001, it happened that there was very disturbing news that we could not avoid relating to. It became a crystallizing point for the piece. This video capture was made a month later on October 20 in Montréal at the International Festival of New Cinema/New Media. It more or less reproduced the same structure as the September performance. It ends very abruptly because we used an hour-long miniDV tape for an hour and eight minute performance, but I think this abrupt and arbitrary ending is not without significance.

Video/Intermedia/Animation

Tom Sherman

Video is the predominant medium of the twenty-first century. Video's power and relevance stems from its unparalleled capacity for mixing and dissolving into other media. Video embodies film, television, performance, and surveillance, and has become the ultimate living and breathing, matter-of-fact medium of all forms of advancing digital telecommunications. High-resolution, real-time video streaming, with synchronous, spatially rich digital audio, is the immediate destiny of wireless digital telephony. Text messaging and still-picture phones are paving the way for full-motion, video-based personal telecom.

Video is a liquid, shimmering, ubiquitous medium that absorbs everything it touches. This liquidity makes video synonymous with intermedia, the art of filling the gaps between media. Today's media culture and media art are composed of complex, hybrid forms of multi-sensory information. Nothing is very pure and one-dimensional these days. Print media, from online newspapers to blogs, feature video feeds. Books talk. Music and advertising are synonymous. Digital cable television functions like a DVD player. Audiences are active, scanning multiple sources of information, usually simultaneously. Artists choose to work in media that overlap and offer multiple paths to and from audiences. Video flows through and around all other media. Video saturates—it really connects.

still: Jeremy Bailey's *Video Paint* (2004)

Contemporary artists infuse their images, sounds, and ideas into the world through video. Dick Higgins, the Fluxus artist and philosopher, wrote in 1966 that "much of the best work being produced today seems to fall between media." The compartmental approach to art and culture, where painting was separate from sculpture, music was devoid of moving images and cinema differed substantially from television, had come to an end. The phenomena of intermedia, in which new hybrid relationships are forged between media and genres, has been the result of artists of all disciplines breaking free of the constraints of their individual practices. The desire to redefine the boundaries of artistic expression has involved collaboration, interaction, and the redefinition of strategies, aesthetics, and audience.

It is no accident that video emerged from television in the mid-sixties, which saw the heyday of Pop art and the birth of Happenings and conceptual art. Video was (and still is!) the ultimate tool for documenting and amplifying these comprehensive, inclusive strategies through instant replay and systematic feedback.

Today's art, more than ever, progresses toward total integration. Video-based collectives are springing up everywhere. Such groups are experimenting with the interaction between visual media, music, movement, theatre, poetry, design, propaganda, the sciences, et cetera. These experiments are most often authored and disseminated in video, that ubiquitous, unparalleled medium for defining psychological, social and political attitudes. Identities are being modified, social gaps are being bridged, and political actions are being initialized as we speak.

In fact, making video is like talking. In its essence, it occurs in real time, permitting our minds to run ahead of the moment. Video is intimate and immediate (quick as light), and it is positively inclusive. Video will be at the heart of all forms of digital telecom in the near future.

Video (intermedia) fills all the spaces between the arts today.

Video (intermedia) features tomorrow today.

Video is just under forty years old. As a technology goes, that is fairly old. Video was spawned by television. Video was first understood to be the visual component of television. Television's picture was video. This initial manifestation of video goes way back to the early days of the twentieth century, when there were experiments in transmitting images from place to place using radio waves. Images of earthly reality were translated into signals and thrown onto little screens that emitted, rather than reflected, light.

The magic of cinema was already old hat. It was great sitting around in the dark with hundreds of other people watching stories unfold in the flicker of the big screen, but some people wanted cinema beamed into their homes in the worst way. Cinema was taken out of the movie theatre and into the home by television, that motion-picture appliance. The first televisions were like floor radios. They had big speakers and tiny round screens. The first TV screens were like oscilloscopes. Besides the fact that television was radio with pictures, there was one very important difference between television and cinema. The television screen was also a porthole onto the world. Television delivered cinema into the home, and it also delivered live events in real time, as they were happening.

From its beginning, television delivered cinema into the home and it extended time and space by connecting its audience to live broadcasts from remote locations. Television was a delivery system for cinema and video. It delivered two very different media into the home, and it delivered the attention of its audience to advertisers and governments.

Television was the ultimate delivery system for audiovisual content in the twentieth century. It was not much of a medium in its own right. It was a network. Television was characterized by a synthesis of cinema and live drama intercut with stretches of video (live and taped); this rich, high-contrast collage was glued together with magazine graphics and lots of text. The beauty of television was its transparency. It was a delivery mechanism for everything that came before it, and it introduced video, which was synonymous with television until the mid-sixties, when video was extracted from television and became a medium in its own right.

The first portable video recorders (Portapaks) were introduced in the mid-sixties. Television had introduced the idea of video instant replay, where a live event was enhanced by instant reviews of recorded action. The Portapak took this power to the street. Portable video is a powerful cybernetic technology. It generates a duplicate, parallel world in real time, and it provides instant feedback through playback. The impact of an event or gesture is amplified through instant replay, and behaviour is modified by the introduction of video feedback. Television used the power of video to transcend cinema. The video dimension of television multiplied time and space at the speed of light and permitted everyone on the network to travel to remote places through the television's window. Events and places and people were fixed in memory through replay. Repetition was used to give weight to highlighted appearances and events.

Over the last couple of decades of the twentieth century, television was fully decentralized. It was spread as video. The VCR was developed to continue television's mission to distribute cinema into the home. Video became synonymous with home movie consumption. Portapaks evolved into cam-corders, personal video instruments for recording everyday life and shaping behaviour through feedback. Appearance could be studied through replay. Personal histories were recorded. Identity was defined. Self-consciousness was overcome. Parties were energized. In the first decade of the new millennium, picture phones finally arrived in the form of webcams. The computer has become the next major network, and, like television, the computer is not much of a medium in itself. The computer is a typewriter, photo lab, movie theatre, video studio, game parlour, et cetera, et cetera. The so-called digital revolution is a cleaner, crisper way of doing many familiar things.

Television is still an important network for promoting and distributing cinema, and for linking audiences to spectacle via video. It also promotes the medium of video through the phenomenon of "reality television." Reality TV is television under the extreme influence of video. Video, as a medium, has a fundamentally real, literal quality. Video, the technology, is an instrument for cutting through fiction and fantasy. Raw video is at the very foundation of the news. The smouldering wreckage of a car bomb, accompanied by the screams of its living victims, cannot be more authentic in any other medium. Video can also be dressed up to look like cinema. In fact, reality television is a cinematic, theatrical distortion of video. In reality television, porn actors and models pose as ordinary people. These "real" people are humiliated for our vicarious pleasure. They are overexposed for what they really are: imposters to be consumed and discarded. Script, for the most part, has been eliminated. Improvisation is recorded and examined during replay. Performance and replay have been adopted as the formal structure of television influenced by video.

Video now straddles the two major networks—television and computer-based telecommunications. The television broadcast/cablecast now shares an audience with the digital video stream. Video, the electronic, digital medium for the conveyance and storage of image and sound in real time, has become the primary medium of both television and the computer. Video, although inherently non-cinematic, has also become the technical base of cinema. This has caused some confusion, for cinema's time and look has never been literal or real. Video is the antithesis of fantasy and fiction. Cinema, in video, is now forced back to its roots, to the live stage, and to animation (both character animation and special effects).

Acting is more difficult under the scrutiny of video's unforgiving critique of reality. Unfortunately, the use of video to make cinema will result in more products resembling reality television. Animation, on the other hand, will flourish in and across the triumvirate (cinema/television/video). Animation's concrete, explicit articulation of imagination will fit nicely in any context provided by cinema, television, or video. *

Fuck film. The dead ideas of film are being heaped onto video. Cinematic history is like a ball and chain. Video, as an inclusive, soluble medium, is having difficulty defending itself from the weight of this affliction. It has become fashionable to declare, "I 'filmed' this or that with my digital camcorder." In this ahistorical time, it has become common to use the nomenclature of film, the predominant medium of the twentieth century, to declare one's existence in the twenty-first. Everyone is going retro.

Most of the curators of film and video at major museums are the strange bedfellows of film chauvinists. They love to decorate the galleries with projections of fragments of film and video formatted in loops. Sometimes museums actually project film itself, providing the public with the luxury of experiencing a nearly obsolete technology. It seems particularly fashionable to shoot in film and then project in video (to get very close to the film look). Although this kind of thing goes against the strengths of the video medium, cinema in the museum is generally called "video" installation.

Interviews with the artists who make video installations often reveal their ultimate goal is to make a feature film someday. They start their film careers in museums because film that doesn't move (in time) and doesn't tell a story can still manage to hold a wall nicely in competition with paintings, an even more arcane medium than film. A lot of video-installation artists are making video paintings these days. They shoot moving images that move very little, sometimes simply re-enacting the content of historic paintings, and project them at cinematic scale on gallery walls, or on hotter, high-resolution plasma screens. Slow motion is the main device of video painting. For the most part this perversion of video is driven by attempts to commodify the moving image as object.

Video, when served straight up (neat), is so direct and raw and explicit, it's almost embarrassing. The camcorder reveals the world with X-ray levels of clarity. There are no illusions. Look at what video has done to television! Reality television is in fact the aftermath of video's impact on television. Beginning with *America's Funniest Home Videos* (which first aired in 1990), we are now subjected to a plethora of extreme, inane behaviour (scantily clad fashion models eating worms, for instance) in the name of reality. Video's direct, explicit clarity drives people crazy. Video has affected all sectors of society (sports, surveillance and security, dating, shopping, cooking, sexuality), and yes, it has affected film.

Unfortunately, video, that ubiquitous, liquid medium of the twenty-first century, has absorbed film and, in its saturation of all things cinematic, it appears to be something it isn't. Video is not film. In this digital era, when computers are everywhere and everything is converging with digital telecommunications, video, too, has become digital. Universities are now offering courses in "digital cinema" (which are of course taught using video camcorders).

Video technology is still in its early days. Video will continue to proliferate and gain power well into the twenty-first century. It will supersede film and television, becoming a leading, discrete medium and part of a major triumvirate of media (cinema/television/video). Video will be the central channel for advancing digital telecommunications technologies of all forms, riding and boosting the energy of the personal-media explosion. In the meantime, film enthusiasts can attach as much cinematic history as they want to video. They can call video anything they like. I'm going to call it video.

*Animation is the hard copy of memory, accessed while it is being rendered by hand, or by hands assisted by machine. In general terms, animation is memory that moves and evolves. People tend to think of animation as evidence of the imagination. In other words, you can see the mind working as a drawing unfolds. This is a misnomer: a fiction. The imagination always remains unseen or unheard. When I state that animation is the "concrete, explicit articulation of imagination," I am taking a shortcut toward creating meaning. I am saying that animation—memory in the act of forming—alludes to something essential, yet unattainable: the imagination itself.

The romantics love the idea that the imagination can be witnessed as the life force of a pencil's line. The body is perceived as an organic mechanism, like a seismograph, which transforms the hidden mind into a drawing that continues to evolve and resolve itself. The imagination thus pours out onto the page or screen. I love this idea myself. But unfortunately animation does not work this way. Animation is not the imagination revealed so directly, so wholly. Animation is the transparent act of manufacturing memory. This process of creating memory, as a kind of performance, is pushed or fueled by the imagination, but the imagination remains hidden, unexposed.

I stated above that animation will flourish in and across the media triumvirate (cinema/television/video) of the twenty-first century. Animation is a complex category of meta-media phenomena, a manner of creative behaviour quite capable of attracting and sustaining attention in all manner of media environments. Animation has marched through cinema, television, and now video, without missing a beat, because it is the concrete process of manufacturing records of psychological memory. Animation is like writing prose or poetry, or writing music—it is an act of composition, of accruing and organizing images, sounds and ideas. It does not matter whether you use a pencil, a camera, or a computer. Any device for writing memory will do, as long as the process of writing (authoring) is evident in a kinetic, in-progress sense.

Our cultures are obsessed with transcription and memory. Family histories are comprised of boxes of letters, photographs, slides, 8 mm and super-8 films, videocassettes, and computer disks. Today we love video because it records and displays memory in real time. In a way it is a full-motion, literal form of animation. Video is composed in real time by a machine that instantly defines point of view. It renders a description of visual and acoustic space, and any subjects therein, in a time continuum determined by the video instrument (at electronic speed, the speed of light). I suppose calling an unaltered video recording an "animation" is a bit of a stretch. Animation in video is conventionally done in post-production, often by removing information. Animation, in this reductive sense, is the manipulation of the pure, unaltered video stream, the cutting and pasting, the shuffling of time, and the visual and sonic emphasis of aspects of the frame. The hand, even in fully automated technological processes, seems integral to the overall nature of animation.

Throughout the years, there have been drawing and painting machines that appear to eliminate the hand from the animation process. The Swiss artist Jacques Tinguely and his Meta-Matic painting machines of the 1950s were quite impressive; and British/American Harold Cohen has been drawing and painting by machine for over three decades. Cohen claims his machines, which are driven by his software called AARON, are artificially intelligent and have an imagination of their own. It is true that Cohen's machines never make the same exact drawing or painting twice, but of course they do have the Cohen style as their governing structure. These machines are Cohen's prodigies. They mimic his style and propagate his aesthetic preferences.

More recently I have been impressed by drawing and painting machines by Canadian artists Jean-Pierre Gauthier and Jeremy Bailey. Gauthier's deceptively simple machines (constructed with electric motors that articu-

late pencil leads via variable, sliding lengths of retractable dog leash) make beautiful, wall-size drawings, seemingly in the absence of the artist. Bailey, a video artist, drives digital paint programs with ridiculously comic performances where he dances in video space while an automatic painting device tracks and notates his movement in the form of an abstract painting.

These four artists are engaged in animation on a fundamental level. While they all take the "look, no hands!" approach to animation, the most interesting aspect of these parodies or simulations of drawing and painting is the declared absence of mind, of imagination, the psychological essence of the creative individual. While Tinguely, Cohen, Gauthier, and Bailey have clearly instructed or programmed their machines to act as though they are drawing and painting autonomously, these artists are in firm control of these acts of animation, the articulation of visual memory that moves and evolves before our very eyes. In the case of these machines that can apparently draw and paint, we love to imagine the possibility that our machines can act creatively, on their own. We enjoy the illusion of automated creativity, and this illusion is at the heart of our fascination with animation in general terms. With animation in all forms, novel or conventional, we love to think we are actually witnessing the concrete materialization of the imagination, the psychological substance of the artist.

So yes, animation as a meta-media category of creative behaviour will continue to thrive throughout a wide range of media contexts. Animation

still: Jeremy Bailey's *Video Paint* (2004)

will flourish across film, television, video, computer networks, and every digital hybrid imaginable. Opportunities for authoring memory that moves and evolves will continue to expand and multiply. And audiences will continue to be fascinated by this movement and evolution of memory. People will mistakenly believe they are witnessing the concrete, explicit articulation of imagination. Animation is a faith-based discipline.

People's minds will be filled, bombarded with drawings and paintings unfolding everywhere they look, in popular and unpopular culture, in advertising and games and propaganda, and in personal communications media of all forms. They will nibble and gulp at this glowing, clamouring conglomeration of memory that constantly moves and evolves and fascinates until they are absolutely saturated with the fabricated images and sounds and ideas of others—hypothetically until the indescribable, unreachable darkness of their own imaginative minds completely disappears. Or, on a more optimistic note, will this continuously unfolding, massive display of memory continue to trigger a search for the imagination, that hidden force that fuels our desire to animate?

A different version of this piece originally appeared as "Video 2005: Three Texts on Video," in *Canadian Art*, Spring 2005

Animated Image, Animated Music

Stephanie Maxwell & Allan Schindler

In this article, we will discuss a multimedia genre we have explored over the past seven years that might be termed "collaborative image/music composition" or, perhaps more simply, "film/music composition." In six such compositions that we have created jointly, and in additional works that both of us have created with other collaborating artists, structural design, textural patterns, and expressive gestures and nuances unfold simultaneously, but not always synchronously, in aural and visual form.

These works have been performed at hundreds of film festivals, concerts, multimedia shows, and other venues throughout the world. Each was premiered on programs of the ImageMovementSound (IMS) festival, a Rochester, New York-based festival that we founded nine years ago and have co-directed along with choreographer Susannah Newman and filmmaker Jack Beck. IMS supports the creation and exhibition of innovative multimedia works by collaborative teams of two or more filmmakers, musicians, choreographers, dancers, and other artists. Many of the hundred or so works premiered on these shows have incorporated procedures related to those that we will examine here.

The source materials from which our compositions derive unite direct-on-film visual animation techniques (i.e. painting, etching, and layering images directly on 35mm film, then digitally processing, filtering, transforming, and editing this footage) and computer-generated musical procedures in which both acoustic and synthetically generated sound sources are sculpted, transformed (sometimes beyond easy recognition), granulated, recombined, and interwoven. The visual imagery and music contribute equally to an aggregate, multi-threaded structural and expressive design. The visual animation has its own self-contained formal and expressive components, and so does the music. The music *could* be (and on a few occasions has been) played independently, as a stand-alone concert piece. Similarly, the screen imagery could "work" as a silent short, or could be fitted to a complementary musical score in post-production. However, the most important element we seek to achieve lies precisely in the interaction, or "dance," between visual and aural threads. The structure of these compositions might be likened metaphorically and somewhat fancifully (if not completely accurately, in scientific terms) to a "double helix": separate but intertwining, complementary strands in shifting roles as point and counterpoint, reciprocal and simultaneous, focus and periphery—a unique, dynamic, hybrid visual and sonic expression. One's experience and under-

 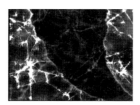 

standing of the music is coloured and influenced by one's simultaneous experience and perception of the imagery, and vice versa. These works do not lie on a continuum between either music or moving image; nor are they based on a shallow structure of eye and ear accoutrements. Rather, these works acquire behaviours that simultaneously draw both visual and aural senses into subjective interpenetrations.

Collaborative process

During the creation of these works animated imagery and music are realized simultaneously, sometimes in leap-frog fashion. The creative energy and working methodology that brings these works to fruition is a concerted, interactive process. We admire such contemporary artists as Reynold Weidenaar, Ron Pelligrino, Joran Rudi, and others who are skilled at both moving image and music composition and are able to produce provocative multimedia works in which visual imagery and music issue from a single fertile artistic imagination. Neither of us possesses such dual expertise or cross-media breadth of conception. While creating our works we remain a filmmaker and a composer, applying our individual technical crafts and, more importantly, our individual artistic imaginations. And this is the most challenging and ultimately most rewarding aspect of our left-hand/right-hand working procedures: to exercise our full creative freedom in devising patterns of sound and visual imagery and colour, but also to play off each other's ideas, to extend, comment upon, reinterpret, and enrich these ideas, and ultimately to develop and shape them into a richly textured fabric that represents her work, his work and our composition.

For both practical and aesthetic reasons, our works are fairly short—typically between four and six minutes in duration. Many of the techniques we employ are time-consuming; for example, experimentation with art media and techniques for creating three dimensional spaces in *terra incognita* (2001) and *Time Streams* (2003); the creation of multiple hand-cut mattes for the "characters" in *passe-partout* (2002); and the process of deconstructing

stills: Stephanie Maxwell and Allan Schindler's *terra incognita* (2001) acoustic sounds and then reconstructing them with alterations. More importantly, however, our compositions tend to be diverse in content but also highly concentrated and condensed in the presentation, development, and eventual integration of these materials.

Ideas and Concepts

The ideas for our works emerge spontaneously rather than through conferencing. Some ideas are abstracted from real experience (the dangling pendents of an aerial mobile abstracted in *passe-partout*), while others are conceptually more formal and approach structural experimentation (e.g. the forms elicited by persistence of vision in *Outermost*). The idea is unscripted and each of us interprets and responds to it through the creation of the imagery and the music. The basic concepts for each of the six works we have produced together are briefly described below:

> *Outermost* (1998): At the edge of a continuum.
>
> *Somewhere* (1999): The limited view; the view through a periscope; off-screen worlds.
>
> *terra incognita* (2001): A voyage to an unknown, dynamic, and uncharted space.
>
> *passe-partout* (2002): Pendants of an aerial mobile each reveal a unique universe of motion, color, light, and sound.
>
> *Time Streams* (2003): The unpredictable and infinite interplay of segments and ribbons of time.
>
> *Second Sight* (2005) (collaboration with painter/graphic artist Peter Byrne): A passage through a mist in which perception is ultimately clarified and sharpened rather than obscured.

Structural Design

The structural designs of these works are non-narrative, non-linear, abstract, continuous rather than sectional, and have been variously likened in their construction to tapestries, mobiles, spider webs, and networks. The works are dramatic, poetic, transparent, multi-threaded, rhythmic, colouristic, textural, and mutable in their effect. Often within a work, images or musical segments suggest an unlimited universe, in which the passage of the audience through the work is but a brief encounter with that universe.

Image Process: Stephanie Maxwell

My imagery emerges out of very strong affinity for the physicality and tangibility of simple art materials and substrates and their translations into manifestations of motion and light energies and plays of colour within a three-dimensional space. In a subjective relationship with the raw materials, I am able to conjure ways to translate my "lived" experience and make it available for others to experience through abstraction.

My techniques involve creating images directly on 35mm film (direct animation technique), the manipulation of objects, copier art, and the "reanimation" of live action sequences. I have discovered how to create "believable"' three dimensional spaces and unusual atmospheres on 35mm film. Since most of the time one's life is spent in a dynamic, abstract, multisensory relationship to the "real world," it is my goal to tap into the ebb and flow of this living abstraction in my art, and to create fictitious settings and events suggestive of, connected to, and in a discourse with, our "real" abstract experience of life. It is also the sheer love of abstraction that fuels me, as well as an interest in discovery and experimentation (I have also been a marine ecologist and spent countless hours underwater).

The concept and the music are my guiding forces during experimentation. I constantly try to invent and discover ways to articulate the guiding concept and to create that unique visual dance with the music. The concept creates a focus. "How can I make it look like...? How can I create the illusion of the space? What is the atmosphere like, and how big is the space? How do things move in this space? What are the physics of this new world?" ...and so on. This process of understanding and creating the filmic illusion is mostly intuitive. The substance and the orchestration of the imagery is a sculpting in time, an act of choreography that manifests itself in rhythmic, dancing, dramatic, and "musical" effects. I endeavour to open a gate into a passage, to transport the viewer into an alternative reality that unfolds through the continual interplay of the images and the music. I enjoy the fact that the image and the music can evoke different kinesthetic sensations: tension, exhilaration, dread, release, interest, stirring, and so on.

My tools, art material, and media are very simple, and some are very unusual: gravure tools; sponges; bandage gauze and tapes; masking tapes; clear and glitter nail polishes; sand paper and rasping tools; an "eyelash separator"; wine bottle corks; prefab drawing stencils; jeweler's tools; salt and pepper; nitric and phosphoric acids; bleach; toothbrushes; airbrush, droppers, and pipettes; probes; burnishers; adhesive transfer graphics; and rubber bands.

The 35mm film imagery is prepared in my studio on a six-foot light table with rewinds at each end. My tools and media sit on top of the light table so that they are close at hand as I work. I am very happy working with the small

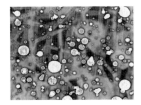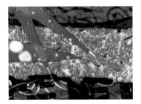

35mm film frames. (Super8 and 16mm are too small, 70mm and IMAX just take more paint.) I mostly work without magnification, as I have learned the precision of working small, and I also let the pressure and motion of both my hands and body direct my painting and other manipulations across the frame "canvas." I experiment and experiment and experiment to establish the visual design and look of the work and the visual expression of the concept and as it integrates with the music.

The handcrafted imagery usually will go through a series of transmutations before the work is finished. The original handmade 35mm footage is photographed using a small feed camera that points downwards to a small three-inch by four-inch light box. During photography of the handmade 35mm frames I can bend, flip and flop, twist and rotate the film in incremental movements that I record frame by frame with a frame-grabbing device. I will also animate small mattes using the feed camera/light box set up. The mattes are made of black-painted paper and they will be used later in post-production for compositing images together.

In addition to the handmade 35mm film, I will also animate small objects (the sponges in *Time Streams* and the speckled translucent crab carapaces in *Second Sight*, for instance), and graphic materials (such as copier art work, drawings, or patterned or textured papers and plastics). The feed camera allows me to shoot in positive or negative, and to manipulate exposure and colour. The camera also features a zoom lens so I can achieve zoom effects and super close-ups (to about the size of approximately one square centimetre). The moving and bending three-dimensional spaces in *terra incognita* were created by recording frames of alternating zoomed-in and zoomed-out positions of progressive frames of 35mm handmade film; the golden "electricity" sequence was shot in the negative using the same zoom-in/zoom-out technique with a small, wrinkled piece of wax paper.

Typically, post-production is the stage at which shots are put together and tweaked to form the coherent, linear plot of a film; but for me it becomes another phase in which experimentation takes place. During post, I am still animating, or "reanimating" as I like to call it. I recombine frames of

stills: Stephanie Maxwell and Allan Schindler's *Second Sight* (2005) imagery. I "activate" the imagery in motion manipulations, and create layered compositions that merge patterns of imagery in spatial expressions within the moving image/music composition. The reanimation process is an active "mosaicking" of imagery that involves a tight and responsive interplay with the music.

Music Process: Allan Schindler

The computer-generated music for our most recent works has been realized in my personal home studio on a $2,000 stock Pentium 4 desktop computer modified with quiet fans and other tweaks to reduce obnoxious computer noise. The software base is all open source - Linux, and GPL (General Public License) music applications such as Csound. All of the specific sound generating, signal processing, mixing, and sound spatialization software algorithms used to generate the music are written by me with the use of highly extensible and customizable GPL software libraries.

After the basic concepts and design of one of our works have been determined, one of the first steps is to begin to assemble a particular "orchestra" to play the music. Most of our works feature "defining sounds," which may include unique or memorable timbres, melodic fragments performed with a particular type of phrasing, rhythmic patterns, textures (combinations of tonal colours in rhythmic patterns), harmonies, and more abstract types of musical gestures, such as pulsating, ringing, or cascading sound sources. These "defining sounds" are the structural pillars of the music. They may recur cyclically throughout the piece, or may emerge at key moments, perhaps in conjunction with a particular visual image or sequence of images. The interplay of these sounds, and their changing interrelationships with the imagery, largely determines the qualities of movement and expression, the energy levels, the kinaesthetic qualities and the suggestive musical colours, shadings, or "moods" of various passages in the work. Most of our works feature four or more of these "defining sounds" ("principal musical characters"), as well as a "cast" of secondary musical ideas (similar types of sound sources that are used less prominently or less extensively), and finally a "chorus" of other sounds that are used only briefly, as "stepping stones" or to enrich some of the textures.

In *Second Sight*, some of the principal "defining sounds" include: a swishing, high-pitched, gong-like sonority (perhaps reminiscent of vibraphone bars stroked vigorously and simultaneously with seven or eight cello bows); synthetic bagpipes, which become associated with a succession of companion tone colours that include a hurdy-gurdy and a duduk; a metallic harp; widely spaced chords of long, pulsating vocal tones that surge and recede in wave-like ripples; and an assemblage of rapid shaking, hissing, and stuttering or "throat-clearing" types of percussive sounds.

The source of these sounds may be purely synthetic (groups of software oscillators, filters, and so on) or else acoustic (digital recordings of isolated tones of orchestral or ethnic instruments, or of environmental sounds such as the pop of a cork or the hum of a refrigerator). However, sampled acoustic sounds are rarely used in their original form, because such recordings "are what they are," and can be difficult to sculpt into convincing phrases or gestures with musically alive note-to-note, event-to-event articulations and connections. Paradoxically, although the music of our works is created largely by typing in code and numbers at a qwerty keyboard, it is important to us that our imagery and music create a strong illusion of physicality. I want the music to sound and feel as though it is produced by scraping, bowing, and breathing, and by the excitation of wood, metal, glass and air.

Often, recorded samples are subjected to digital analysis-and-resynthesis procedures: a sound is deconstructed into data that represents its noise and pitch components, and then resynthesized from this data, but with some of the components altered or eliminated, or combined with components from another sound. Sometimes only fragments of recorded samples are used and then reshaped: in *passe-partout*, spitting sounds were created from just the attack (first fifty milliseconds or so) of wood flute samples; in *Second Sight*, isolated vocal consonant and vowel phonemes ("p," "t," "oo," and so on) spliced out of vocal narrations of poetry are rhythmically combined into a digital form of scat singing.

Another element in the development and manipulation of the musical material involves the use of algorithmic compositional procedures. Deterministic procedures are used to generate extensions, variations and permutations, while weighted distribution or randomizing procedures can create more substantive transformations. Subjecting source material to such manipulative procedures often suggests possibilities that otherwise might never occur to me. The spitting sounds in *passe-partout* are not always effusive; at times, with some massaging and a few loops through the transformative algorithmic machine, they can take on a more reflective— even elegiac—quality, at least to my ears.

Working with these "defining sounds"—developing and extending them, varying their articulations, transforming and combining them and, most importantly, pairing, associating, or counterpoising them with Stephanie's images—begins to suggest larger patterns of movement, articulations of thirty or forty-second segments, paradigms for motility and balance, and, finally, definition for the music and the work as a whole. Like the characters of a prose work whose personalities become almost real to the author, these "defining sounds and images" begin to become collaborators in their own right. We often sense an intuitive affinity (or work hard to develop such an affinity) between particular visual and aural elements and textures. As noted earlier, however, we generally do not strive for a direct, moment-by-moment correspondence between the visual and aural animation. Sometimes these patterns *do* "arrive" together. But at other times they may overlap, or the visual imagery may surge as the music "relaxes." These constantly evolving and shifting interconnections comprise the dancing element within our film/music compositions, and for us are perhaps the most fascinating and rewarding aspect of our collaborative work on these compositions.

Conclusion

The ultimate goal of all the processes discussed above is to transport our viewers/listeners, briefly but memorably and meaningfully, into imaginary (but seemingly, while you are "there," very tangible and "real") worlds that burst with possibilities, associations, and connections. There, ideas, events, and arrival points may occur simultaneously or overlap, lighting up and then receding, recurring or recombining; this is also a realm in which distillation, transparency, and focus gradually define or clarify how and why all of these little mosaic puzzle pieces fit together.

Demoscene and Digital Culture

John Sobol

One day, a few years ago, as I sat in my office in Toronto's Design Exchange, toiling away as co-director of one of Canada's new media festivals, I became aware of a sudden commotion a few desks over. I turned to see our in-house computer programmers, graphic designers, and 3-D animators—all just out of high school and hence extremely knowledgeable about all things digital—trembling with excitement as they crowded around a computer monitor. Venturing over to see what was up I was informed that they had stumbled upon something so mind-blowing that—from their geekish perspective—it was almost unimaginable. "Look at this!" they cried in unison. So I looked.

What I saw was one of the most imaginative and beautifully rendered computer animations that I had ever encountered. The screen was alive with intricate shadows and reflections, all effortlessly morphing from one complex 3-D form into another; subtle flavourings of colour and movement were layered within this abstract phantasmagoria, accompanied by an ambient electronic soundtrack. I was awed. But I still hadn't fully understood what made it so special.

"It's real-time 3-D," I was told in an almost reverential tone by a teenage computer animator. "It's a 64k file. The whole thing is 64k," added a wet-behind-the-ears programmer in wonderment. I looked at them in confusion.

photo: ASSEMBLY 03.
Image courtesy of ASSEMBLY Organizing / Pekka Aakko; ASSEMBLY BigScreen and computers (2003)

Although I was co-directing a new media festival, my expertise had never been technical. I generally try to understand *why* things are happening as opposed to *how* they are happening, and this certainly applied to my interest in new media. So when informed that I had been watching a computer render a 64kb executable file in real-time I did not immediately grasp the significance of this statement.

But slowly the wheels began to turn. I thought of the three real-time 3-D projects we had commissioned and the immense file sizes of those projects. I considered the aggravating clunkiness of typical real-time 3-D visualizations, which stuttered and balked even on our million-dollar SGI Onyx II machine. I recalled how a highly compressed mp3 file still comes in at about 1 mb per minute of audio, which meant that if the soundtrack of the seven minute animation I had just seen was an mp3 file then it would be 7mb in size. But the whole file was only 64k, approximately one percent of 7mb. And that wasn't even counting the extraordinary visuals. *The thing was tiny.* It took a split second to download and the computing power of a child's toy to run and yet the quality of the resolution and visual effects was mind-boggling, far outstripping our own genuinely high-quality output. Remarkable.

"What is it?" I asked, starting to catch on.

"A demo," came the reply, "called *Poem to a Horse*, by Farbrausch." Needless to say I was stumped. But since that day I have become an observer—at a distance—of *demoscene*, a youth-driven digital subculture whose members have produced countless eye-catching animations—*demos*—for their own amusement and underground glory, without the slightest interest in mainstream acceptance, recognition, or remuneration. To this day it amazes me just how profoundly obscure this artistic community remains. I have often mentioned demoscene to extremely well-informed individuals working in the digital sphere only to be met with utterly blank looks. When I explain it to them, and above all when they see these demos in action, they are usually rendered speechless.

So before I go on, I want to invite you to go have a look for yourself. You can find *Poem to a Horse*—as well as many other demos by Farbrausch—on the shadowy collective's simple website, www.farb-rausch.com. But that's just the tip of the iceberg. To tap into the full demoscene, you've got to visit www.pouet.net, www.scene.net, or www.ojuice.org, which are the primary demoscene portals. There you will find innumerable demos, though not all of them will be of the same calibre as those by Farbrausch, which is one of the most celebrated demoscene collectives (along with Future Crew, Complex, and the quasi-parodic Elite). But at 64k a pop, you can afford to try out as many as you wish, even with a slow dial-up internet connection. The only caveat is that most of these demos will play only on Windows machines.

Because demos are not interactive, they resemble traditional animations more than many computer-based works. However, nobody actually draws demos. Visual effects are achieved by writing thousands of lines of carefully crafted code. The result is a work of art that exists as lines of C++ or Machine Language. When that code is processed by a PC, it is transformed into an audio-visual experience in "real time." In other words, there is nothing but the code—which is an insubstantial potency—and its actualization by the machine in the moment. There are no cels, no paints, no storyboards, not even any imaging software; no jpgs, no gifs, no Combustion, no Maya, no Flash. There is only the algorithm and the silicon chip. And us.

But where do demos come from? And what is the demoscene? Here, in a nutshell, is the tale of its evolution.

Back in the early eighties, the likes of Amiga, Atari, and Commodore 64 were the home computers of choice. Then, as now, games were the most popular applications. And then, as now, kids who bought these software games were determined to copy and share them illegally. To prevent this retail piracy game, manufacturers put their best programmer-minds to work developing copy-protection software, which they integrated into their products. But then, as now, rebellious teenagers soon began cracking these security codes. Once cracked, a game was copied and shared.

The key event in the genesis of demoscene took place when someone (exactly who remains a mystery) decided his or her (most likely his) cracking achievements merited memorializing. So, having cracked a particular game's coded shell, he inserted his own "tag" into the game's short audio-visual introduction, in the form of a unique bit of code producing a cool visual effect. Subsequently, all pirated copies of this cracked game would bear visual evidence of his programming prowess, nerve, and creativity. Soon, cracking games and adding customized intros—the more complex and innovative the better—was all the rage among a select group of brilliant and obsessive teenage nerds. Reputations were made as floppy discs containing cracked games circulated by mail, until eventually this ragged underground experienced a mild schism. Those who valued above all the ability to crack games gradually migrated to a distinct scene known as warez. Those who cherished the visual tags that were being added to cracked games ended up in the demoscene, where their cracked intros eventually evolved into demos.

Siebren Versteeg's *Dynamic Ribbon Device* (2003)

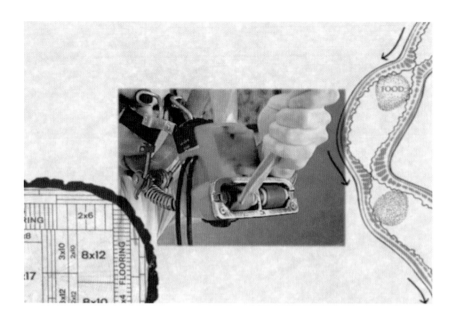

above: Eric Henry's *Wood Technology in the Design of Structures* (1997); below: Richard Linklater's *Waking Life* (2001).

Lewis Klahr's *Daylight Moon (A Quartet)* (2002)

above: William Kentridge's *WEIGHING and WANTING* (1998); below: Kentridge's *Felix in Exile* (1994),
courtesy of Marian Goodman Gallery

above: Janie Geiser's *The Secret Story* (1996); below: Geiser's *Lost Motion* (1999)

Izabella Pruska-Oldenhof's *Light Magic* (2001), courtesy of Canadian Filmmakers Distribution Centre

Jude Norris's *Red Buffalo Skydive* (2001), courtesy of Vtape

above: Libby Hague's *Our Town* (2001), courtesy of Vtape; below: Wrik Mead's *grotesque* (2002), courtesy of Canadian Filmmakers Distribution

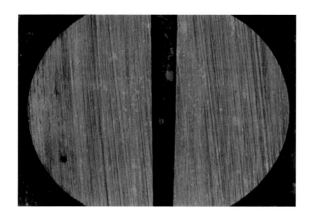

Stephanie Maxwell and Allan Schindler's *Somewhere* (1999)

above: The Brothers Quay's *Street of Crocodiles* (1986); below: Quay's *The Comb* (1991),
courtesy of Atelier Koninck / Zeitgeist Films

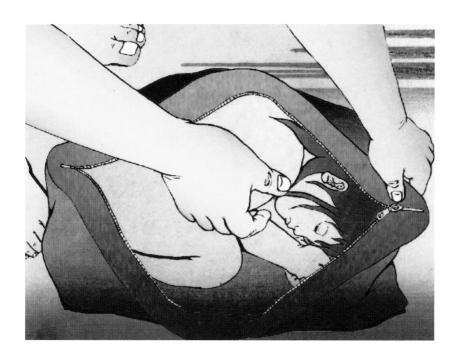

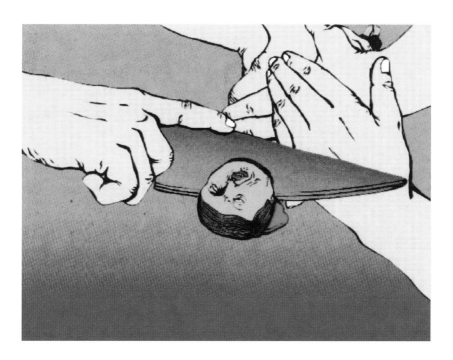

above: Tabaimo's *Japanese Bathhouse—Gents* [2000]; below: Tabaimo's *Japanese Kitchen* [1999]
©Tabaimo / Courtesy of Gallery Koyanagi

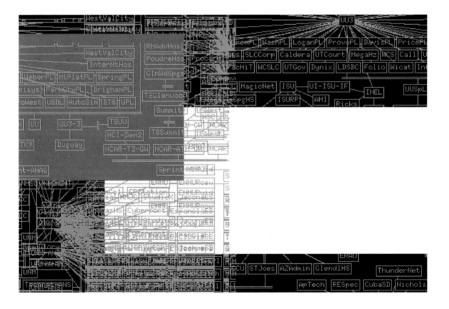

above: Oliver Hockenhull's *Boilt Pixels* (2001); below: image by Jodi.org

Daniel Barrow's *Every Time I See Your Picture I Cry* (2005)

Jeremy Blake's *Winchester* (2002). Sequence from DVD with sound for plasma or projection, 18 minute continuous loop, courtesy of Feigen Contemporary

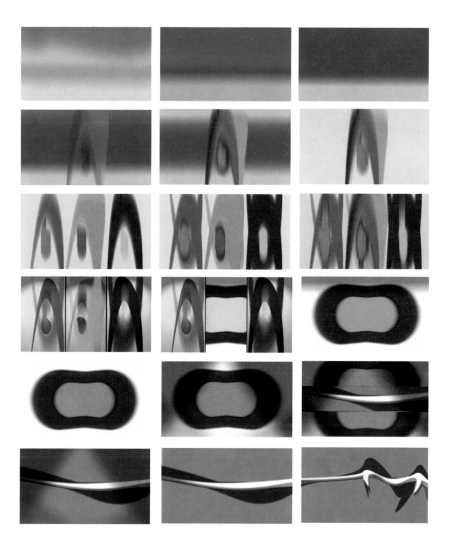

Jeremy Blake's *Berkshire Fangs* (2001), courtesy of Feigen Contemporary

LeCielEstBleu's *Puppet Tool* (2003)

As the technology evolved, so did the animations being produced by these self-taught teenage artist-coders. And the medium's canvas has exploded in its short history too. Today's cheap 3 gigaherz processors are *50,000 times* more powerful than the puny processor of the Commodore 64. In many cases, the first known instances of specific computer animation effects can be traced to demos and the programming skills of many "sceners" are such that they have lucrative jobs with leading game developers. James Schmalz, for example, specifically sought out sceners when he founded his company, Digital Extremes, which has since sold over eleven million copies of its "Unreal" computer games.

In the early days, intros and demos were shared, critiqued, and celebrated in electronic magazines like *HUGI* or *PAIN*, which were distributed on floppy disks by mail among the demoscene cognoscenti. Nowadays, the web makes global distribution effortless. And yet the essence of the scene has always been creation and presentation of demos in a "live" setting, called a compo. Compo is short for competition, but a compo is much more than just a creative contest. It is also a tribal gathering, a party, a professional symposium, a training ground, a star-search, and a sublimated testosterone-driven psychedelic teenage mindfuck. For years now, entirely under the radar of the popular media, thousands upon thousands of teenagers have been hauling their hard drives and monitors and headphones and keyboards and servers and ethernet cables to empty arenas in Denmark, in Germany, in Finland, and elsewhere (northern Europe is the hub of demo culture). There they stay up for days on end, typing code elbow-to-elbow amidst brain-rattling techno beats, splashed by hypnotic flashing lights until—perhaps aided by mind-altering substances—they collapse in tranced-out exhaustion and quasi-hallucination. These compos, like The Gathering or the scene's revered mecca, ASSEMBLY (held annually in Helsinki) are attended almost exclusively by adolescent boys, who often work together in teams of three—a programmer, a graphic artist, and a musician. It's a massive nerd convention—but more than that it's a carnival and art fair, in which all entries are eventually screened and winners are declared. It's an adolescent escape, a home away from home, far in the future, yet rooted in the time-worn need for freedom, fun and escape into esoteric realms of the imagination.

Demoscene is an extremely arcane subculture characterized by endlessly clashing perspectives, trends, and technological innovations. Many sceners are convinced that demos are dead and have been for a while. They argue variously that the scene has been corrupted by greed, ignorance, or filthy lucre. The web is replete with massive message boards containing profound and petty critical writing by, for, and about sceners, most of which goes way over my head. But I think a few useful conclusions can be drawn about demoscene even by one such as myself, only marginally initiated into its many mysteries.

I think demoscene is important for a number of reasons beyond the beauty of the work and the creative power of the sceners themselves. The patterns—social, expressive, communicative, economic—embraced by the demoscene community perfectly correspond to the values that I believe are inherent to what I call—for lack of a better term—digital culture. These values include collective improvisation, public collaboration, a rejection of copyright, free distribution of artworks, borderless tribalism, peer-to-peer knowledge sharing, and a celebration of endlessly iterative processes over the cataloguing of fixed artifacts. In this sense, demoscene exists as a challenge to mainstream literate culture, whose values—including the ownership of ideas, the legal immutability of creative products (i.e. no sampling or remixing allowed), selling to individuals rather than sharing within a community—all stand in contrast to digital values. And yet demoscene is not self-consciously challenging anything, because it doesn't need to. Sceners don't need to fight the restrictive bonds of literate capitalism because they are masters of their own digital domain. And as they are well aware, it is a huge domain. And it's growing every day. Every hour. Every second.

So the scene continues to evolve, far from the limelight. But I think it likely that in years to come, as mainstream economic models and systems of social organization begin to more aggressively reflect and resist the revolutionary power of networked digital culture, it will be visionaries whose mindsets were shaped in subcultures like demoscene who will ultimately contribute the most ambitious and coherent new strategies to our society. Having mastered futuristic visual vocabularies, developed extended global communities of catalytic and creative peers, and remained at the forefront of the technological curve, demosceners—like other members of creative digital subcultures—are poised to discover new opportunities amidst the clash of cultures that is rapidly bearing down upon us.

Our Town

Libby Hague

In Libby Hague's short video *Our Town* (2001), simple animated drawings and scrolling text are combined with video images of an unfinished suburban housing development. The video images are doubled and presented in two different monochrome fields, so that these views, behind the drawings and text, call to mind a red-green 3-D movie seen without the 3-D glasses.

Voice of a young girl:

your mother went to sea sea sea
to see what she could see see see
but all that she could see see see
was the bottom of the deep blue sea sea sea

Our town was the wide world. Everything was new and smelled like lumber and dirt. Our mothers opened the doors in the morning and we ran out to play in the construction sites and came home when we were hungry or hurt.

Sometimes we jumped from one side of an upstairs hall to the other. If you fell, you would fall to the concrete basement floor and die. The adults had no understanding of us kids and we kids had no understanding of the adults.

We didn't know yet how anyone would grow up or how anything would turn out. Kids, moms, and dads, we were all stuck here together. There weren't many ways to leave.

Molly is tiny. She's seven or maybe eight years old. She stares in her mother's silver mirror. Wherever she is, she doesn't want to come back. She wants a prince, a magic carpet, and a happy ending. She cries as she admires her reflection in the mirror. She has a set of manicure tools. She uses cuticle remover and little cuticle sticks to push back the skin and make perfect half moons. She files her nails to perfect ovals and puts on clear polish because she is too young to wear coloured polish. She is getting ready.

Molly's brother Lenny is a graceful bully. He experiments with pain in a modest way. Later he goes to jail, but right now he has locked himself in our house. A small crowd gathers and he bites the finger of the girl who tries to slide back the lock chain. Amazed, we wait to see how much trouble you get into for something like this.

Just quiet ferocity + nylons

Molly and Lenny's mom is a tense woman. As if it was a bedtime story, she told us that long ago the nuns tied the girls in bed at night to keep them from touching themselves. In the daytime they taught the girls to sew neat little stitches, smaller and more perfect than a machine. I imagine a room of girls with their heads bent over white handkerchiefs, their needles moving back and forth and back and forth.

Claire's mother is small, pretty, and tidy as an acorn. She makes us cocoa and cinnamon buns because she wants us to like her daughter. But Claire goes out with high school boys. She is perfect and therefore we will never like her.

The retarded girl is just as isolated, just as threatening somehow. Lenny knows the words that make her cry. The kids laugh and run away and the retarded girl is left in the middle of the street. She is crying and her nose is running. She can't see her way to the sidewalk.

Molly and Lenny's dad. I try to imagine him as a kid. Because he is pink and fat, I see a clumsy boy who wants new toys, who isn't clean. Sweaty. Sentimental. Ineffectual.

still: Libby Hague's *Our Town* (2001), courtesy of Vtape

Marilyn arrived from down south somewhere. She doesn't have a winter coat. Just quiet ferocity and nylons like the high school girls. She says it's mind over matter and if you have character you don't need a coat. Her dad is the janitor at the school. Everyone else's dad works at a desk in an office. No one has been inside her house. It has no flowers, no bushes. The house just sits there.

When their dog dies, Molly and Lenny's mom stops taking her medication again. Before long she turns on the radio, takes the gun, and goes downstairs. I can only picture this to the point where her finger starts to pull the trigger.

Maybe Molly and Lenny heard the shot. Maybe they didn't. Anyway, they are in the living room. They have closed the door and are watching cartoons with all their might. They will never talk about it. The police and emergency crews arrive.

1 mississippi
2 mississippi
3 mississippi
4 mississippi
5 mississippi
6 mississippi
7 mississippi
8 mississippi
9 mississippi
10 mississippi
ready or not you must be caught

The kids stand around outside. Claire, Marilyn, and the retarded girl are there, as well as the new couple from across the street who don't have kids. Everyone is watching the police. It's a lot like watching TV. That the mom is dead is something strange, we don't know what to feel. Except for your own parents, adults aren't especially real to us, like the other kids are. Adults are sort of flat. It's weird to see them cry. They have lost their "We know best" voice and something sharp has replaced it. Molly's dad cried, "It's not my fault. It's all ruined. You can't protect someone twenty-four hours a day."

The kids hang around outside. In a town where nothing happens, we are thrilled by how intense the afternoon has become. Molly and Lenny are different from us. We are trying to figure out what all this means.

still: Libby Hague's *Our Town* (2001), courtesy of Vtape

Red Buffalo Skydive

Jude Norris

Jude Norris's paintings, videos, and installations often involve animals important to the Cree culture. In *Red Buffalo Skydive* (2001), she juxtaposes two apparently unrelated elements: a beautifully rendered rotoscoped loop of a young buffalo breaking into a run, and her impromptu account of an encounter with a determined paraplegic skydiver.

Woman: (laughs) You know what the trouble is?

Man: What?

Woman: Yesterday, I was like, really happy, and in a really good mood, and full of laughter, and today, I don't feel happy, and I have no laughter.

Man: I think that's good. I think—just listen to it. Just get really close to the mic.

Woman: OK. Like that? Is that good? So I hitched down here, and the second ride I got, which took me most of the way, was this guy in a little blue pickup truck, and he, um, he was paralyzed, from the waist down—he got shot—but he could drive, and he was a really good driver, and when we got to... we were coming through Hope, he was telling me this story about, uh... (sound of someone coming into the room)

Second Man: Sorry to interrupt.

Woman: (laughs)

Second Man: Call me when you're finished.

Woman: (laughs again) He was telling this... (more laughter). Just let me carry on (still laughing). I have to start all over again?

Man: No, it's OK. Keep telling the story.

Woman: No? OK, so he, um, he was a skydiver. He *is* a skydiver. He started skydiving when he was a kid.

Man: Who? The guy who got shot?

Woman: Yeah. His parents took him the first time, when he was like twelve or something. Oh yeah (moves closer to the mic). And, uh, after he got shot, he said it took him about, I don't know, what, six or seven years before he could get up the nerve to go skydiving again, and then when he did, the first ten jumps—*eight times out of ten*—he broke his legs. But he still would just keep going right back up again.

Man: He was paraplegic?

Woman: Yeah. And, um, the one time, the first time it happened, he said he broke his leg, and he said you—'cause you got so much adrenaline and stuff pumping through you, you don't even know you're hurt—he was trying to talk them into taking him back up to do another jump before the ambulance got there to take him away, because he figured (laughs) he'd have just enough time to do one more, but the person who he has to hook himself onto, someone when he, when he's falling, they wouldn't let him.

So he finally figured out that, um, if—well obviously, right?—if he just kept jumping like that he was gonna keep breaking his bones, so now he jumps into the lake and lands in the lake 'cause its a softer landing, but if the parachute lands on top of him he'll drown, right, 'cause whoever's waiting for him down there can't get there quick enough, so he jumps out of the plane, *in his wheelchair*, with his wheelchair attached to him, and the parachute attached to him, and right before he hits the water he's got it just barely timed out so that he can unhook himself from the wheelchair, and from his parachute, right before he hits the water, so the parachute'll just float off and land beside him.

Man: What about the wheelchair?

Woman: (laughing) I don't know what happens to the wheelchair...

stills: Jude Norris's *Red Buffalo Skydive* (2001), courtesy of Vtape

A Clarification

Lewis Klahr

When I was asked to contribute a short essay to this book, I was flattered but ambivalent, unsure whether I fit in. For many years now, I have considered the relationship between my films and animation to be, at best, tangential. Although I'm usually described as an animator, I've taken to publicly declaring that I don't consider myself to be one. The consternation this aesthetic Zen koan causes is extremely useful—it's meant to unsettle an audience, force them to rethink their basic assumptions, and discard what they thought they could take for granted about the orientation of my films. It also defines very clearly what my priorities are and pushes collage and appropriation to the foreground, an emphasis that I believe offers a more fruitful gateway to my work. The expectations of *collage* can help a viewer more deeply engage in and better follow the formal decisions contained in my films. The expectations of *animation* will not.

But isn't "cut-out animation" or even "collage animation" an accurate label for my films? Well, yes and no. My declaration is a polemical half truth—but what interests me is the part that is true! What's at stake here is how wide one wants to throw the net of definition around animation. Are all films created frame by frame animation? Maybe. But are all films created frame by frame considered animation? Within the experimental film tradition, pixillated, time lapse, and optically printed films are all constructed frame by frame and are not considered animations or normally included in animation history.

We've entered a grey zone of genre definition here, where things overlap and hybridization rules, which is one of the reasons I feel more comfortable being defined as a collage filmmaker. This idea is much more inclusive, especially since cut-out animations are not the only type of collage films I make, and these other kinds of collage films are not minor pieces within the body of my work. To give two recent examples, *Govinda*, the penultimate film of my feature length series *Engram Sepals (Melodramas 1994-2000)* is a found-footage film. Likewise, two of the films in my latest series, *Daylight Moon (A Quartet)* (2002) are explorations of two-dimensional source material shot in real time through a magnifying glass. No cut-outs. No frame by frame construction.

Another important distinction is that animation history, as much as I love, respect, and admire it, has rarely been a touchstone of inspiration for me. The bulk of my work is conversant with Hollywood film history via the funhouse mirror of experimental film. Films by Kenneth Anger, Bruce Conner,

Ken Jacobs and Jack Smith that fracture Hollywood storytelling and turn it to their own elliptical purposes have had far more impact on my aesthetic than the abstractions or cut-out animations of Harry Smith.

Finally, it's important to point out that I got involved with cut-out animation by default—not because I was in love with the form, but because I was in love with the materials and the access they give me to memory and history and a kinetic interface between the personal and the cultural. My films engage in a kind of archaeological detection that requires empathetic projection into other eras to explore *the pastness of the present*. Can one ever separate the past from one's vantage point in the present? Likewise, I can't separate my use of cut-outs from animation. But the question of emphasis remains and is far from a meaningless one. Perhaps a more accurate and satisfactory description would be *re-animation*.

still: Lewis Klahr's *Pony Glass* (1997)

Eric Henry: The Thing that Doesn't Seem Tasty

Daniel Cockburn

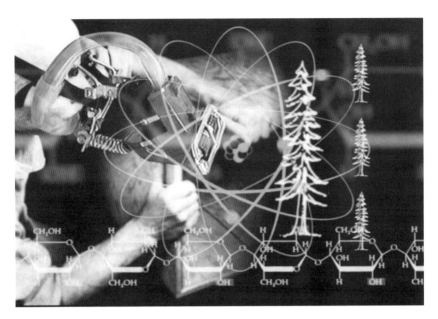

"Man did not, and does not, naturally eat wood." So begins what seems to be an educational video on the science of human digestion, complete with pleasantly cold female narrator and intricate disco balls of spinning molecular diagrams. But instructional texts generally teach why things are the way they are, how things work. What kind of teaching aid would bother to take as its subject a hypothetical impossible scenario (human digestion of wood) and explain why it is impossible? For that matter, what kind of science video begins with a quote from *Madame Bovary*? ("She longed to die, and yet she longed to live in Paris.")

But the on-screen demonstration of a certain apparatus provides a clue: it is like the mutant child of a scuba mask and a lawn mower, and we see it put to use in the loud, laboured consumption of a wooden spoon. The video and the narrator take this in stride, and when on-screen statistics show the extent to which this nature-surmounting invention has been employed by the human race, we realize what is going on: This is an instructional video from a parallel universe, one in which people have fulfilled their wood-eating desire by the hubristic application of technological progress.

For the most part, *Wood Technology in the Design of Structures* is a resolutely two-dimensional artifact (Henry: "the movie essentially unfolds on a giant piece of paper"[1]). Created on an Apple Macintosh using After Effects,

still: Eric Henry's *Wood Technology in the Design of Structures* (1997) it's a reverie of textbook clippings and diagrams, still images and text, sliding past and through each other. The detailed layering invokes a sense of motion from the compositions' mostly-static components, and a sense of beauty as the offspring of classic portraiture and contemporary graphic design.

The images' soothing flow may lull you into a false security, confident that you have decoded this cryptic piece of video art as a satire on the misdirection of technological progress—and indeed, that is borne out by "the record down through the ages of the millions crushed, having precipitated the collapse of their own houses and apartment buildings"—but there is something more. The ghost of Mme. Bovary's alienated desire hangs over the proceedings (as does the video's subtitle, "How To Live Happily Ever After"), waiting patiently for the climax. The narrator then seems to lose track, spending a brief time parsing a seemingly random sentence ("I wish I liked jazz," the onscreen words shaded so as to suggest it as a possibly deviant descendant of the simpler ancestor "I like jazz.") before proceeding to a state of ecstasy just as quickly usurped by a scepticism of the same breathless transcendence that we thought she was suddenly experiencing, that we thought the images were suddenly expressing:

> Consider... that, seated next to you, I can be gripped by the acute longing to get to the room that you're sitting in. Perhaps if one of us left the room and came back in, we would get a different result. Perhaps on the second try you would light up, I would light up, and we would both don vests made of flowers and do little dances and be racked with great sobs of joy, having shed the notion that life is elsewhere, that there is always something missing.

But something must indeed be missing; one wonders what particular void *Wood Technology* was made to fill. Cinema in its early days strove to either establish credentials by slavishly imitating prior arts or to carve out its own identity by isolating its differences from any existing arts. Things have calmed down since then, and we've accepted fairly pragmatically that neither approach makes a lick of sense, that synthesis is the necessary outroad. Experimental film and video art have undergone the same initiation rite, their supporters falling all over themselves to define their difference from cinema/sculpture/visual arts, and their detractors viewing them (or, more likely, not viewing them) as pale imitations of the real deal. If cinema is the shadow under which video art must toil (and many would say it's not, but to me it is), then *Wood Technology* embraces this shadow while working toward something unique.

What is the nature of this embrace? A clue is to be had in a sequence showing the demise of one of the "millions crushed," staccato editing and bursts of blade-whirring leading up to a composite shot of a house collapsing. We move in closer to see a set of still-rotating blades amidst the rubble, slowing to a stop after which all is silence. The distanciation within this sequence—we witness a death merely by inferring it from a tangential event, see the cause only via the effect—is a classic cinematic tactic (from Robert Bresson to Wes Anderson) newly rendered in the digital realm.

Unity of form and (dis)content is a tempting siren song; it promises perfection and in fact often delivers it. The fine print, however, is that "actual perfection may be smaller than pictured." Occam probably got it right: entities are not to be multiplied beyond necessity, particularly in seven-minute videos, but his razor improperly wielded can shave away all the meat as well as the fat, paring videotapes down to little units as unremarkable as they are tight. Eric Henry doesn't multiply his entities, and neither does he repeat them; he reiterates them in various styles and contexts. The spinning blades of the devouring-device's initial appearance are very different from the spinning blades of the death-by-house-crushing, and the viewer's range of associations is richer for it.

Most contemporary video artists, if setting out to make *Wood Technology*, would be content to create a fantasia of appropriated imagery, such as constitutes the bulk of the video. It is significant, however, that Henry sought to fill the remainder with images of his own creation—which themselves contain objects of his own design. It shouldn't seem necessary to say "take heed, fringe filmmakers: he wanted to make a movie about a prosthetic wood-eating device, so he actually built one"—but it does. Misdirected and dangerous the wood-eaters' hubris may be, but all too rare is Henry's parallel hubris, his willingness to adopt whatever means he considers necessary and then to coax them all into the service of expressing a single theme: appropriation, animation, prop-building, location shooting, original music, sound design, and those unfashionable tools of screenwriting—even and especially the climax, which most video art shuns as though it were the bourgeoisie's most insidious tool of oppression.

This climax offers a recontextualizing of the video's supposed thesis. What seemed to be a clearcut satire on desire's place in progress and consumerism becomes something much thornier, a parsing of desire's syntax. Henry wonders:

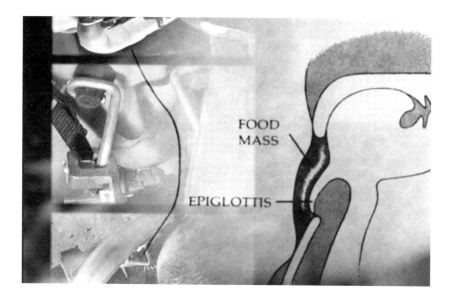

How is it possible in our culture to say something like, "I could really try to like Jazz?" Why would you try to like something that you don't like? How is it that people can believe in the desirability of something that they fail to experience themselves? There's some sort of meta-desire that says "must try to eat the thing that doesn't seem tasty."[2]

The desires and doubts evoked by *Wood Technology* put a bit of a lie to its closing argument. Why would I respond so strongly to this piece if I did not feel there was indeed "something missing?" And why would Henry have made it if he did not feel the same? The video is neither dystopian (as it seems at first glance) nor utopian (as it seems at second). Rather, it's meta-utopian. It posits that utopian dreams are the obstacles to our happiness, and that the absence of such aspirations is a necessary criterion of an ideal world. My desire to see more videos like this one would, in a perfect world, be unnecessary. Until then.

Daniel Cockburn
March 21, 2005

Endnotes

1 Tim LaTorre, "ResFest NYC: A Conversation with Eric Henry, Director of *Wood Technology in the Design of Structures*," <www.indiewire.com/people/int_Henry_Eric_971024.html>.
2 Ibid. www.erichenry.com

still: Eric Henry's *Wood Technology in the Design of Structures* (1997)

Wrik Mead: Animating the Jitter and Tilt of Erotic Anguish

Bart Testa

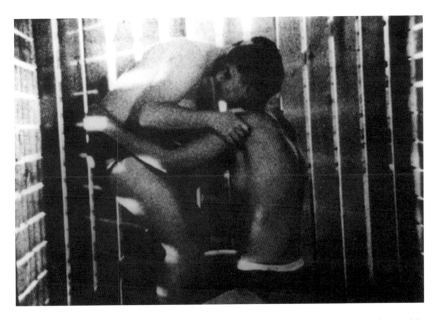

Wrik Mead emerged in the early 1990s as an experimental filmmaker with a specialized subject matter and a developed style and format, the latter rooted in step-printed animation to which he has remained perennially faithful. Writing what is still, surprisingly, the single substantial essay on Mead in 1995, Mike Hoolboom refers to him as "one of Canada's best-known chroniclers of the [gay] closet."[1] Mead started as a Super-8mm filmmaker who often used a cut-up animation technique. Although he would continue to shoot in Super-8mm, in 1992 he switched his exhibition format to 16mm blow-ups, and began to use the intervening re-photography of his shoots for manipulations to develop his mature style. The larger format opened the way to his regular presence at major short film platforms, such as the Toronto International Film Festival's Canadian programs and the Images Festival. Images gave him a retrospective in 1997 under the title *Homo Eroticus: The Films of Wrik Mead*, accompanied by a small Pleasure Dome catalogue authored by Scott McLeod and Julia Creet.

Mead's best films of the 1992-1995 set that established his presence stage simple and extreme situations within a single enclosed *mise-en-scène*. In *Warm* (1992) a solitary naked man undergoes some inner torment and a weakness (he has trouble standing upright) that lasts some four minutes until he is released into the embrace of another man who is scarcely

still: Wrik Mead's *[ab]normal* (1995), courtesy of Canadian Filmmakers Distribution Centre glimpsed, an event that lasts about a minute. The film is wholly typical of its maker: full of sexual anguish longing for release and concluding with a healing embrace that Mead is liberal in offering his tormented protagonists. The variations, as in *Frostbite* (1996), consist of a protracted approach to the scene through an exterior—in that case a frozen wood outside a cabin. Mead's interpreters, such as Mike Hoolboom and Scott McLeod alike, see him as a filmmaker of gay "identity allegories." The figure of a man trapped in a confining space—in *Closet Case* (1995) as well as *Frostbite* and *Warm*— is seen as a man in the allegorized "closet," and the embrace or encounter liberates him and his desire. One should add that these are highly human- istic and wordless allegories, and one could also construe the erotically tormented protagonists as suffering from some other, perhaps spiritual or existential torment. However, the figures are unusually handsome and naked, and the erotic reading is compelling. Mead eschews a complex or even specific psychology.[2] This perhaps explains why in 1994 he could, with- out much variation (but with less success), play out a similar scenario with a woman protagonist in *Homebelly*.

The other critic contributing to the *Homo Eroticus* catalogue, and Mead's collaborator on *guise* (1997), Julia Creet makes two observations worth recalling about the filmmaker's reception, which was by the late 1990s quite well defined. Creet claims that Mead was much more straightforward than most experimental filmmakers and therefore his reputation in the experi- mental community was suspect and, further, that his films made gay and lesbian audiences uneasy because there is something rather "creepy" about his style. Both these claims should be related. On the first point, Creet missed the obvious reason experimental programmers and critics like Hoolboom recognized Mead as one of the family, namely that the film- maker was so successful at revisiting and re-tasking one of the trickiest classic avant-garde genres, the psychodrama or trance film.[3] The form dates back to the 1940s and Maya Deren's *Meshes of the Afternoon* (1943). One of the seminal works of queer cinema was another psychodrama of the 1940s, Kenneth Anger's dream film *Fireworks* (1947), and the likely template for Mead. He does not create the kinds of complex Surrealist scenarios of the type Sidney Peterson pioneered with trance films like *The Potted Psalm* (1946), or the heroic quest-narrative subjectivism of the Brakhage-Baillie lin- eage of the 1950s and 1960s, preferring the direct and intensified tension-release pattern of the psychodramatic phase of the trance film. Mead cannot measure himself for an antic kind of desire, dispersive come- dy, or flowing associationalism; nor has he found much attraction to Anger's ironic use of metaphors, which undercut even the sadomasochistic climax of *Fireworks*. On the other hand, Mead feels a magnetic attraction to the crueler erotic solemnities of psychodramatic expressionism—of which *Warm* and *Frostbite* are powerful examples. This is a mode that is extremely difficult to execute, especially repeatedly, without a disastrous deflation of conviction or a lapse into self-parody. (The latter does threaten all three of the tableaux of *(ab)normal* (1995), co-directed with Isabelle Auger, which are simply too tricked out to carry the conviction of his best work, and lack a persuasive containing structure. The failure of *(ab)normal* to lead the filmmaker into the direction of an extended format indicates that Mead was not ready to abandon the intensities of his single tableaux for a more complicated form.)

The reason Mead's films seem a bit "creepy," as Creet remarks, is likely two-fold. The first is thematic and iconographic. Mead never depicts erotic desire without the accompaniment of an anguish expressed in convulsions, which would seem to be the covert object-matter of his expressionism.[4] The other is that Mead pursues an aggression toward the film image itself, devising various procedures that merit comparison to two of his close contemporaries in Toronto's avant-garde cinema, Gariné Torossian and Carl Brown.[5] In Mead's case, these stem from animation because he never allows his takes as shot to appear in the finished film without re-rendering them into a jumpy staccato between aching stasis and ellipsis. Mead's combination of pixillation, jump-cutting, irregular film stock use, shooting through glasses and gels and lighting set-ups, and recently using mattes, amplifies already overwrought performances with jittery or cruelly static image-surface effects. When they work best, these effects transform his oppressively composed psychodramatic tableaux into strong expressionist articulations.[6] They also make for films that are more than a little scary and that abrade the filmmaker's high-empathy humanism and affirmative queerness, which means that while Mead *does* makes bold affirmations of gay desire, they are never simply comforting affirmations. The tension between his directly humane themes and his abrasive style can, at his best, produce the peculiar and strong paradox of his films.

We can try to pull these observations together and suggest that the tight format Mead prefers is often painful to watch in such energetically stylized iterations, and it's as if his cruel and tragic sense of "the closet" does not allow for some hoped-for amelioration of its pain. Quite the contrary, Mead does not refigure desire except through a tearing kind of anguish, which is what frequently gives his films their horrific colouration. Rather than some experience of naturalizing affirmative willing to social change that could accommodate gay desire (which is what Creet's gay and lesbian film audience may prefer to see), Mead's films express the tragic solitary condition of desire and a desperate need for out-and-out redemption. The embraces in Mead's films are not an achievement of permission for bodies to clutch, but a convulsive act of corporeal salvation—a release from desire's solitude. These convulsive acts constitute Mead's obsessive iconography in the 1990s. They mark the ends of his films accordingly as very sudden and very suddenly the end. There is no time in these films for elaborate joy or extended pleasure—they finish with blunt and shuddering release. The effect of the whole execution can be, therefore, more than one bargained for sitting through an evening of queer cinema, disturbing even what Mead's films seem set to say, or perhaps lend to the more facile paraphrases of his interpreters. All this makes Mead's best films stronger than their rather obvious themes and makes them recognizable as "experimental films" in viewing and reviewing contexts where users of that term sometimes forget the potential tension and distress avant-garde cinema occasions.[7]

The collaboration with Julia Creet, *guise* (1997), coming after the powerful *Frostbite*, was a notably gentled effort. Basically a performance piece (Creet wrote and acted) with an arch metaphor and a deft punchline, *guise* offers a simple allegory: A naked woman rises from the earth, born into a tableau with a painted backdrop out of a floor of leaves, in a pixillated passage. She crouches and stumbles with weakness until she starts to put on armor, piece by piece, and is able to stand strong and erect. But the suit becomes too heavy and restrictive and she then abruptly removes it. Shot at some distance and from a high angle, Creet gives a deftly cartoonish performance, and Mead's shooting and processing give the act his familiar stuttering meter. The allegory may be a bit pat and the voice-over text, in tidy rhymes, produces an effect akin to a children's story. This is not a film that ends in release, however, but in a joking irony. The naked woman begins dressing all over again with a long-sleeved fetishistic rubber glove that appears out of the ground. The success of the film is that it is not at all "creepy" but funny and accessible, without falling into self-parody.

Mike Hoolboom remarks, in connection with *(ab)normal* (1995), that the film "signs a shift, it is at once a summary work and a fully elaborated treatise which moves beyond his previous work." However, if Mead was using *(ab)normal* to work his way out of his highly contained tableau format, or beyond the genre of psychodrama played out by a single solitary protagonist or couple—defining features of his films before 1995—then Hoolboom has

 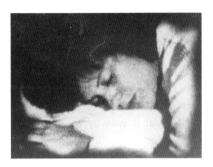

reason to be disappointed. *Fruit machine* (1998) and *camp* (2000), each of which deals with a real historical subject, also mark attempts to expand beyond the hermeticism of his characteristic form, but with mixed success.

Fruit machine is a tale from one of those ridiculous and sinister incidents in Cold War Canadian history that form part of the political lore of the country's pre-Trudeau dark ages. Scientists were enlisted in 1959 by the RCMP to devise instruments to unmask homosexuals in the Canadian Civil Service.[8] One of these scientists was a Carleton University psychiatrist, Robert Wake, who devised the "Fruit Machine."[9] Mead dramatizes Wake's work using two tableaux, the first set in the lab. Wake tests a young man using a long questionnaire (heard in voice-over) while the boy looks into a scope at slides of naked men—placed by rapid montage as inserts into the tableau. As Wake then walks and skates the Rideau Canal home from his government office, Mead inserts more shots of naked men and images of hands manipulating the dials of a machine until they climax in a short and fast montage, apparently a depiction of Wake's inner life. In his apartment, the second tableau, Wake, still in his lab coat, pours a drink and then, in a comic surprise, pulls his test subject from his briefcase. Now the boy is dressed in full leather gear and Wake kneels before him adoringly, putting his face to the other's crotch in a short series close-up dissolves. Despite the nice pulsing of the editing of the found naked-man images, they go on too long, and the disclosure of so simple a hypocrisy leaves *fruit machine* feeling facile, which is the flaw that *guise* so narrowly avoided.

The most ambitious of his recent films, *camp* (2000), finds Mead grafting his own *mise-en-scène* and treatment of footage onto an historical exposition, complete with documentary footage and voice-overs, concerning the Nazi concentration camps and gay prisoners. The combination points to Mead's challenge in devising extended multi-shot forms that can get beyond his sustained tableaux (the problem that has largely defeated him since *(ab)normal*). The documentary footage cannot be integrated with Mead's

stills: Wrik Mead's *Frostbite* (1996) and *Homebelly* (1994), courtesy of Canadian Filmmakers Distribution Centre own shots, which are once again staged in very long takes, but the problem becomes more intriguing here. The film begins conventionally, with an expanse of expository voice-over embedded in industrial music, while archival shots pass by. Then, he inserts a very long take of a man's face in a severely masked frame. A scratched title informs us that he found a way to survive in the camp and we infer from his staring eyes and slight movements that it was by being buggered by the guards. The next sustained passage, presaged by a voice-over, is a long take of scalpel inscribing a thin young man's torso with words listing the "cures" the Nazis applied to gay subjects. The final extended passage, and the longest, is a naked man shown alone and then embraced by another—apparently both are prisoners.

The problems with *camp* are two. The first is our confusion of the status of the images, some of them witness to a past, the archival ones, while other are enacted as if in a present tense. In this topical setting the problem of performance is always going to be vexed. The second is that for all its charged erotic physicality—his men are almost always handsome and desirable and again here they are naked—and its obsessive isolation of specific and single figures, Mead's style runs to the abstract, to the allegorical. The figures have no individual psychologies, but rather exemplify states of being, so they cannot concretely experience historical events or circumstances, which is exactly what is required of them in *camp*. Because Mead's figures' spiritual affects are expressed in physical terms—and this is why and how Mead is essentially an expressionist filmmaker (he makes over bodies as a way of figuring interior states)—his is not a mode that combines well with the forms of concrete historical anecdote or with footage that witnesses to the look and texture of real events. *Camp* leaves one wondering about the status of the men we see in Mead's own footage. They so closely resemble the expressionist figures in *Warm* and *Frostbite*, whose torments are allegorical-existential, that we may be left to infer that the tormented states of Mead's allegorical men are the *same* as the men who are camp prisoners, which could be a morally abhorrent inference.[10] But we are also left to infer, alternately, that reenacting the conditions those men suffered abstracts their experience and beatifies them as martyrs in a gesture of empathy, for what concludes the film is a desperate embrace. What perhaps secures this alternative interpretation is that one man stitches a pink triangle into the bicep of the other man, whom he embraces, twinned motifs that have, by this point in his career, become the most intense signs of Mead's redemptive will.

Cupid and *stage fright* (1999), short single-tableau pieces, are returns to form. Cupid, cast as a beautiful young man with white fluffy wings, appears in a matted frame at a bar smoking and drinking. He then starts shooting his arrows, when a naked male figure takes two of them in hand and hurls them back, puncturing the god himself. A phallus rises from his loincloth and, like some *anime* tentacle, wraps around him as he swoons past the bottom of the frame to the floor. Now, this is an ironic piece that does suit Mead. His heavy expressionist sense of sex has never before made room for the impish god, but here Cupid is. Mead double-deals the soundtrack with a medieval chant and bar sounds. That he enacts a sharp reversal of a gay Cupid icon as the punch line suggests some sense on Mead's part of the Baroque iconography of the "Defeated Cupid," such as those painted in polemical response to Caravaggio's very famous "queer" Cupid, *Amour Victorious (Love the Winner)* (1602-03).[11]

Stage fright is one of Mead's most harrowing films, and his most cruelly ironic work. A figure costumed somewhat like a clown and ambiguously as to gender (the performer is Carol Anne Gillis) enters a theatre stage, stands stock still before a restless audience (heard, not seen), slowly bends forward, and vomits in medium close-up. The performer slowly exits to boos from the crowd. Then a giant vaudeville hook pulls the figure back on stage, and animated ropes tie her hands, pulling her arms outward as the crowd shouts and heckles. The clown struggles while being pelted from the crowd with garbage (another antique touch) until she is struck in the face. Tears flow and makeup runs and the clown pulls anguished faces. The crowd changes mood and begins to applaud. Mead then pulls back in a zoom as the figure falls or bows into a crouch, then relaxes and, after a moment, says "Thank You" in a heavily amplified, and—surprise!—female voice. Mead's decision to use old-fashioned elements, a beautifully realized set and lighting, and allusions to vaudeville and the clown performer (out of Picasso by way of Fellini), generates a remarkably allusive work. Mead is back on familiar ground—solitude, anguish, cruelty, expressionism—but here the allegory is stronger, and much less easily read.

Mead's three most recent films—*Hand Job* (2001), *Manipulator* (2002), and *grotesque* (2002)—are allegorical parodies that develop motifs suggested in slightly earlier films. Belatedly, Mead arrives at an ironic mode which, for him, is a kind of release from the intensities of his 1990s cycle of psychodramas. While *Manipulator* and *grotesque* continue in the mode of *stage fright*, *Hand Job* is a departure is several respects. *Hand Job* is a title with a pun. It suggests that Mead's films are hand-made (which they are—excepting the short, commissioned portrait video *Hoolboom* (1999), he has resisted the lure

of electronic processing). And it is the only film he has made so far that alludes to film—a bit surprising given his numerous references to theatre and television.[12] The film also centres on a self-administered hand job. In the grubby texture and dulled coloration of the image, the film pretends to be old-fashioned footage—Mead managing the measured framing of a series of deftly edited shots with a care that contrasts sharply with the wan appearance of *fruit machine*. The shots are arranged in a decoupage of close-ups (something unprecedented for Mead) that show a man proceeding from the street to an old-fashioned leather seat. There he dons glasses, and the film begins a series of cross-cut shots, one series showing a gay porn film, rather the worse for wear, of two muscular young men embracing (by now recognizable as Mead's image of utopic bliss, or at least utopic comfort). The other series shows the man pulling out a handkerchief and reaching into the crotch of his pants—and we see now that he is wearing an old-fashioned checkered suit with a vest—to give himself a hand job (though Mead discretely shows nothing). Cut to a very large cock getting a hand job on the porn screen, in a luminous solarized image that flares into white. Back and forth as the porn footage appears increasingly abraded until it fades out, and the last shows the man's hands folding onto his lap. This is a brilliant encapsulation of a now-antique porn-film experience, with its

still: Wrik Mead's *Hand Job* (2001), courtesy of Canadian Filmmakers Distribution Centre

steady, cautious approach to a seat, its rituals and its glimpses into a mate-
rially abraded, flickering and inaccessible paradise of love. It is Mead's most
mournfully ironic film and, though just four minutes long, one of his fullest
and most unusual.

still: Wrik Mead's *grotesque* (2002), courtesy of Canadian Filmmakers Distribution Centre

Endnotes

1. *Cantrill's Film Notes*, Nos. 77-78 (November 1995), 44-45. The other critic to write about Mead, Barbara Goslawski, published a steady stream of short notices, most of them for *Take One*.

2. To put this another and more complicated way, Mead is pre-psychoanalytical. His gay subject matter is presented in a simple and unified fashion and the anguish of his figures' desires is expressed with kinaesthetic directness and without much modulation.

3. Hoolboom, for example, recognized this feature of Mead's films instantly.

4. The cruel cutting in *Frostbite*, the extrusion of phallic tentacles and the even tighter boxing of the lesbian couple in *(ab)normal* are examples of the often grotesque images expressing deformations of desire that Mead customarily deploys.

5. It should be added immediately these three filmmakers otherwise hold almost nothing in common. Torossian ever inclines toward composing a highly composite, often cut-up film image set into a highly agitated montage. Brown deploys a very steady and restricted set of shots in each film in a highly measured repeat-and-vary montage while fiercely agitating-recomposing the image surface through improvisatory photo-chemical effects of his own invention.

6. The likely influence here is the Czech surrealist animator Jan Švankmajer, who similarly sometimes applies such techniques to live-action footage, though his more famous works utilize puppetry (and stop-action object-animation). The Brothers Quay did much to popularize the Czech's work through their own applications of Švankmajer's techniques.

7. The experimental erotic film, whether straight or gay, has rarely provided a comforting erotic spectacle, and this goes back to Surrealism and forward to such erotic works as Rubin's *Christmas on Earth*, Schneemann's *Fuses*, and Smith's *Flaming Creatures*, not to mention the 8mm "transgressive avant-garde" of the eighties and nineties, exemplified by Nick Zedd and Lydia Lunch, that form the horizon—however close or distant—against which Mead developed his filmmaking.

8. The sinister side of this, as Mead points out, is that this led to the dismissal of some 8,200 workers by the late 1960s. In the Cold War, homosexuals were regarded as a security threat because they were likely subject to blackmail by foreign agents, and the RCMP was tasked to expose them before that happened. The ridiculous aspects of this scientific endeavour join them to others, such as the CIA-sponsored LSD experiments conducted in Montréal during roughly the same period.

9. This is the second time Mead has used Dr. Wake in a film. The first was in 1992 when he placed a tape recording reporting Wake's work over an animated couple in *Haven*.

10. Or not. Mead includes mention of the post-war status of imprisoned homosexuals, still regarded as criminals under the Allies. The pink triangle that was stitched onto the prisoners' clothes Mead shows in a long close-up being stitched into the bicep of one of the two men by the other in the film's concluding passage. The incarceral gaze extends from the Nazis to the rest of Western society, which now (one could say) and again writes the homosexual stigma onto the flesh, continuing the fascist imposition of a badge in a covert and perhaps less brutal but nonetheless cruel continuation of oppression. If taken in this sense, Mead intends a very bitter expression of how the post-war period still writes its condemnation of gays.

11. This famous painting used a naked and leering twelve-year-old boy, rumoured to be the painter's lover, as Cupid and engendered a scandal, including several countering paintings, which led to lawsuits, etc.

12. *Stage fright* is an obvious case in point with respect to theatre, but Mead's reliance on tableau constructs and stylized performance are both redolent of theatre. Television figures in several films, most notably in the heterosexual couple segment of *(ab)normal* which includes a TV and sound from "Wild Kingdom."

Janie Geiser

Chris Gehman

The films of Janie Geiser begin, with *Babel Town* (1992) and two earlier films not in distribution, as film adaptations of her work as a creator of puppet theatre, and rapidly develop into highly complex and layered cinematic works. In their use of found materials to evoke a mysterious charge of emotion and memory, the films may call to mind the boxes of Joseph Cornell or the collages and objects of Bruce Conner, but Geiser's works are less fragile than Cornell's, less entangled in the psychopathology of American society than many of Conner's.

Critics are too quick to hang the label "dream-like" on anything that evokes narrative, but cannot be completely explained in logical terms. In the case of Geiser's films, however, the incompleteness of memory and dream really do seem to offer a model for their sense and construction. The repeated appearance of certain figures, the interactions between one figure and another, and the movement of the figures in relation to the spaces they inhabit, all encourage us to try to read these films in narrative terms, while resisting all attempts to reduce them to the logic of story.[1] Cause and effect are seldom clear, but webs of association and moments of connection develop, usually accreting around one central figure who becomes a kind of protagonist.

If *Babel Town* can be considered Geiser's first film (in the sense that it's the earliest one she continues to screen publicly), it is also the *last* in which an uncomplicated photographic space would be employed throughout. Using puppets, the film shows the story of a girl who leaves her family home

still: Janie Geiser's *The Red Book* (1994)

and returns to find that she has grown too large to enter it again. The filming of the puppets and sets in this film is conventional enough; it is the puppet performance and the fragmented narrative itself which provide the film's interest. Already in her next film, *The Red Book* (1994), Geiser seems to have identified a problem first posed by Josef von Sternberg, who objected to the "dead space" between the camera and its subjects. Von Sternberg famously brought this space into play by placing layers of screens, scrims, and sundry bric-a-brac throughout the depth of the image. Here, Geiser began to use the film frame not as a simple field for the representation of a performance, but as a composite or laminate space constructed using in-camera multiple exposures. Geiser shares with von Sternberg a love of foreground patterns and apertures which create partially obstructed views. However, the space she creates is more complex, since it is often composed using multiple layers of exposure rather than merely filling the space between camera and subject. It is characterized by the simultaneous use of flat images and images which create an illusion of depth, and not simply by the baroque complication of a single diegetic space.

The Red Book also marks a shift from "live-action" photography of puppets in motion to frame-by-frame animation, although Geiser continues to combine single-frame shooting with continuous shooting in many films. Here, white line drawings on black, or a screen representing a grid, are exposed over the red face and body of the female figure who appears as the film's quasi-protagonist. (It's a colour film, but the colour scheme is restricted to black, white, and red.) There seems to be a feminist idea underlying the film, a protest against an alienating scientific visualization of women's bodies, with its tendency to conceptually divide a whole body into parts. The technique of the overlay, the multiple exposure, becomes a device for calling attention to the distinctness of a figure from the pattern into which it may be placed. Animation also plays its part throughout: At one point, for example, a drawing of the woman is perforated, frame by frame, by dotted lines, and then pulled apart, dismembered by huge, intruding white hands.

This tendency to create a laminate space continues throughout Geiser's subsequent films. There are a number of fundamental devices which recur: the addition of layers of flat overall pattern (drawings, wallpaper, fabric, etc.) to figural images; the use of mattes—often moving, opening and closing—that restrict exposure to one area of the frame, at least for that particular layer of exposure; the combination of flat surfaces (playing cards, fabric, book pages, etc.) with 3-D objects (clocks, toys, blocks, etc.) in shallow 3-D "sets"; and transitions made through fades, defocusing, and grad-ual overexposure. In many cases, the overlap of one or another optical layer, or the softening of transitions through fades, defocusing and changes in exposure, weakens the role of the cut. This can create more of a sense of continuous flow than of a series of discrete shots, though the films certain-ly do not refuse montage altogether (as, for example, do most of Caroline Leaf's films).

The use of these devices is developed in *The Secret Story* (1996), which also sees a shift to the use of found objects over drawings (*The Red Book*) or puppets (*Babel Town*) made by Geiser herself. In *The Secret Story*, these found objects, often worn, chipped and dented by years of use, immediate-ly seem to place the film in the past, in the realm of memory rather than in the cinematic "present" of the two earlier films. Again, the film gravitates around the figure of a woman: This time, it is a wooden figure printed with hands clasped in front of her, eyes cast upwards. Her attitude evokes prayer, sorrow, or beseeching, and each of these interpretations is support-ed by other elements in the film. A religious environment, for example, is suggested repeatedly: by the figure of a nun, by a printed child's block labeled "S sin," and by the woman's final dissolution as she goes out of focus and the exposure increases to near white. We see a flood, war, a man falling to the floor and being examined by a doctor—is she a grieving wit-ness or a victim in the series of calamities that unfold around her? And then there is the strong sense of an everyday feminine space, represented by shadows of clothes hanging on a line cast on the thin brown paper of a sewing pattern, and by the many floral patterns superimposed over the scenes. *The Secret Story* seems to invite us to read it somehow as a version of a woman's own memories (perhaps from Geiser's family home in Louisiana?).

From *The Secret Story* onward, Geiser's films become more and more polished and assured. *Immer Zu* (1997) is entirely in black and white, with its cryptic narrative, heavy atmosphere and vaguely familiar, foreboding movie music all evoking mid-century American crime films. *Immer Zu* gives us drawings of an injured man and a woman who shares secret messages with another man. As if providing a metaphor for its own cryptic narrative, the film returns repeatedly to images of coded messages hidden in unexpected places, such as watches, test tubes, and the high heel of a woman's shoe.

Lost Motion (1999) and *Spiral Vessel* (2000) represent the extreme ends of Geiser's current diegetic approach. *Lost Motion* offers what seems to me the most complete narrative in Geiser's films, while *Spiral Vessel* offers a

set of non-narrative variations on a set of found objects and images.[2] In *Lost Motion*, the film follows a worn, painted toy "businessman" figure through a series of tableaux. He is haunted by images of a woman and a bed. The bed is associated with the image of a travelling case being closed. Is he keeping a rendezvous with her, only to be disappointed? Has she left him, or is she merely absent on a trip? After moving through a series of relatively open spaces, including a train station where he appears to be looking for someone, he enters a darker, more menacing space of obscure machines, supported on the soundtrack by a grinding drone, and watched surreptitiously by a leering doll's face. Here, the man encounters a woman, then another, both nude, seductive, chipped plaster figures, and a sexual liaison ensues. The earlier, more "wifely" woman's image intrudes into the frame in composite as a guilty reminder: as a separate inset image; superimposed over the nude figure's own face; and, in a dramatic moment, "Xed out" in a few short bursts of single-frame articulation. In these brief shots, frames showing her face are superimposed with frames showing a linear fabric pattern, pictured diagonally from lower left to upper right, then from upper left to lower right, in alternating frames. The result is an image of her face over which a flickering "X" appears through the phenomenon of the persistence of vision (a kind of articulation between frames developed in

still: Janie Geiser's Lost Motion *(1999)*

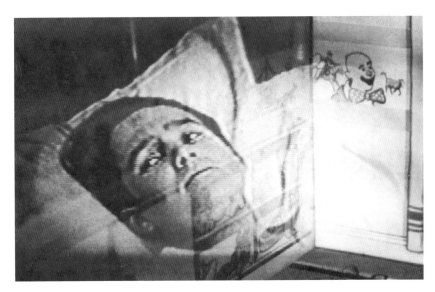

detail in the films of the French filmmaker Rose Lowder). In a final variation, the face of one of the nude female figures is added to the composite,
expressing the male figure's confused desires. Following this encounter, he
floats, in superimposition, out of the mechanical space and past images
returning from earlier in the film. The film ends with an image of a little
kitchen set containing an empty table and chair, which have been glimpsed
before. And, finally, the empty chair alone, framed from above by a circular
iris. The sense of absence and desolation expressed at the film's close
seem bound to the male figure's choice between wife (perhaps) and seduc-
tress, and the failure of his sexual adventure to compensate for the first
woman's loss or absence.

Spiral Vessel, by contrast, is highly refined in its use of colour, pattern,
and composite space, but appears not to attempt a unified narrative. The
film combines several sets of imagery: wooden puzzle pieces that come
together to make up simple line drawings of figures, faces, and body parts;
fine nineteenth-century engravings of scientific vessels and instruments;
detailed photographic images of leaves, with their vein structures clearly
visible; and cloth or wallpaper patterns derived from plant forms. The
wooden puzzle figures come together and come apart, and the film makes
use of moving, opening, and closing mattes throughout. Like *The Red Book*,
Spiral Vessel hints at a critical view of a certain way of seeing, an overly
rational image of the world understood through fragmentation.

Geiser's recent use of re-filmed video images to manifest the "puppet"

still: Janie Geiser's *The Fourth Watch* (2002)

figures in films such as *Ultima Thule* (2002) and *The Fourth Watch* (2002) reminds us that the development of media is not unidirectional. The composite moving image is not new. It has been part of cinematic practice since it began: Think, for example, of the countless trick films of Georges Méliès, Ferdinand Zecca's *Histoire d'un crime* (1901), Edwin S. Porter's *Dream of the Rarebit Fiend* (1906), or, later, the intricate fantasy sequences animated by Ray Harryhausen for features such as *The Seventh Voyage of Sinbad* (1958) and *Jason and the Argonauts* (1963). Filmmakers have been using video to make films since the 1960s, and Geiser brilliantly draws video images (often of old films!) into her composite film space, creating a kind of Chinese box of media transformations and cultural memory. This mediated version of "live action" also creates an additional composite temporality in which frame-by-frame animations are layered with images originally shot in live action, then re-filmed by Geiser from a video monitor, a process that creates interference via the rolling bar of the video raster, shifts in contrast and colour values, reframing, etc. The films made using figures derived from video combine an elegance of motion and construction with an increased sense of distance from the material.

The power of Janie Geiser's films grows not only from the complexity of their organization of screen space and time, their technical finesse, and their ability to sustain a certain mood from start to finish, but also from their general commitment to an aesthetic of composition from multiple, simultaneous fragments. The experience of a subject who feels incomplete—or whose parts are all present but no longer fit together, like those of the woman in *The Red Book*—must be among the most universal experiences among people in the contemporary world. (So much so that expressing this idea as I am here, in a simple verbal formulation, I'm acutely aware of how banal it sounds.) Geiser's films use images to speak out of, and to, that experience in a way that discursive language cannot.

Endnotes

1. It may seem an odd point of comparison, but in this sense perhaps Geiser's work with animated puppets, drawings, and found objects could be said to intersect at some point with the increasingly elliptical live-action dramas of Claire Denis, whose films appear, one by one, to become less and less "complete" in traditional narrative terms. Denis's concern with the fragmentation of identity and the body (as in the 2004 film *L'Intrus*, which concerns underground organ transplantation) also coincide in some way with Geiser's construction through minute fragments.

2. I can't help but wonder, however, if this might be a matter of gender: Would a woman be likely to find *The Secret Story* or *The Red Book* equally "complete"? *Lost Motion* is somewhat anomalous among Geiser's films in having a male figure at its centre.

Scratchatopia

Steven Woloshen

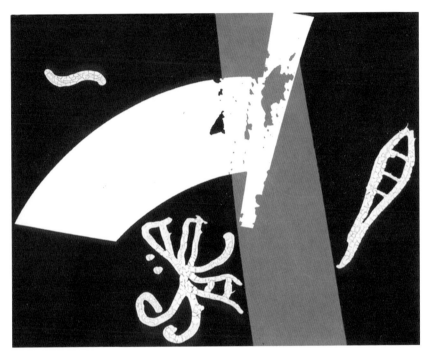

Whenever my funds are low, I take a job as a driver on large-budget Hollywood motion pictures. It pays the bills according to my own secret "trickle-down" theory: the money you pay at the cinema's box office feeds the Hollywood machine, which in turn fuels future Hollywood productions, which in turn goes into my pocket, then into my scratch films. On this particular occasion, I built a small portable scratch box loaded with fifty feet of 35mm black leader. The box was made entirely from scrap wood, plastic, and glass. It weighed two pounds and fit squarely between the two front seats of a rented seven passenger car. I knew I would have some "down time" in my sixteen-hour day to work on this film. (I think spontaneous urges and desires are the best part of handmade filmmaking. I've always worked whenever I wanted, and now, *wherever* I wanted!) It was vitally important to me that this scratch box be visible at all times to my passengers. On this production, there were six producers, a Hollywood actor-turned-director, and four well-known Hollywood actors (not all these passengers rode at the same time—this would be a major *faux pas*, as well as highly impractical).

still: Steven Woloshen's *Bru Ha Ha!* (2002), courtesy of Canadian Filmmakers Distribution Centre

Usually, automobile conversation (if any) covers the weather, the population of the city, or how we are stealing jobs from foreign technicians. This time, when the scratch box was spotted, the conversation would be directed to the dark and mysterious world of abstract filmmaking. Between the years of 1996 and 1998, I tried my hand at commission sales work. As a salesman, I learned that the client would always direct his/her attention to the sealed envelope on the desk next to the application forms. When they inquired, it could eliminate any hesitation on their part and they felt inclined to fork over the money to me. It's the same thing in a car. The ride is long and the passenger is usually bored. I could either compliment them on their last film, or just shut my mouth and drive (this would force them to break the silence barrier).

Question: What's that?

Answer: It's a portable scratch box. I'm making a short experimental film recounting my thoughts, feelings and experiences as a driver on this film production. I like to work on it while I'm on "stand by" behind the wheel of the car.

This first response opens the door to further questions because it's packed with many mysterious, noncommittal buzz words. It answers the question, while also suggesting that I'm not neglecting my job title or its responsibilities. The conversation continues. The passenger (hopefully a producer) is getting a little nervous at the prospect of an unlicensed "behind the scenes" documentary of his project.

Question: Do you have our permission to do this?

I love this question. It reminds me that independent filmmakers speak for themselves, while Hollywood producers always speak as a corporate body - never quite sure what they remember or what they may have agreed to (unless it's in writing... maybe).

Answer: Certainly not! I haven't told anybody about this. You're the first person who's seen it. You're looking at the near-final result now. I don't know how long it's going to be or when I'm going to finish it. As you can see, I'm just scraping the black emulsion off the film with this knife. I thought I would give it the same title as the film production we're working on.

Now, I'm really baiting him for a response. I'll get it, too. I've pushed all of his legal, creative, and copyright panic buttons. For a short period of time, he will be forced to forget about his multimillion dollar production. Now, he's worried about his driver who is zooming down the highway at 110 km/h. He had better have an air of diplomacy. All this time, he's wondering where the camera is mounted on the scratch box. "Cameraless animation," I concede, "is created without the aid of a motion picture camera." Suddenly, my passenger is beginning to understand the possibility of an *other* film world that could exist parallel to his own knowledge and experience. He has been given a small window into a world he has never heard of. Now, the real conversation begins...

My feeling is that experimental, cameraless animation is more than just a shared experience on a big screen. I think it's a rare and wonderful opportunity to travel (and to bring a person down the road with you) and come face to face with the obstacles that cloud our vision. Cameraless animation is one of those rare filmmaking occasions when you have the privilege to have all your materials and raw elements *at your fingertips*. Showing this process and its products to other people is a thrill as well. Cameraless animation is *also* the essence of *risk*. With every frame, you hope and pray that you can achieve your results, and, with this—one of many car encounters—you'll reach out to someone without getting yourself fired, sued, or reprimanded.

Sand

Percy Fuentes

Sand, Percy Fuentes's first film, was shot and post-produced digitally using a combination of drawing and animated sand, then transferred to 16mm film for distribution. Much of the film is narrated by a female voice in Japanese, which is translated using English subtitles. These are excerpts from the narration and dialogue.

Girl's Story

When I was ten, me and my sister climbed onto our roof at night and listened to old records through our neighbor's window. She fed me candy. They don't really see her when they drive by. They see something different. Some nights she brings them here. Some nights... like tonight. He smiles at me as they enter. I somehow manage not to throw up when I smell him. He doesn't see me or my sister. She's got a picture of her boyfriend on the fridge. His shoes litter the entrance. All brand name and expensive. Like a woman. I heard his brother is a fag. When I was fourteen, I heard the sound of old records when I climbed onto the roof.

Overseas

My aunt posed in front of our neighbour's red Camaro and sent the picture to our relatives overseas. Now they think we are rich, and ask us for money to spend in shopping malls.

still: Percy Fuentes's *Sand* (2001), courtesy of Canadian Filmmakers Distribution Centre

Teacher Dialogue

Student: I lived next to a German family once. They were all pretty fat. Cory said they were on welfare 'cause they didn't have any food in their fridge. But they were still fat.

Teacher: Really? You know it's not really nice to call—

Student: —they offered me moose meat sausages. It had dog hair in it. Those fuckers.

Teacher: Oh, Copper! You're so delightful.

Voice # 1:

I was awake when my dad died. My mother screamed and pulled my sister out of bed to help.

I heard him screaming in a slurred manner for painkillers as the paramedics took him. I remained paralyzed in my bed unable to cry out. The light under the door pulsated rhythmically to the footsteps of everyone. It slowly transformed to a single line of white light as everyone left. I can't remember how long I stayed awake in the dark that night.

Make a name for yourself

When we were young, our mom lent me and my brother out to her friend Mitsy. Mitsy used us as some type of alibi so that she could get her "medicine" back from her black boyfriend.

Mitsy: Before we go in, you have to make a name for yourself. Chris, what do you want your name to be?

Chris: Um... Bruce.

Mitsy: What do you want to be called, Jason... Hurry up!

Jason: Thomas?

Mitsy: Okay then. Bruce and Thomas... Reyes.

Chris: Thomas? Like Thomas Wells.

Jason: Shut up, stupid!

Mitsy: See, Bruce and Thomas were the ones that you saw driving with me in my car.

Anthony: They looked older.

Mitsy: No. That's them down there.

Apartment Building

The trendy girl upstairs is dying her hair again and admiring herself in the mirror. The Vietnamese boys in the apartment below are getting ready to go to the arcade to meet their friends. Some of their friends are in the alley selling their bodies to a middle-aged white man. The youngest one was called a "gook" today by a white kid with a cold sore.

The family down the hall has a toilet filled to the rim with urine. There are spots of blood on the bottom. The daughter's bed smells of stale urine. Anna Salnes changes her husband's bedpan. They have lived here for twelve years. Mr. Salnes remembers the uptown theatre, the place where they had their first date. He regrets not having children. Anna occasionally questions if he still remembers who she is, but she knows that he can. His eyes tell her.

Marcus and Henry stay up all night making mix tapes. Marcus thinks that punk died when Sid Vicious died. Henry knows that punk died when Mötley Crüe did a version of "Anarchy in the UK." They were both born in 1982. Everyone with taste knows that *Blowout Comb* is the slickest hip-hop album of the nineties.

The mother in apartment #185 feeds her two mulatto kids junk food and rents them horror movies. The other day she thought about whether Father Valdez would like liquor in his cereal.

A Good Dream

... It's kind of like waking up from a good dream. You can't wait to go back to sleep to find out what happens next.

Darkroom

The test strip showed that twelve seconds would be a satisfactory exposure... "Satisfactory"—he once used that word jokingly to describe me. This was our first picture together. There was a problem with the camera so the image is difficult to see. Three, two, one... and into the next chemical. I once said it was easier for me to forget people than forgive them. Seeing these pictures makes it so hard. Why do I look at them then? A picture of his house out my bedroom window. When I came home from work, I would check if his room lights were on. It shows that he was waiting up for me. I checked tonight. All I could make out is his closed blinds. He's probably sleeping soundly. It obviously doesn't bother him tonight.

That day in February, the time in my backyard, and the night in the street were all worse than this time. In fact, I can't quite remember what started those fights. Just call. Tell me how much I mean to you. Don't do this to me again. I won't forget you. I won't forgive you. I need some sleep.

Every Time I See Your Picture I Cry

Daniel Barrow

Daniel Barrow lists his credits on *Every Time I See Your Picture I Cry* as writer, direc-tor, animator, and performer. This strange array is actually quite appropriate: Barrow performs with a microphone, prerecorded music, an overhead projector, and images on clear acetate, which he manipulates by hand. *Every Time* is "the interior dialogue of a bitter and jaded garbage man/failed artist as he wanders through the city streets, collecting garbage in the early hours of the morning."

I'm not saying that I think I'm shriveled and ugly, but I started worrying about aging and decay when I turned thirteen, and this anxiety has been escalating ever since.

Talking about it, I can see how this could really bore people. It's kind of like saying, "I know I'm not a supermodel, but I'm not a dog either." It's that kind of boorishness. When other people fish for compliments or seek encour-agement from me in this way, I feel like saying, "Yeah, you're about average. Good call!"

Anyway, it's not like I was any better looking in the past, and even if I had been, I'd never go back. There's nothing happy for me there. I have greater perseverance now. I can manage contemporary hostilities and aggressions in a way that I couldn't on the playground.

I know I'm not the only one. Everyone remembers getting their ass kicked. Some more than others. In fact, it could have been a lot worse for me. I could have been fat, phenomenally stupid, and smelled like tuna fish.

Elliott Bellringer was tormented more than any other kid at school. The sneering contempt and schoolyard abuse Elliott endured for years was so intense, I think it bordered on martyrdom. And apparently it was even worse at home. The horror of his life in grade school can't be overemphasized. On rainy days, Elliott's parents sent him to school wearing a garbage bag. (You know I didn't make that up.) Every single day for Elliott must have been a living nightmare.

At least I can say that I didn't participate in the abuse. If I have ever been cruel in my life it has always been in retaliation.

There were all kinds of rumours about his family and I imagine most of them were at least half-true. There was the usual back-fence talk of incest, but there were also bizarre stories of Elliott being molested by ghosts, or that his house was haunted by space aliens. I know these allegations weren't taken seriously because no one ever intervened, but everyone instinctively knew to back away from the Bellringer house in fear.

In winter, it was rumored that Elliott was forced to stay up all night flicking the outdoor Christmas lights on and off. I can remember driving past the Bellringer house at night, watching fearfully as the lights blinked with no apparent pattern—wondering if I might decipher (or ignore) some digital cry for help—some forlorn, Morse code scream or surrender.

I'm alternately drawn and repelled by the idea that there is poetry to squalor. The theme of complete loneliness in stories is, to me, compelling, but the idea that life is only a test of our endeavour to cope with the depths of human misery is outrageous. I know I am capable of much more.

Occasionally, people like Hellen Keller come up with an interesting comment like, "Our greatest challenges in life will one day be known to us as our greatest teachers." But in truth, no wheelchair-bound person has ever learned so much that they encouraged others to seek out the experience first-hand.

I sincerely wonder whatever happened to Elliott—partly out of morbid curiosity, but also partly out of genuine concern. The last time I saw him, he was a teenaged Satanist—but only the most commercialized, Iron Maiden variety; which I now realize is much scarier than the real thing.

Four Works

Siebren Versteeg

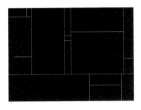 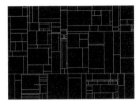 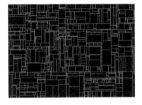

Long Division (2005)

This code-based, generative animation draws lines that divide, and divide again, the space of its field of projection 50,000 times (to the point of near saturation). Each run is unique and takes approximately forty minutes. Using a modified, pre-existing program, the randomly determined image is projected onto the floor. It consists of a rectangle of light that receives single pastel lines that gradually subdivide the space in a manner that is visually reminiscent of Mondrian's *Broadway Boogie Woogie* (1942-43). As the image becomes more complicated and the lines shorter, the animation appears to accelerate, and the image transmutes into an aerial map for a city becoming denser and denser. As Maureen Sherlock writes in her forthcoming catalogue essay, "Siebren Versteeg's work implicitly understands that in making the algorithms that structure our world visible, he allows us to imagine it differently, and that against the seamless science of the hidden, equality turns on another very different logic: in division rather than consensus, in a multiplicity of concrete acts and actual moments and situations."

Dynamic Ribbon Device (2003)

Dynamic Ribbon Device uses an internet connection to appropriate a live news feed from the Associated Press, which is then integrated into a piece for plasma screen. The AP headlines are reformatted to resemble the Coca-Cola trademark, and slowly scroll in that trademark's place. The entire visual field of the plasma screen is the glowing red field of Versteeg's slick

above: Siebren Versteeg's *Long Division* (2005); below: Versteeg's *Dynamic Ribbon Device* (2003)

rendering of a Coke can, complete with algorithmically generated conden-
sation droplets and simulated ice crystals. Commerce meets information.
The piece links to an external web page which uses .asp technology to tear
text from APWire. The delivered content is dynamic and could be programmed to deliver textual content from nearly any web-based source.

Emergency (2002)

Code-based, generative animation for plasma or LCD screen. Birds swoop
over a pastoral landscape. At the bottom of the screen is a road that is
sometimes empty, sometimes contains a few emergency vehicles, at other
times a chaotic traffic jam of fire trucks and ambulances, tiny in the bucol-
ic landscape, moving always from left to right, all accompanied by the
appropriate sirens. The number and frequency of the emergency vehicles is
controlled algorithmically and is unpredictable.

> *Emergency* is a beautifully scaled program that recalls the reality effect of
> Dutch landscape painting, quintessentially Vermeer's View of Delft (ca.
> 1661-64) itself possibly a technically facilitated image made with a mobile
> camera obscura. Vermeer's work, influenced by both Kepler and Huygens,
> takes place at the intersection of what was then called (art)ifice and a
> nature defined mathematically, not religiously. Unlike the Italians, Vermeer
> does not frame his landscape, it is a continuous line of sight—some of
> which is absent and none of which is resolved in a single subject position
> outside the painting. Its structure belongs to mapping and not the theatre,
> its framing devises are mobile like the cinematic pan. The Dutch of the time
> were, after all, on the move, expanding a mercantile empire for middle-
> class burghers. Freeing themselves of Rome and Spain was also freeing
> themselves from myth and dramaturgy: by their ships shall you know
> them! Using a photograph taken by Versteeg on the flat terrain of Martha's
> Vineyard, the landscape transforms the shoreline into a twentieth-century
> road filled with traffic, the vessels of the new burghers. The program gen-

stills: Siebren Versteeg's *Emergency* (2002)

erates an endless traffic jam more in line with Godard's *Weekend* (1967) and its collision of fiction and realism, as Versteeg's miniature cars and ambu-lances with sirens screeching careen down an endless highway to nowhere. Above the pastoral tree line, birds on a drunken holiday somer-sault in a loop-de-loop sky, while an imaginary art world fights traffic to be seen at the de rigeur watering hole by the people they were trying to avoid during the week. Into this horror story, Versteeg steals a little humor—at least the birds are free to travel until the pesticides get them. — Maureen Sherlock

Delf (2001)

A shadow puppet theater is created by placing a candle behind, and paper in front of a laptop computer screen. A custom program randomly animates a floating portrait of the artist in a zero-gravity state.

> What I mean is that the idea of detached bodies floating in space, of differ-ent sizes and densities, perhaps of different colors and temperatures, and surrounded and interlarded with wisps of gaseous condition, and some at rest, while others move in peculiar manners, seems to me the ideal source of form. — Alexander Calder on his mobile works

stills: Siebren Versteeg's Delf (2001)

Change/Translate/Represent

Oliver Hockenhull

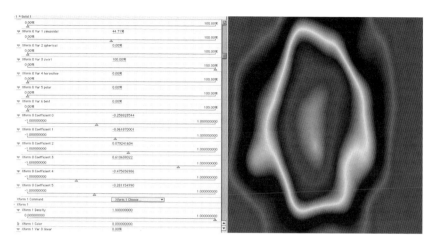

Code is conditions and interpretation, a deciphering, shared assumptions and cookie cutters.

The transforms of binary information, of a database of inputs, becomes solely a palette of variation awaiting specific designations.

My work in computer-generated animation—the *Boilt Pixels* series (2001) and the *Cosmic String* series (2002)—was conceived via the placement of seed numbers into parametric generators[1]: graphic equivalents of x, y, and z axes, and colour definitions. Key frames were interpolated using motion math, new x, new y, new z points, colour definitions, and pre-defined end points. The seed numbers were pinched from calculations derived from the dynamics of quantum fluctuations in a vacuum. These works were part of a long-term study into the relationship of binary language to life processes and animated imagery.

My first works in digital animation, in 1999, were studies in L-Systems[2], essentially morphogenetic algorithms. (In lay language, growth patterns, mathematically interpreted, of skeletal frames—in the case of L-Systems these algorithms are the numbers of the stems, branches, leaf patterns, etc. of plant.) These earlier experiments applied constraints and possibilities to 3-D forms, playing, riffing, morphing off of the reiterations that make up growth. These 3-D environments were then animated and image-sequenced to video.

still: Oliver Hockenhull's *Boilt Pixels* (2001)

Our typical response to a disturbing new environment is to re-create the old environment instead of heeding the new opportunities of the new environment. Failure to notice the new opportunities is also failure to understand the new powers... — Marshall McLuhan

The binary code as a vehicle for a manner of thinking—an associative emergent cloud floating in a startling open sky. How so? By the dependence on equivalences, by an indeterminate nature—impossible similitude pushed through continual (extravagant and ultimately baroque) electronic switches, allowing and disallowing in computative procedural commands—stamping a passport to the strange.

The code of the binary needs to be engaged with directly from the perspective of the most basic rhetoric—that of yes and no; a profound yet simple logic that can emulate the most complex of analog presentations. It was Leibniz, the founder of modern symbolic logic, who developed the system that John von Neumann would use 300 years later to build the first digital computers. Leibniz was a visionary whose keen desire was to emulate the *Visio Dei*—the all-at-onceness of the vision of God—inclusive of all pattern and randomness.

In these works, I am using the binary as an animate art. The subject is the processing of the data, and the data necessarily reflects a connective quality and a dial-o-matic aesthetic. The dynamics imposed, and other relative time-based visual tags, are the performances of the untoward and of chance-based operations conditioned by constraints. The art is the artifact of numbers. The image an incitement to speak using a rhetoric of uncertainty and potential.

When the unity of code and representation, code for code's sake, numbers as active and dynamic variables, are both subject and object of attention, the message of anthropomorphic representation is undermined. The transform is a support in weightlessness, a coping method of syncretic potential in an era of fundamentalisms and blinkered certainties, a sort of Proun[3] of the hypermedia age, of data architectural processes.

Multiplicity which is not reduced to unity is confusion. Unity which does not depend on multiplicity is tyranny. — Blaise Pascal

Credits

The original source code used to generate and animate these fractals was created by Scott Draves, a brilliant programmer who lives in San Francisco. His source code is available for use under the open source software model and can be downloaded at www.andrewdavidson.com/aeflame/download.html. For more information about Flame, as well as a gallery of still images (and a few animations), go to Draves's Flame page: www.flam3.com/.

The After Effects port of Scott's code was made by Drew Davidson, a programmer who lives in Raleigh, North Carolina. Drew went far and beyond a basic AE port and embellished aeFlame with some exceedingly handy features and settings. The aeFlame code was then taken by Evan Wies and ported to the Macintosh.

Endnotes

1. One of a set of independent variables that express the coordinates of a point.

2. Deterministic L-systems: simple string rewriting. In 1968, Aristid Lindenmayer, a biologist who worked with yeast and filamentous fungi, published a description of L-systems (Lindenmayer systems). These were string rewriting systems that could be used to describe the growth of a filamentous cyanobacterium (blue-green alga) called Anabaena. Rewriting is a technique for defining complex objects by successively replacing parts of a simple initial string using a set of rewriting rules or productions (Prusinkiewicz and Lindenmayer, 1990). However, the application of L-systems took a large leap when the strings generated by the production rules were interpreted using turtle graphics by Smith (1984), so that a simple axiom and production rules could code for a relatively complex plant. This was further developed by Prusinkiewicz, Hanan, and Lindenmayer in their extensive work modeling plants and trees.

3. El Lissitzky was the creator of the concept of Proun, a word derived from the expression Proekt Utverzhdeniya Novogo (Project for the Affirmation of what is New). These nonobjective compositions broadened Malevich's Suprematist credo of pure painting as spiritually transcendent into an interdisciplinary system of two-dimensional, architectonic forms rendered in painted collages, drawings, and prints, with both utopian and utilitarian aspirations. Blurring the distinctions between real and abstract space—a zone that Lissitzky called the "interchange station between painting and architecture"—the Prouns dwell upon the formal examination of transparency, opacity, colour, shape, line, and materiality, which Lissitzky ultimately extended into three-dimensional installations that transformed our experience of conventional, gravity-based space. Occasionally endowed with cryptic titles reflecting an interest in science and mathematics, these works seem engineered rather than drawn by hand—further evidence of the artist's growing conviction that art was above all rational rather than intuitive or emotional. "Thanks to the Prouns, a monolithic Communist city will be built on this foundation and the people of the whole world will live in it" (El Lissitzky to Malevich, personal letter 1919).

stills: Jim Trainor's *The Moschops* [2000]

The Moschops

Jim Trainor

M: First I was a reptile; then I was a mammal-like reptile; then I was a mammal. When I was a Moschops, another male bashed into me and broke my rib. I wanted to tell him, I thought you were my friend. But back in those days, the bones of our ears were still part of our jaws, and we couldn't hear a thing.

F: We all lived on a grassy plateau. We kept our babies in little herds. Gorgonopsians nipped at them, but we chased them away. We didn't love each other exactly, but we all slept together in one big, stupid pile.

M: I was proud of my big head and my broad feet that held firm to the hard earth. When I saw another male, I pushed hard against him. My skull fit tight in the pit of his broad shoulders.

F: When our blood warmed up, we'd go wallow in the flooded gully. We pushed trees over and shit where we sat. We loved horsetail caps, the skins of water plants, the rotten piths of fallen trees. When one of us died, we barely noticed it.

M: You bashed a male with your head, but that night he'd be dozing right next to you. One little male never got to have sexual intercourse. I eyed him tenderly though my throat flared red with anger. I hit him 'til the females flipped over, all dreamy indifference.

F: The afternoon sun made our openings swell. We loped to the lake to watch the males fight. We had sexual relations with the winners. Then it was back to the swamp for some water plants.

M: One hot day, I chose a big male and galloped toward him. I pushed and pushed until my hemipenes inverted. I didn't notice the little male squatting behind a cycad. His skull, my side, my sinuses sticky with blood.

F: For three days he listed like a broken wing. He hung around the egg pit but we edged away like crabs. On the third day, the gorgonpsians found him. There weren't many mud puddles on our plateau, but he found one, and he got in it.

M: I wanted to tell them, all those battles, but I never hated anyone! The mud hardened across my eyes as I watched my world turn yellow and flat. Were those males battling, or were they insects, stuck in sap? Nothing on earth has a right to live, only a chance, a chance.

Contributors

Contact information for artists' distributors, galleries, or representatives is provided on page 281.

Daniel Barrow is a Winnipeg-based media artist working in performance, video and installation. He has exhibited widely in Canada and abroad. Recently, Barrow has exhibited at Three Walls Gallery (Chicago), DAZIBAO (Montreal), and the Images Festival (Toronto). Since 1993, Barrow has used an overhead projector to relay ideas and short narratives. Specifically, he creates and adapts comic book narratives to a "manual" form of animation by projecting, layering and manipulating drawings on Mylar transparencies. Barrow variously refers to this practice as "graphic perform-ance, live illustration, or manual animation." Barrow's forthcoming performance, *Every Time I See Your Picture I Cry* will once again use an overhead projector in this way, to trace and develop the internal dialogue of a melancholic cartoon character.

Zoe Beloff grew up in Edinburgh, Scotland. In 1980 she moved to New York to study at Columbia University where she received an MFA in Film. Her work has been exhib-ited internationally at venues including The Museum of Modern Art, the Whitney Museum of American Art, the New York Film Festival, International Film Festival Rotterdam, Pacific Film Archive and the Centre Pompidou. Beloff works with a vari-ety of cinematic imagery; film, stereoscopic projection performance, interactive media, and installation. She has worked with a number of artists from other disci-plines, including composer John Cale, sound artist Ken Montgomery, and the Wooster Group theatre company, who collaborated with her to create the CD-ROM *Where Where There There Where*. In 2003 Beloff was awarded a Guggenheim Fellowship to create her installation *The Ideoplastic Materializations of Eva C.*, based on accounts of a medium who could apparently conjure up fantastic images. She is currently working on her second stereoscopic 16mm film, *Charming Augustine*.

Jeremy Blake is well known for his DVDs, C-prints, paintings and drawings that present visual semi-narratives combining the representational and the abstract. The hallucinatory transmutations in Blake's opulent DVDs unfold in seamless and dream-like loops that preclude a beginning or end. Using various graphics pro-grams, photographs and film footage, he laboriously renders and alters his images with countless layers of line and translucent colour using techniques inherited from conventional drawing and painting, as well as lighting and editing effects suggestive of film. Blake has exhibited extensively in museums and galleries worldwide, and his works are in numerous public collections, including the Centro de Arte Caja de Burgos (Spain), the Museum of Contemporary Art (Los Angeles), the San Diego Museum of Contemporary Art, the Whitney Museum of American Art (New York) and the Museum of Modern Art (New York). In 2002 he was invited by director Paul Thomas Anderson to create abstract sequences of art for the film *Punch-Drunk Love*. He also produced a series of album covers and inserts for Beck's CD *Sea Change*. He is represented by Feigen Contemporary in New York.

David Clark is a new media artist known internationally for his award-winning *ais-forapple.net* project. Clark is also a filmmaker with two feature films currently in development. He teaches at the Nova Scotia College of Art and Design University in Halifax and is developing their graduate film program, slated to launch in 2006. Two more net art projects are in the research stages: *Sign After the X*, a site that will explore the myriad implications behind the letter X, with collaborator Marina Roy, and *88 Constellations for Wittgenstein (To Be Played With the Left Hand)*, a web/film hybrid. The latter will examine the logic of coincidence and connection to create a non-linear portrait of influential philosopher Ludwig Wittgenstein (1889-1951) and the number eighty-eight, the number of constellations in the sky and keys on a piano. Clark has not abandoned the gallery setting for the screen world, however—recent solo exhibitions include *Screen Play* at Gallery TPW (Toronto) and *Chemical Vision* at Museum London (London, Ontario). The Maryland Institute College of Art in Baltimore will host a David Clark retrospective in 2005.

Daniel Cockburn is a Toronto-based filmmaker, video artist, and writer. His work has been exhibited at various venues since 1999, including the Images Festival (Toronto), IMPAKT Festival (Utrecht), and Berlin's Transmediale. He will be the subject of a video artist spotlight at SAW Video's Art Star Biennial in 2005, and his recent typewriter performance *Visible Vocals* will be published in book form in late 2005 as a two-volume set by Parasitic Ventures Press. His video work is distributed by Vtape (Toronto).

Percy Fuentes is a 28-year-old Filipino Canadian filmmaker born and raised in the Province of Saskatchewan, where he eventually attended a local prairie film school. His films and videos have been screened at numerous international film festivals. This young man is a hermit and is rarely seen in the out-of-doors. He is quiet, socially inept and should never be approached. Mr. Percy occasionally makes a film and or video. Sometimes the films and or videos are of the animated kind. His hobbies include modifying cheap Polaroid cameras and referring to himself in the third person. Mr. Percy is currently a citizen. *Sand* is distributed by the Canadian Filmmakers Distribution Centre (Toronto).

Janie Geiser is an internationally recognized theatre director/designer, filmmaker and illustrator. She has made a significant contribution to the field of contemporary puppet theatre through her innovative original works, which have toured nationally and internationally, and she has been recognized with numerous awards, including an Obie and a Guggenheim Fellowship. Geiser's films have been presented at the Whitney Museum of American Art, the Guggenheim Museum, and the Museum of Modern Art, as well as at the New York Film Festival, the International Film Festival Rotterdam, the Images Festival (Toronto), the Ottawa International Animation Festival, and other venues. Geiser is also a nationally recognized illustrator whose work has appeared in the *New York Times Book Review*, *The New Yorker* and *The*

Wall Street Journal. Her theatre pieces have been presented at The Walker Art Center (Minneapolis), the Museum of Contemporary Art in Los Angeles, PS 122 (New York), and other venues. Her films are in the collection of the Museum of Modern Art in New York and are distributed by Canyon Cinema (San Francisco), the Film-Makers' Cooperative (New York), and Canadian Filmmakers Distribution Centre (Toronto).

Chris Gehman is an independent filmmaker, curator and critic based in Toronto. His films include works in animation and other forms of frame-by-frame construction, and they have been exhibited at numerous venues, including the Ann Arbor Film Festival (Michigan), the Onion City Festival (Chicago), Cinematheque Ontario (Toronto), the Semana de Cine Experimental (Madrid) and the international touring program *Super-8: Film as Art.* His writings on film have appeared in periodicals such as *Cinema Scope, Millennium Film Journal, Take One* and *Broken Pencil*, and he has contributed to anthologies on the films of John Porter and Philip Hoffman, as well as to the *Canadian Film Encyclopedia* on-line. From 2000 to 2004, Gehman was the Artistic Director of the Images Festival (Toronto), and prior to that he was Assistant Programmer and Programme Guide Editor at Cinematheque Ontario, where he oversaw the design and production of anthologies on the films of Robert Bresson and Joyce Wieland. His films are distributed by Canadian Filmmakers Distribution Centre (Toronto).

Lia Gangiatano is Founder/Director of PARTICIPANT INC, a not-for-profit art space on the Lower East Side of New York. During four years as curator of Thread Waxing Space (New York), she curated numerous exhibitions, screenings, and performances, including Spectacular Optical, and solo exhibitions by Sigalit Landau, Lovett/Codagnone, BØrre Sæthre, and Luther Price. She is currently editing a book about the history of the space, *The Alternative to What? Thread Waxing Space and the 90s.* Formerly Associate Curator at The Institute of Contemporary Art, Boston, she co-curated exhibitions including Dress Codes and Boston School. She is the editor of numerous publications, including *New Histories* and *Boston School.*

Libby Hague <www3.sympatico.ca/libbylibby> is a visual artist who has exhibited in North and Central America and Europe. She looks to science fiction, comic books, and anime for inspiration and has specialized for several years in installation works involving hundreds of watercolour, printed, and photographic pieces. This work now operates as a story board and image archive for her work in video. Her recent work has looked at the relationship between marginalized and mainstream communities, at the animals and people lost to us in one way or another, and suggests that our connections and responsibilities here define us. Hague has been at work for the past three years on an animated film called *Close to Home*, set for completion in 2006. Her videos are distributed by Vtape (Toronto).

Pierre Hébert was born in Montréal near the end of the Second World War. In 1965, he dropped his studies in anthropology and started working as an animator at the National Film Board of Canada, where, until the end of 1999, he directed more than twenty shorts and a feature, *La plante humaine* (1996). From the mid-eighties, Hébert has been involved in many multidisciplinary projects, working with musicians, choreographers, and writers. He is now an independent artist and filmmaker, and forms a duet with the American electronic musician Bob Ostertag in computer-assisted live animation and video processing performances called "Living Cinema," which have been performed extensively in Canada, the United States, Mexico, most of Europe, and Japan. (A video based on these performances, *Between Science and Garbage* (2003), was an outcome of this project; it is available on DVD from the Tzadik label.) In 2004, Hébert was the recipient of the Albert-Tessier prize, the Québec Government's annual award for lifetime accomplishments in cinema. Most of Hébert's films are available from the National Film Board of Canada; information on his collaborative performances with Bob Ostertag can be found at <www.detritus.net /ostertag/home.html>.

Eric Henry is a San Francisco-based filmmaker, animator, and teacher. His work has screened at the Institute of Contemporary Art (London), the Metropolitan Museum of Art (New York City), the Cannes and Sundance Film Festivals, and many other venues and events around the world. His projects include *Wood Technology in the Design of Structures* (Best Experimental Video, 1998 Atlanta International Film and Video Festival), and the ground-breaking animated featurette *DJ Q-Bert's Wave Twisters* (Sundance, 2001).

Oliver Hockenhull is a prolific Vancouver media artist. He is also a screenwriter, communications theorist, and lecturer. He has completed six feature length works and numerous dramatic and experimental shorts. These have received critical acclaim through screenings at venues including the Museum of Modern Art (New York), Massachusetts Institute of Technology (Boston), the new Canadian Embassy in Berlin, and The Melbourne International Film Festival. In 2003-2004 Hockenhull was visiting artist/lecturer at Northwestern University in Chicago. He has also been deeply involved in the study, theory, and application of new media imaging and authoring technologies and has been a research associate with the Centre For Image and Sound Research in Vancouver, and a director/resident at The Banff Centre for the Arts. As a member of WebWeavers Network Society he contributed to getting online the first cultural web site in Canada. His early and groundbreaking hypertext documents have been used in courses at The University of Virginia Institute for Advanced Technology in the Humanities, the University of California, Santa Barbara, Victoria University (New Zealand), and at The Institute for Social Theory at Keele University (England).

William Kentridge has gained international recognition for his distinctive animated short films and for the charcoal drawings he makes in producing them. Kentridge has also worked in theatre for many years, initially as set designer and actor, and more recently, as director. Since 1992, he has collaborated with Handspring Puppet Company creating multi-media pieces using puppets, live actors and animation. Since Kentridge participated in Documenta X in Kassel (1997), solo shows of his work have been exhibited at the Museum of Modern Art (New York) and Museum of Contemporary Art (San Diego). Kentridge sees his work as rooted in Johannesburg, South Africa, where he continues to live today with his wife and three children. He is represented by the Marian Goodman Gallery (New York).

Lewis Klahr has been called the "reigning proponent of cut and paste" by critic J. Hoberman of *The Village Voice*. Klahr has been making films since 1977, and is known for his idiosyncratic experimental films and cutout animations, which have been screened extensively in the United States and Europe, including at the Whitney Biennial (New York), the New York Film Festival, the International Film Festival Rotterdam, the Toronto International Film Festival, and many other venues. Four of his films are in the permanent collection of New York's Museum of Modern Art. His epic cutout animation *The Pharaoh's Belt* (1994) received a special citation for experimental work from the National Society of Film Critics. His short film *Lulu* was commissioned by Copenhagen's Gronnegards Theatre for their critically acclaimed 1996 production of Alban Berg's opera, and he has created special effects and animation for television show openings, music videos, commercials, and Michael Almereyda's feature film *Hamlet* (2000). Since moving to Los Angeles in 1999, Klahr has also worked as a screenwriter; he collaborated on the rewrite of the feature *The Mothman Prophecies* (2002). His films are distributed by Canyon Cinema (San Francisco), the Film-Makers' Cooperative (New York), Lux (London), and Light Cone (Paris).

Rosalind Krauss is University Professor of Modern Art and Theory at Columbia University. Professor Krauss's attempts to understand the phenomenon of modernist art, in its historical, theoretical, and formal dimensions, have led her in various directions. She has, for example, been interested in the development of photography, whose history—running parallel to that of modernist painting and sculpture—makes visible certain previously overlooked phenomena in the "high arts," such as the role of the indexical mark, or the function of the archive. She has also investigated certain concepts, such as "formlessness," "the optical unconscious," or "pastiche," which organize modernist practice in relation to different explanatory grids from those of progressive modernism or the avant-garde. Recent books include *Formless: A User's Guide* and *Bachelors* (both MIT Press, 2000).

Lev Manovich <www.manovich.net> is an Associate Professor in the Visual Arts Department, University of California, San Diego, where he teaches courses in new media art and theory. He is the author of *The Language of New Media* (MIT Press, 2001) and *Tekstura: Russian Essays on Visual Culture* (Chicago University Press, 1993), as well as many articles which have been published in 28 countries. Manovich lectures extensively on new media; since 1999 he has delivered more than 180 lectures in North and South America, Europe, and Asia. His awards include a Mellon Fellowship and Guggenheim Fellowship (2002-2003).

Laura U. Marks is a theorist, critic and curator of independent and experimental media arts. Her current research interests are independent media in the Arab world, and connections between computer art and classical Islamic art. She is the author of *The Skin of the Film: Intercultural Cinema, Embodiment, and the Senses* (Duke University Press, 2000) and *Touch: Sensuous Theory and Multisensory Media* (Minnesota University Press, 2002), as well as dozens of essays. She has curated programs for film and media festivals worldwide. Dr. Marks is the Dena Wosk University Professor in Art and Culture Studies at Simon Fraser University, Vancouver.

Stephanie Maxwell is Professor in the School of Film and Animation at the Rochester Institute of Technology (Rochester, New York). She earned her MFA in Film at the San Francisco Art Institute. Her animated works are exhibited in international film and television programs and festivals, and collected by museums as works of art. Stephanie's web site is www.rit.edu/~sampph; her email address is sampph@rit.edu. Clips from these works may be viewed on Stephanie's web site at www.rit.edu/~sampph/Works.html. Audio samples can be found on Allan Schindler's web site under "List of Currently Available Compositions—Film/musical compositions" at www.esm.rochester.edu/allan/.

Wrik Mead is one of Canada's most distinctive experimental filmmakers. His films are psychodramas—first-person narratives of desire and accommodation. They are a mix of painstaking pixillation, fairy-tale allegory and queer identity, and are preoccupied with the materiality and tactility of film itself. Mead's fantasy narratives offer provocative, ugly/beautiful, often unsettling explorations of desire and longing, isolation and confinement, ritual and transformation. In 1997, a retrospective of his work was presented at the Images Festival (Toronto), followed by a national tour. Mead's films have screened around the globe; recently his work was part of a major touring program of Canadian experimental film in Italy. Wrik Mead's films are distributed by Canadian Filmmakers Distribution Centre (Toronto).

Morishita Akihiko is a media artist who makes experimental films and videos, and presents performances. He teaches Media and Design at Kobe Design University, and is active as a critic, curator and organizer. He was the Director of the Idemitsu Mako Exhibition Project and Co-organizer of The Idemitsu Mako Exhibition: 1 Create —I Create Myself,'" which appeared in Kobe, Osaka, Fukuoka and Tokyo in 2002. Morishita recently contributed the article "Art Aspires Dialogues" to the book *Visual*

Dialogues (Workshop for Architecture and Urbanism, 2005). Many of Morishita's films and videos are distributed by Image Forum (Tokyo).

Jude Norris is a multi-disciplinary Cree Métis artist who uses video both in the form of independent shorts and in video installations. Her approach to this medium relates directly to her practice as a painter and sculptor, and her affiliation with Plains Cree culture; her work incorporates an awareness of video's physicality, incorporating painterly use of colour and framing, and using the luminosity of the recorded image as a symbolic element. She has used slow motion and/or a circular editing style to stretch or emphasize the viewer's relationship with time, using video to mirror culture-based perceptions of reality and aspects of ritual. Norris's work employs digital technology to extend fundamental elements of traditional story-telling into a colonial, postmodern realm. Her videos are distributed by Vtape (Toronto).

The Brothers Quay are identical twins who were born in Pennsylvania in 1947. Stephen and Timothy Quay studied illustration in Philadelphia before going on to the Royal College of Art in London, where they started to make animated shorts in the 1970s. They have lived in London ever since, making their unique and innovative films under the aegis of Koninck Studios. The Quays' work also includes set design for theatre and opera. In 1998 their Tony-nominated set designs for Ionesco's *The Chairs* won great acclaim on Broadway. In 2000 they made *In Absentia*, an award-winning collaboration with Karlheinz Stockhausen, as well as two dance films, *Duet* and *The Sandman*. In 2002 they contributed an animated dream sequence to Julie Taymor's film *Frida*. Most recently the Quays have made four short films in collaboration with composer Steve Martland for a live event at the Tate Modern in London and are in postproduction on their long-awaited second feature, *The Piano Tuner of Earthquakes*. The Quays' films are distributed in North America by Zeitgeist Films (New York).

Steve Reinke is an artist and writer best known for his work in video, which is widely screened and exhibited. His work is in several collections, including the Museum of Modern Art (New York); Centre Pompidou (Paris); MACBA (Barcelona); and the National Gallery of Canada (Ottawa). He has taught at University of Wisconsin, Milwaukee, the School of the Art Institute of Chicago, Cal Arts, and the University of Western Ontario. Recently, Coach House Books published a collection of his scripts, *Everybody Loves Nothing: Video 1996—2004*. His work is distributed by Argos (Brussels), Lux (London), Video Data Bank (Chicago) and Vtape (Toronto). He is represented by Robert Birch Gallery in Toronto.

Allan Schindler is Professor of Composition and Director of the Computer Music Center at Eastman House. Several of his works are available on compact disc, and several are published by Semar Editore (Rome) and Worldwide Music Incorporated

(USA). Schindler also has served as a Music Editor and consultant for several pub-lishing houses, including McGraw-Hill, Random House, and Alfred A. Knopf. Allan's web site is <www.esm.rochester.edu/allan/allan.bio.html>.

Tom Sherman is an artist and writer. He works in video, radio and live performance, and writes all manner of texts. His interdisciplinary work has been exhibited inter-nationally, including shows at the National Gallery of Canada, the Vancouver Art Gallery, the Musée d'art contemporain (Montréal), the Museum of Modern Art and Ars Electronica (Linz). He represented Canada at the Venice Biennale in 1980, and in 2003 was awarded the Canada Council's Bell Canada Award for Video Art. He per-forms and records with Bernhard Loibner in a group called Nerve Theory. His most recent book is *Before and After the I-Bomb: An Artist in the Information Environment* (Banff Centre Press, 2002). He is a Professor of Media Arts at Syracuse University in New York. His videos are distributed by Vtape (Toronto).

John Sobol is the author of four books, including *Digitopia Blues—Race, Technology and the American Voice* (Banff Centre Press, 2002). He has performed across North America and Europe as a musician and toured his one-man show Two Million Years of Technology across Canada. Between 2003 and 2005 he was the co-director of Digifest, Canada's largest new media festival. He has created numerous multimedia projects, including *Globalhood* and *The Cosmic Questions Media League*. His website <www.johnsobol.com> contains an extensive media archive of works he has created over the past 25 years.

Tabaimo (Tabata Ayako) was born in 1975 in Hyougo, Japan and is now recognized as one of the leading young artists in Japan. She is best known for her animations, which are entirely drawn by hand, then coloured and edited digitally. These anima-tions are exhibited within elaborate architectural installations. Tabaimo's undergraduate thesis project, *Japanese Kitchen* (1999), was awarded the blue ribbon at the Kirin Contemporary Art Awards, a competition for emerging artists; she was the youngest person ever to receive this award. She was also the youngest artist to be selected for exhibition at the Yokohama Triennale, in 2001. At the age of 26 Tabaimo was appointed as a professor at the Kyoto University of Art and Design. Her work has been exhibited at many key contemporary art galleries and festivals in Japan and abroad; these include the Hara Museum of Contemporary Art (Tokyo), Kobe Art Village Centre, Images Festival (Toronto), Sao Paulo Biennale, Walker Art Center (Minneapolis), and many others. Tabaimo is represented by Gallery Koyanagi (Tokyo).

Tess Takahashi is a PhD candidate at Brown University in the Department of Modern Culture and Media, where she is writing a dissertation on medium specificity and the cinematic avant-garde. She has worked with artist Susan Schuppli on her DVD *Phony*, and published an essay on Schuppli's work for *Pick Up!*, a catalogue pub-lished by the Art Gallery of Hamilton in 2003. She has also written and lectured on video art and contemporary experimental documentary, including public lectures at the Art Gallery of York University on the work of Walid Ra'ad and an essay on the work of Julia Meltzer and David Thorne in a forthcoming collection entitled *For Interpretation: Experiments in Documentary.*

Bart Testa teaches Cinema Studies and Semiotics at the University of Toronto. He is the author of *Spirit in the Landscape* (Art Gallery of Ontario, 1989) and *Back and Forth: Early Cinema and the Avant-Garde* (Art Gallery of Ontario, 1992), and co-editor of *Pier Paolo Pasolini in Contemporary Perspective* (University of Toronto Press, 1994). His essays have appeared in several recent anthologies, and in journals including the Canadian Journal of Film Studies. His reviews have appeared in the *Globe and Mail, The Literary Review of Canada,* and on CBC Radio's *Definitely Not the Opera.*

Jim Trainor has been making animated films since he was thirteen. (That was 1974.) His best-known films are *The Fetishist* (1997), which is about a sociopathic boy, *The Bats* (1998), and *The Moschops* (2000), both of which are part of the series The Animals and their Limitations, as is the live-action monkey-film *The Magic Kingdom* (2003), which was included in the 2004 Whitney Biennial. Most recently, he has been making video portraits of unusual people, and a long comic strip, *Sun Shames Headhunting Moon.* He teaches at the School of the Art Institute of Chicago.

Siebren Versteeg lives and works in New York. He received a BFA from the School of the Art Institute of Chicago and is pursuing an MFA from the University of Illinois, Chicago. His work has been exhibited widely, with recent exhibitions at Rhona Hoffman Gallery (Chicago), International Biennale of Contemporary Art (Prague), The 25000 Cultural Transmission Center (Beijing); Chicago's Museum of Contemporary Art, The Wexner Center for the Arts (Columbus), ExitArt (New York), The Renaissance Society (Chicago), and Beacon Project Space (New York). In 2004, he attended The Skowhegan School of Painting and Sculpture. In 2005, he was Artist in Residence at Smart Project Space in Amsterdam.

Steven Woloshen was born in Montréal in 1960. His first exposure to filmmaking was in 1972: A local community program encouraged young people to make films without the aid of camera or raw stock of any kind. In 1980 he was admitted to Concordia University in Montréal, where he specialized in 16mm independent film techniques. His films include *Curse of the Voodoo Child* (2005), *Two Eastern Hair Lines* (2004) and *Ditty Dot Comma* (2001). Woloshen's films have screened at countless international film festivals, and a retrospective of his films was presented at the 2003 Ottawa International Animation Festival. He currently lives in Québec and has been a member of the Directors' Guild of Canada since 1991. Woloshen's films are distributed by Canadian Filmmakers Distribution Centre (Toronto).

Distributors and Galleries

Argos
Werfstraat 13 rue du Chantier
B-1000 Brussels, Belgium
tel: +32 2 229 00 03
fax: +32 2 223 73 31
email: info@argosarts.org
web: www.argosarts.org

Birch Libralto Gallery
129 Tecumseth Avenue
Toronto, ON M6J 2H2, Canada
tel: 416 365 3003
email: info@robertbirchgallery.com
web: www.robertbirchgallery.com

Canadian Filmmakers Distribution Centre
37 Hanna Avenue, Suite 220
Toronto, ON, M6K 1W9, Canada
tel: 416 588 0725
fax: 416 588 7956
email: cfmdc@cfmdc.org
web: www.cfmdc.org

Canyon Cinema
145 Ninth Street, Suite 260
San Francisco, CA 94103, USA
tel/fax: 415 626 2255
email: films@canyoncinema.com
web: www.canyoncinema.com

Feigen Contemporary
535 West 20th Street,
New York, NY 10011, USA
tel: 212 929 0500
fax: 212 929 0065
email: Gallery@FeigenContemporary.com
web: www.feigencontemporary.com

The Film-Makers' Cooperative
c/o The Clocktower Gallery
108 Leonard Street, 13th floor
New York, NY 10013, USA
tel: 212 267 5665
fax: 212 267 5666
email: film6000@aol.com
web: www.film-makerscoop.com

Gallery Koyanagi
8F, 1-7-5 Ginza, Chuo-ku
Tokyo 104-0061, Japan
tel: +81 3 3561 1896
email: mail@gallerykoyanagi.com
contact: Kaori Hashiguchi

Image Forum
2-10-2 Shibuya, Shibuya-ku
Tokyo, Japan
tel: +81 3 5766 0116
fax: +81 3 5466 0054;
email: info@imageforum.co.jp
web: http://www.imageforum.co.jp
Light Cone

12, rue des Vignoles
75020 Paris, France
tel: +33 (0)1 46 59 01 53
fax: +33 (0)1 46 59 03 12
email: lightcone@lightcone.org
web: fmp.lightcone.org:8000/lightcone

LUX
18 Shacklewell Lane
London E8 2EZ, UK
tel: 44 (0)20 7503 3980
fax: 44 (0)20 7503 1606
email: info@lux.org.uk
web: www.lux.org.uk

Marian Goodman Gallery
24 West 57th Street
New York, NY 10019, USA
tel: 212 977 7160
fax: 212 581 5187
email: goodman@mariangoodman.com
web: www.mariangoodman.com

National Film Board of Canada
P.O. Box 6100, Stn. Centre-ville
Montreal, QC H3C 3H5, Canada
tel (Canada): 1 800 267 7710
web: www.nfb.ca

Video Data Bank
112 S. Michigan Ave.
Chicago, IL 60603, USA
fax: 312 541 8073
tel: 312 345 3550
email: info@vdb.org
web: www.vdb.org

Video Pool Media Arts Centre
#300 - 100 Arthur St.
Winnipeg, MB R3B 1H3, Canada
tel: 204 9499134, ext.1
fax: 204 942 1555
web: www.videopool.org

Vtape
401 Richmond Street West, Suite 452
Toronto, ON M5V 3A8, Canada
tel: 416 351 1317
fax: 416 351 1509
email: info@vtape.org
web: www.vtape.org

Zeitgeist Films Ltd.
247 Centre Street
New York, NY 10013, USA
tel: 212 274 1989
fax: 212 274 1644
email: mail@zeitgeistfilms.com
web: www.zeitgeistfilms.com

Index